ABERDEENSHIRE: DONS
(FORMERLY

AN ILLUSTRATED ARC

CW01653730

When first approached to provide a foreword for this well-used publication my initial thoughts were to wonder what I could say about these books that has not already been said.

It is true that this splendid series provides a fascinating and invaluable insight into the Architectural history of the areas which they address and, I am delighted to say, Ian's latest edition of the Aberdeenshire Guide is no exception.

From the low lying coastal areas of Formartine to the rugged hills of Strathdon, and all points in between, Aberdeenshire has a diverse and fascinating history written in its numerous fine buildings and monuments.

This excellent book, with its wealth of information, helps bring to life this rich built environment to the reader providing further depth and texture to the buildings featured.

It is a book to which I frequently refer and whether for systematic and specific study or simply pleasurable reading, this guide will reward its readers well.

SHOLTO HUMPHRIES
PRESIDENT
Aberdeen Society of Architects

© Author: Ian Shepherd
Series editor: Charles McKean
Series consultant: David Walker
Cover design: Luise Valentiner, Trigger Press
Index: Oula Jones

The Rutland Press
ISBN 1 873190 55 7
1st published 1994
2nd edition 2006

Cover illustrations
Front *Craigievar – owned by The National Trust for Scotland (RCAHMS)*
Back (from top) *Pitcaple (RCAHMS); Pitmedden House and Great Garden (RCAHMS); Railway carriage summer house, Oyne (Norman); South doorway at St Mary's, Auchindoir (Shepherd)*

Typesetting by Luise Valentiner, Trigger Press
Picture scans and maps by the Royal Commission on the Ancient and Historical Monuments of Scotland
Printed by Alden Group Limited, Oxford

British Library Cataloguing in Publication Data.
A catalogue record for this book is available from the British Library.

The maps in this volume have been reproduced from Ordnance Survey based mapping on behalf of HMSO. © Crown copyright 2006. All rights reserved. Ordnance Survey Licence number GD03127G/01/06.

Shepherd

The land and the plough: Forgue

This most architectural shire ...
Lord Cockburn, *Circuit Journeys*, 1842

Lord Cockburn's view of Aberdeenshire, a substantial part of which is covered in this volume, elevates it to a primary position in Scottish architectural history. For here is to be found an extraordinary concentration of architectural wealth, of a depth and quality unsurpassed in Scotland.

True, the present development maelstrom which the Aberdeenshire environs of oil-rich Aberdeen have experienced for the last 30 years has not so far produced many buildings of a quality to excite a contemporary Lord Cockburn. However, if nothing else, this effect of a city state *par excellence*, Aberdeen, well illustrates the contrasts to be found across Donside and Strathbogie. The pressures of economic expansion ripping through the eastern parts of the district can be set against the problems of rural recession to be found in the western parts, up to 50 miles inland.

***No towns**, few villages, no stack of any manufactory, nothing but agriculture, which ... delights the eye of taste.*
Lord Cockburn, *Circuit Journeys* (1842) on Aberdeenshire

Rural restraint: Achath farmhouse, Cluny

Aberdeenshire Council

Aberdeenshire is an intensely lived-in landscape, in which the houses and farms conform to the lie of the land which generations of their inhabitants have helped to transform. In J R Allan's words: *man, nature and the plough in good community.* It is an essentially Lowland experience, the rolling north-east plain being the largest extent of flat land north of Yorkshire. Its character and culture have been as firmly wrought by the plough as have the dyked fields and level parks.

This landscape was shaped above all by such farmers and their families; not only those who lie in countless thousands in the numerous silent kirkyards and who, last century, double-dug the waste to create their now-ordered parks, but those of the earlier millennia, who cleared the first forest, picked up stones, and erected monuments such as recumbent stone circles whose immanence still compels respect.

Yet the landforms are often distinctly Highland in feel. The ship-like bulk of Bennachie with its distinctive tors dominates the skyline from so many vistas, while the rivers – Don, Deveron, Ythan – have often carved secret dens and silent pools. The land falls in a series of steps from the highest foothills of the Grampians in the west, through the rounded hills of Kildrummy and Rhynie to the rolling grain girnel of the Garioch, to finish in a vast coastal sand system, set between the Don and the Ythan.

There is an abundance of mysterious names – Garioch, Balquhindachy, Clatt, Aquhorthies, Bennachie, Forgue – many reflecting Gaelic roots in the time of the Scottish takeover of the ancient and vigorous Pictish kingdom, which enhance the feeling of a self-contained province.

The towns above all reflect the materials from which they are built. The varied geology of north-east Scotland provided an often bewildering range of stone: not one but many types of granite, as well as whinstones, sandstones, serpentine and even slate. Of these settlements the jewel is Huntly, adjacent to the great palace of the powerful and headstrong family of the Gordons. The town's fortunes waxed and waned, partly in tune with those of the Gordons, but its evolution through the centuries can be clearly traced today. The smaller towns scattered throughout the Aberdeenshire countryside – Inverurie, Oldmeldrum, Insch, Alford, Ellon – were local market centres and reflect the prudence, modesty, restraint and occasionally the meanness of their early burghers.
They, and the host of smaller villages, were also formerly centres of cottage industries, particularly knitting and weaving. In the late 18th century Ellon supplied 100 pounds' worth of stockings to Aberdeen merchants each week. Sizeable woollen factories developed in rural settings at Garlogie and Goval during the 19th century.

Several of the great families of Aberdeenshire are imprinted on Scotland's history, particularly those two mirror-images of gaiety and sobriety, Catholicism and Protestantism, the Gordons and the Forbeses. (Architecturally they can be

*... **This is the East coast** with winter*
Written into its constitution
And so is very productive of men
Who do not wait for good
In case there is none.
George Bruce, *Praising Aberdeenshire Farmers*

Granite towns: doorpiece, Church Street, Huntly

Aberdeenshire Council

seen to have been in opposition too: Huntly-Druminnor / Tolquhon; Wardhouse / Haddo-Castle Forbes.) Magnates such as these who had emerged following the decay of the great earldom of Mar in the 15th century made much of the district their cockpit in which to act out both local and national conflicts. Prior to this, Mar and Strathbogie had featured strongly in the Wars of Independence; they were also to play a part in the Troubles of the mid-17th century, and in the Jacobite risings of 1715 and 1745. The principal players in these dramas - the Gordons, Forbeses, Frasers, Keiths, Bissets, Hays, Burnetts and Leslies – also left an inheritance of truly astonishing architectural richness.

RCAHMS

Above *Rural grandeur: the House of Fetternear.* Below *Kildrummy: the great donjon*

Shepherd

In this process the external view was always important to Aberdeenshire, whether imposed unavoidably as in the Anglo-Norman motte-and-bailey castles, or, later, looking out and far afield to northern Europe and France. This view could come in several ways, from the activities of adventurers such as Alexander Stewart, Earl of Mar, who, with Robert Davidson, the *warlike* Provost of Aberdeen, ran a most efficient piracy operation on Dutch vessels in the North Sea during the early 15th century, to *Danzig Willie* himself, William Forbes of Craigievar, who, by early in the 17th century, had amassed a fortune from the Baltic trade, or the classic north-east scholar-soldier General Patrick Gordon of Auchleuchries, who died in 1699, *the Emperor of all the Russias watching and weeping over the deathbed ...*

Castle Country has justly been adopted as the slogan of Aberdeenshire. It refers to such early, outstanding fortalices as the vast enceinte of Kildrummy or the gaunt, enduring towers of Dunnideer and Hallforest, and, perhaps less appositely, to the exuberant, inspiring chateaux of the Renaissance which punctuate this landscape. These include *concealed* Midmar, *majestic* Craig, *sublime* Craigievar, *ethereal* Udny, and, above all, *grandiloquent* Fraser, as well as the clusters of mock-military mansions of the later 16th and 17th centuries such as Auchanachie, Davidston, Glenbucket. The work of two important families of master masons can be traced at the best of these: the Bels, George (Midmar), I [John] (Fraser), and David (Pitfichie); and Thomas Leper, who having worked at Fraser in 1565 was also responsible for Tolquhon's palace-plan in the 1580s, and James Leper (Castle Fraser) in 1614. The grandest Aberdeenshire palace is, of course, the consummate block at Huntly, but Monymusk also has considerable style. Here, and at Tolquhon, were pleasaunces, the forerunner of the great garden at Pitmedden. In all an extraordinary range of Aberdeenshire lairds' responses to new fashions and caprices, met often with subtlety and joy.

Religious life is perhaps rather less well represented, but such pre-Reformation traces that do survive as Auchindoir or Monymusk retain a distinct serenity. There are many ruined survivors of the simple rectangular kirks of the 16th and 17th centuries but the population increase of the 18th century was followed by a tideline of country kirks, c.1790-1800, dedicated to preaching, augmented a generation later by Free Kirk boxes.

The style and prosperity of the bygone rural clergy are clearly visible in the many manses (cf Tullynessle, Keig or Tarves) which regularly outshine the adjacent kirks in grace and comfort (although the best kirks, eg Kildrummy, Tough, Glass, Bourtie are bright,

Shepherd

Castle Fraser: a Bel achievement

RCAHMS

Left *A muckle kirk: Blairdaff before its gutting*. Below *Methlick manse, refined display*

Aberdeenshire Council

Shepherd

Above *Fintray burial vault*
Right *Improvement archetype: East Lochside, Skene*

tranquil and ageless). In the classic country triumvirate of laird, minister and dominie, much less of an income gap often separated the laird from the minister than divided the minister from the teacher who was often made session clerk to eke out his salary.

Other characteristic features of Aberdeenshire kirkyards include mortsafes (of a particular Aberdeenshire type) and watchhouses and burial vaults indicating the impact of resurrectionists servicing the medical school in Aberdeen. It is unfortunate that so many fine 18th-century slabs should still be in danger of damage and disappearance beneath the mulch of over-enthusiastic grass-cutting.

RCAHMS

***The natives of this county** are regarded throughout Scotland as an unusually active, vigorous, and enterprising race of men. Many of them emigrate to the south, and pursue the road to prosperity with great success.*
R Forsyth, *The Beauties of Scotland*, 1806

To many Aberdeenshire lairds Improvement became a system almost as strict as that of any monastic rule. Its two 18th-century pillars locally, who had a national impact, were James Anderson of Monkshill, Udny, and Sir Archibald Grant of Monymusk. By 1877 at the eponymous holding of Drumdelgie the tenant and his father had *reclaimed 450 acres, built 11 miles of stone dykes and laid endless tile drains.* For the poorer tenantry, that is the great majority, any spare money went into the farm and then the steading, hence the modesty of most 19th-century farmhouses.

The population increased markedly during the first three decades of the 19th century. The wealth generated from Improvement during the 18th and 19th century helped to pay for the construction of many new mansions, classical (Haddo, Wardhouse, Williamston, Thainstone, Whitehaugh) as well as the more expected baronial (Auchmacoy, Candacraig, Cluny, Breda). These were created by noteworthy architects such as, locally, John and William Smith, Archibald Simpson, A M and A G R Mackenzie and, nationally, William Adam, William Burn, and G E Street.

The rural slump of the 1870s was prolonged, some would claim until the 1950s, and the great houses suffered as a consequence: Fetternear 1919, Lessendrum c.1920, Newe 1950, Fintray and Tonley 1952 and Wardhouse 1950s.

Classical elegance: Thainstone House

Aberdeenshire Council

A curious but none the less welcome local phenomenon, one of conspicuous consumption, has been the boom in tower-house restoration during the 1970s and 1980s – Harthill, Leslie, Midmar, Tillycairn, Pitfichie and Terpersie.

The district had been traversed by important through-routes from earliest times: Aberdeen-Inverness, Deeside-Donside-Moray / Banff. The 19th century saw the development of turnpikes, the Aberdeen / Inverurie canal and several railways. The early iron bridges are particularly important and especially vulnerable to inappropriate *restorations* by insensitive roads engineers.

Buildings of the 20th century are currently less memorable, although there are a few Arts & Crafts gems such as Place of Tilliefour and Tillyhashlach, an important series of granite war memorials marking the apogee of Aberdeen granite carving and a small number of Modern Movement Buildings, the largest of which, Inverurie Hospital, is quite exceptional. There are also several good examples of council-house building in local stone on a generous scale in Inverurie and Huntly.

Post-war, the picture is skewed by the, to all intents and purposes, new town at Westhill and the oil-related expansion stoking up, steroid-like, Aberdeen and *twal mile round*. Some buildings of wit and character have emerged, such as the Dowell Schlumberger Technology Centre at Westhill and the Archaeolink Prehistory Centre at Oyne. The area has also benefited from the presence of the Scottish Sculpture Workshop at Lumsden, the Council's enlightened *Percent for Art* policy and its biennial Design Awards.

Despite the thistles and ragwort of modern set-aside, the alien iridescence of rape or the sub-urbanising tendencies of housing developers, the settled landscape of Donside and Strathbogie remains bewitching. It is still possible to be transfixed by the perfect conjunction of building and setting – whether a noble house such as Udny, set about with greenery, a quiet kirk on a sunny brae, Bourtie, or the Square in Huntly, a symphony of practical grace. There is much to discover and to savour in *this most architectural shire*.

Shepherd

Aberdeenshire Council

Top *Garlogie tollhouse*
Above *Arts & Crafts, Ramornie, Ellon*

Below *Dowell Schlumberger Technology Centre, Westhill*
Bottom *Archaeolink Prehistory Centre*

Shepherd

Shepherd

Late baronial: Beaton Hall, Methlick

New buildings
Reference is made to 15 new buildings that have been erected since the first edition of this guide (Gordon: 1994). They are described in the margins and identified in the captions by a lower case letter in order to allow their locations to be established by reference to the end map (page 224). Many of the buildings won awards in the biennial Aberdeenshire Council Design Awards.

Organisation of the Guide

This guide follows the ancient provinces of the north-east, Strathbogie, Mar, including Midmar and Formartine, and the Garioch. It begins in the capital of Strathbogie, Huntly, and proceeds first down the Deveron into Forgue and Cairnie and then up the Bogie to Rhynie. The area around Insch and Kennethmont is then described. The great axis formed by the River Don is followed from west to east, from Upper Strathdon down to Alford and Keig. Moving north of the Bennachie range, the Garioch, with its capital, Inverurie, is examined followed by the remainder of the area flanking the Lower Don from Kintore west to Cluny then south by Midmar and Skene. The final sections take in Oldmeldrum and the eastern lands of Formartine, embracing Tarves, Methlick, Ellon and Logie-Buchan on the Ythan, Belhelvie on the coast and, at last, Newmachar.

Text Arrangement

Entries give the name, address, date and architect (if known). Generally, dates given are those of the design of the building (if known). Text in the small column illustrates the history or character of Aberdeenshire.

Map References

References in the index refer to page numbers; numbers on maps to numbers against building entries in the text. Maps are intended to be used as a guideline only.

Access

Although many of the buildings described are public and easily accessible, many are private. Readers are asked to respect that privacy.

Sponsors

The support of Aberdeenshire Council, the Russell Trust, the Landmark Trust and the Heritage Lottery Fund through the Royal Commission on the Ancient and Historical Monuments of Scotland and the Recording Your Heritage Online project, is gratefully acknowledged.

The Improvement landscape: Monymusk

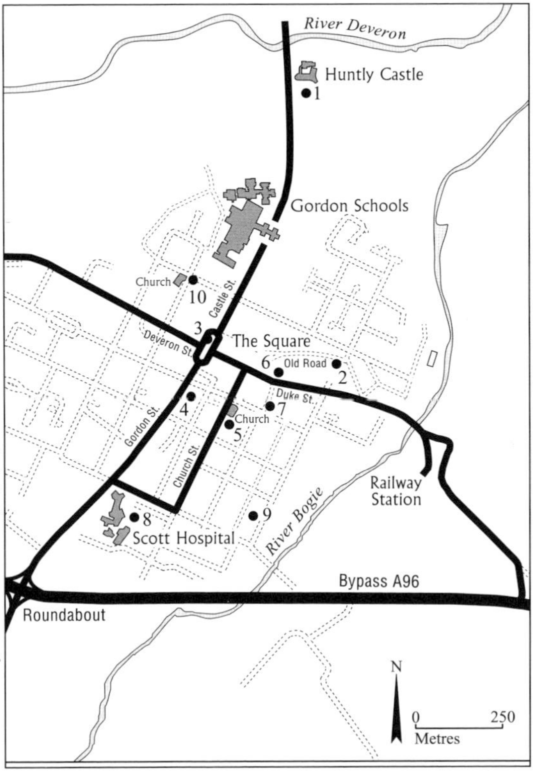

Reproduced from Ordnance Survey based mapping on behalf of HMSO. © Crown copyright 2006. All rights reserved. Ordnance Survey Licence number GD03127G/01/06.

***Vpon the River of Dovern** ar castelis, Touris, palices and gentil menis places nocht few, in quhilkes ar cheif and Principal, Strathbolgie, the principal place of the Erle of Huntley and Rothemay...*
Bishop Leslie (1578) in P Hume Brown, *Scotland before 1700 from contemporary documents*, Edinburgh, 1893

HUNTLY

Huntly is hill-girt and river-wrought: the rivers Bogie and Deveron enclose two sides of the town which lies in a wide bowl of rolling, upland country. It stands athwart two major routeways: that from Strathdon to the coast and the east/west one from Aberdeen to Moray, and takes it name from the Gordons of Huntly, who hailed from Berwickshire and from whom, in 1445 or 1449, the first Earl of Gordon was created. The third Earl, Alexander, received, in 1506, a charter which confirmed him in his lands as long as his *chief messuage be named the Castle of Huntly.* This is therefore the heart of Gordon country, the family who were the major Catholic landowners in late medieval Scotland, and a source of inspiration and grief in equal measures. Created a burgh of barony in 1545, the regular grid-plan derives from the 1776 scheme of the Duke of Gordon.

There are so many Huntlys – the castle complex by the Deveron, the old town straggling up the hill from the Bogie, the grand

Huntly in its bowl

Shepherd

Symbols on the grand doorpiece ascend in importance from the lintel bearing four shields: Huntly, monogram of first Marquess and his wife; his father-in-law's arms (Lennox) and the date 1602. Above are the achievements of the first Marquess and Marchioness of Huntly; then James VI and his wife, Anne of Denmark; in the square panel above were the Five Wounds of Christ with the Resurrection in the oval. Over all stood the warrior archangel, Michael. In 1640 covenanting iconoclasm removed these symbols of Gordon's Catholicism. The noble fireplace in the palace block repeats this hierarchical arrangement: Huntly, Lennox, James VI and I, sacred symbols, while the one in the lady's great chamber bears portrait medallions of George, first Marquess, and Henrietta Stewart.

Glory in you is like the Sun which giues
Eternall splendour, yet is often hid,
Ore-shadow'd in some clime, when yet he liues
Reviving still: the world cannot forbid
Glory, her beams: but like fires hid in night.
Expresle at last a more refulgent light
Grace then the Muses, who can giue you light
Oblivion it selfe can never hide,
Respect those sacrifices, by whose might,
Demigods soone are wholly Deifide:
Onely giue pardon to me who can giue
Nothing else yet, to make you longer liue.

Acrostic to the *Right Honorable and Noble George Lord Gordon sonne and heire to the Right Generous and Potent, the Marquess of Huntley by* Abraham Holland, 1622

Above right *The majestic frontispiece*
Below *Huntly: Gordon splendour*

RCAHMS

new burgh with its eclectic square, surrounded by solid, often rather fine 19th-century development, with the modern expansion to the west and south.

Historic Scotland

1 **Huntly Castle**, from 12th century
A radiant phoenix among the castles of Aberdeenshire, it began life in the 12th century with the building of the Peel of Strathbogie, an earth and timber castle revetted by a great wall at its base which sheltered Robert Bruce during the Wars of Independence; the motte is still visible. By about 1400, a massive L-plan stone tower was begun as a replacement. This tower was burnt by the Earl of Moray as part of the contest between James II and his unruly subject, the Black Douglas. A grand castle, it saw many visits from royalty, including the attendance, in January 1496, of James IV at the marriage between the pretender to the throne of Henry VII, Perkin Warbeck, and Lady Catherine Gordon, *the White Rose of Scotland*. This *great olde tower* was eventually destroyed internally in 1594, in retaliation for a revolt of the sixth Earl.

In 1550, George Gordon, fourth Earl and Chancellor of Scotland, visited France with Mary of Guise, James V's widow; by 1556, his *new wark*, a grand palace-block (fr *palatium*, hall), perhaps drawing inspiration from this visit, had been created on the south side of the courtyard. Following the fatal encounter, for George and one of his sons, with Queen Mary at Corrichie on the Hill o' Fare (1562), Huntly, which, being a Gordon house, had become the focus of Roman Catholic opposition to the Reformation, was damaged and looted; the treasures carried off included the silk tent in which Edward II had slept before Bannockburn, given by Robert Bruce to St Machar's Cathedral in Aberdeen; other furnishings went to the Kirk o' Field, the house in Edinburgh where the Queen's husband, Lord Darnley, was mysteriously murdered.

This was but a temporary set-back for this resilient, exuberant family which, in the century between 1540 and 1640, counted as the richest in Scotland. George Gordon, the sixth Earl, who was created first Marquess of Huntly in 1599 (after a period abroad following his injudicious rebellion in 1594), completed the palace, his *full fayre house* by 1606. This is the chief delight of Aberdeenshire, the château of the Gordons, Cocks o' the North, and a splendidly sophisticated place. An immense inscription commemorating the marriage of George to Lady Henrietta Stewart is triumphantly emblazoned across the whole 17.7 metre width of the upper works, framing a range of delicate oriel windows (1599-1602) inspired by the Chateau of Blois – all in glorious rose-red ashlar. Within is the finest heraldic doorway in the UK and a range of finely carved fireplaces. (The oriels themselves became the inspiration, 300 years later, for the wing constructed by that latter-day self-aggrandiser, Alexander Forbes Leith at Fyvie (see *Banff & Buchan* in this series).

Within the great palace and set over the earlier vaulted basement and dank prisons are a ground floor devoted to kitchen, service cellars and, within the huge round tower, the steward's suite from which access to the lord's private chamber above could be had. The two principal floors, which are approached by a ceremonial staircase entered from the heraldic doorpiece, comprise a progressively more private sequence of chambers, the lord's on the first floor, his lady's above, ending in the great bedroom stack of the south-west round tower.

Further work was carried out in the early 1640s, for the second Marquess, by George Thomson, who had been responsible for rebuilding the *imperial crown* on the tower of King's College, Aberdeen (see *Aberdeen* in this series). Inevitably standing for the King's party in the troubles of the Civil War, Huntly was occupied by the Covenanters in 1640, held by Montrose against Argyll in 1644 and, in 1647, starved into surrender, the garrison being exterminated. Gordon himself was taken in December 1647, housed briefly in his chateau and beheaded in Edinburgh.

Thereafter, its history was one of neglect and patronised decline until *rescued by antiquarian* sentiment last century (colour page 25).
Historic Scotland; open to the public

Historic Scotland

The grand doorpiece

***Near to the village** stands Huntly-castle, the ancient seat of the Gordon family, whose chief residence has long been at Gordon Castle, near Fochabers .... The first-mentioned is a large building, but has nothing that merits a particular description.*
Francis Douglas, *A general description of the east coast of Scotland from Edinburgh to Cullen*, Paisley, 1782

RCAHMS

Gordon Schools

Houses in Huntly at one time were called *The Rawes* (being built in rows) as in the local proverb: *Ne'er misuse a Gordon in the Rawes o'Strathbogie.*

Below *Gordon Schools, 1930s style (built 1956) extension*
Bottom *Linden Centre*

Shepherd

Shepherd

From the castle the town is approached via a tree-lined avenue, leading to **Gordon Schools**, 1839-41, Archibald Simpson; 1888 additions, a Marshall Mackenzie (Matthews & Mackenzie), founded on the site of castle port by the Duchess of Gordon in memory of the fifth Duke; Simpson's work is serene and Jacobean, two storeys of ashlar sandstone, symmetrical about a centre pend arch crowned by an ogee-capped octagonal tower. Mackenzie's additions blend well (colour page 26).

Other buildings include, on west of avenue, old **Public School**, 1895, Marshall Mackenzie, with secondary department as addition by William Kelly, *c*.1912, strong, two-storey Tudor, with three asymmetrical gables to front, mullioned windows and heavy chimneys. Around this is wrapped a single-storey 1930s style (built 1956) extension with good granite bow and a two-storey hall with tall concrete pilasters. Latest building is a discrete three-storey flat-roofer, in creamy brick and glass.

On east side of avenue, the **Linden Centre**, 1903, R G Wilson, a goodly granite ashlar block, three bays to street, the second-floor centre a triple window with three elongated voussoirs; the south front has two gabled triple bays and centre door.

The old town or Tillysoul, the village in whose celebrated inn Huntly was arrested. Tirriesoul or Tilliesoul: 3 July 1545, Earl George had charter under the Great Seal by which *Villa de Tirriesoul* was erected into a burgh of barony.
Old Road, the ancient, narrow main street, winds, canyon-like, up the ridge from the river;

essentially small scale, it has an antique feel, as if the (mostly 19th-century) houses were cleft into the hill.

2 **32 Old Road**, 18th century
Characteristic squared granite blocks with cherry-cocking, two storeys and attic with small widely spaced windows and coped chimney. Swept dormers recent. Link to earlier, single-storey cottage with tiny windows in gable; very serene.

RCAHMS

Police Station, 5-11 Castle Street, 1930s
Subtle, elongated granite ashlar two-storey front to street with two end bays set back by splays, having symmetrical-but-offset array of openings at centre.

20, 22 Castle Street, 1793
Two-storey, four-window house in dark granite cut large and square, Huntly-style. Semi-elliptical pend arch.

30 Castle Street, late 18th century
Strong blocks of granite ashlar and small windows give sense of age and solidity to this house. Renovated, 1984.

Shepherd

30 Castle Street

A very pleasant village ... *It has a clean, beautiful, thriving look, and without asking a single question, one can see that manufactures are carried on in it to a very considerable amount annually.* Linen manufacture was introduced about 45 years ago by an Irishman, Hugh Mackveagh, and silk stockings *made from the waste purchased from the silk and silk gauze weavers. They manufacture the finest silk into knee-garters, mitts and breeches-pieces. They have also a small tannery and a manufacture of white and brown threads.*
Francis Douglas, *A general description of the east coast of Scotland from Edinburgh to Cullen*, Paisley, 1782

Huntly *is now a place of no particular manufactures and the trade is merely local and confined to the immediate neighbourhood. The town appears to be rapidly declining ...*
Pigot's *Directory*, 1837

Left 32 *Old Road*
Below 5-11 *Castle Street*

Shepherd

The Square in the late 19th century

By 1900 *[Huntly] had four woollen mills, a hosiery factory and a large agricultural implements manufacturer. It served a wide area as a market and shopping centre, attracted many holiday visitors, and enjoyed the patronage of the Dukes of Richmond and Gordon.*
S Wood, *The Shaping of 19th-century Aberdeenshire, 1985*

3 **The Square** in Huntly is one of the most pleasing townscapes in Scotland. It has a lived-in, human yet gracious feel which derives in part from the mix of granites and other local stones which catch the steely northern light, but mostly from the outstanding combination of grandeur (Clydesdale Bank), novelty (Gordon Arms) or sheer Gothic exuberance (Brander Library) of the buildings themselves. Most typical are plain, Georgian houses in coursed granite with cobbled pends and flagstoned area to rear. Many of the later Huntly houses are good, restrained two-storey, three-window affairs, like their country cousins, the Improvement farmhouses; quietly rewarding.

Duke of Richmond Statue, The Square, 1862, Alexander Brodie
A sandstone duke, the fifth, standing, side-whiskered and robed on tall, squared battered plinth, with red granite panels erected *as a memorial of Charles Gordon Lennox, fifth Duke of Richmond by the tenantry of the Lordship of Huntly, 1862.*

Clydesdale Bank

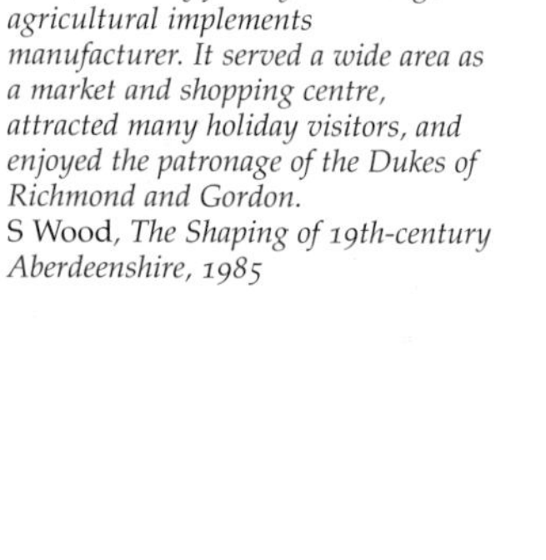

Clydesdale Bank, 2 The Square
Gordon Street, 1842, Archibald Simpson
Accomplished granite ashlar North of Scotland Bank on a prominent corner site. Two strong, sophisticated facades – that to Gordon Street has a complex, three-arched centre with four windows above; that to the Square, three windows, central door with chimney gable over comprising alternating podia and panels in a powerful, tiered arrangement.

3 The Square (Boyds)
Striking two-storey-and-attic, massive granite ashlar building, glazed for shop, the mansard carried between heavy skews with ball finials and the single ground-floor window set between tall rusticated, round-headed pilasters.

Fountain, The Square, 1882
Erected in memory of James Robertson, Bank Agent, Huntly, b.20 January 1789, d.4 February 1877, by his widow, the fountain consists of a square bullfaced granite plinth which carries on each side a polished granite basin and which supports four polished granite colonnettes enclosing keystone arches. Moulded crown above all: trying much too hard.

7 The Square, 1885
Classically granite; only four ground-floor pilasters survive of original scheme. First floor rises to cornice and parapet with ball-finial ends and small centre pediment with bull's eye. Additions of slated mansard; four round-headed dormers.

8 The Square
Four diagonally shafted chimneys on the front of a restrained three-storey-and-attic, four-window granite ashlar block.

Post Office, 15/16 The Square, 1934-5, Ministry of Works
Tall, limpid three-storey, five-window in granite ashlar. Ground floor channelled with two Doric columns at door; coped chimneys. Altogether a clever, eclectic blend for its date.

Brander Library, 1883-5, J Rhind
A narrow, high and ship-like neo-Perpendicular confection in granite with Auchindoir freestone dressings. Four-light mullioned window in entrance gable to Square. Grand staircase and library hall with open timber roof. The result of a gift to his native town by William Brander Esq of London.

Huntly Hotel, 18 The Square, late 19th century
The impression of overflowing the site comes from being partly set back behind the front of No 22 and the extensive use of sandstone dressings and glazing which creates a very open frontage. Two storeys in coursed granite

Below *Post Office*
Middle *Brander Library*
Bottom *Huntly Hotel*

Shepherd

Shepherd

Shepherd

with large splayed three-storey corner block rising to octagonal turret. Four double bays to Square and Castle Street; individually fine, but rather uncoordinated details.

22 & 23 The Square, mid/late 18th century
Two storeys with four bays, one of which is a cobbled pend with keystoned arch, in regularly coursed granite. Mansard attic part of restoration for sheltered housing, 1980s, by Gordon District Council.

Shepherd

24 & 30 The Square

24 & 30 The Square, (?) *c*.1760
For William Forsyth. A real feeling of age flows from this three-storey, six-window facade to the Square with its moulded centre pend arch (now door) and serene semicircular wallhead gable with chimney, all in good granite ashlar.

26 The Square, *c*.1870
Improbable painted granite shop and flats, first-floor windows framed by continuous hood-mould, with dentated cornice above and dormers and cast-iron ridge cresting above them. Moulding and angle-turret confection with weather vane carry building round corner into Deveron Street to terminate in a one-bay gable frontage.

Gordon's Temperance Hotel (site),
The Square, late 18th/early 19th century
Now gone; formed a high, bold corner to Deveron Street. Began suitably severe in squared granite, three windows to ground, two to first, but at attic level broke out into monumental chimney head subsequently

The Square in the 19th century, Temperance Hotel at second right

NESLS

flanked by extravagantly glazed, insect-eyed, canted dormers (similar to those on corner of Deveron Street and George Street). A great loss.

32 The Square, earlier 19th century
Thackstanes at bases of chimneys reveal humbler origins for this simple granite house. Altered to bar, 1984.

RCAHMS

Gordon Arms Hotel

Gordon Arms Hotel, 32A The Square, late 19th century
Large hotel in coursed, dressed granite dominated by canted five-light projecting bay window above central porch; stringcourse between first and second floors becomes parapet of bay and also supports semicircular plaque with re-used crest.

The centre of the second floor is slightly advanced and rises through the eaves to form a truncated pyramid roof with a cast-iron crown. Three tiny hipped dormers and vestigial angle turrets: getting better as it ascends.

1 Gordon Street, *c.*1844
Two storeys of sturdy granite ashlar; turns corner by means of a convex angle corbelled to square at the wallhead and a blocking course. Elaborate, upswept chimney gable with two stringcourses on frontage, nodding to Simpson's Clydesdale Bank chimney gable.

Gordon Street

Shepherd

Nos 7-11 Gordon Street, early 19th century
Very plain granite ashlar, with four windows at first floor and rectangular fanlight on centre door.

Stewart's Hall, 15-17 Gordon Street, 1875, James Anderson
Solid Victorian shop frontages and plain first

Shepherd

Above *Stewart's Hall*
Right *23-25 Gordon Street*

floor transfixed by improbable four-storey tower with corbelled angle turrets and truncated pyramid roof, all built in Syllavethy granite with freestone dressings from Rhynie; hall for 650 within. Rebuilt after fire, 1886/7, Matthews & Mackenzie; the bequest of Alexander Stewart, a local solicitor.

21 Gordon Street, Nelson Street, *c*.1840
Very spare, pleasing treatment of both corner frontages, particularly in the broad pedimented gable to Gordon Street. Fine granite ashlar with curved corner corbelled to square at first floor. Dormers late.

Shepherd

4 **23-25 Gordon Street**, *c*.1819,
(?) Archibald Simpson
It is not clear why George Lawson built such an imposing building with seven arched ground-floor windows to Gordon Street. Above them, ashlar takes over, rising to a strong cornice and blocking course; the whole has neo-Greek overtones, very swank. Altered for bank, 1874, J R Mackenzie.

Bank of Scotland

Shepherd

Bank of Scotland, 2 Gordon Street, 1863, William Henderson
Finely detailed two-storey, three-window Georgian anachronism in finely jointed granite ashlar, very calm, with consoled doorpiece and blocking course.

Crown Bar, Gordon Street, 1898
Spirited frontage in narrow courses of grey granite, entrance on splayed corner with curvilinear return to square over; prominent band courses between floors, rising to bold modified Dutch gable.

10 & 14 Gordon Street, early 19th century
Both corner sites, No 10, two storeys of vigorously cut granite ashlar and a curved corner. **No 14** turns corner neatly into Granary Street by means of one-window door curve, slightly recessed.

Shepherd

Huntly Business Centre, 2000, Acanthus Douglas Forrest (colour page 25)

Shepherd

61 Gordon Street

59-61 Gordon Street, mid/late 18th century
No 59 four-window, door asymmetrical with scrolled pediment and pilasters and pedimented gable over; **No 61**, a four-window cottage intriguingly adorned with Gibbs surround to door, quoined and keystoned windows and quoins at angles. Swept modern dormers sympathetic.

Huntly Business Centre, 85 Gordon Street
High and narrow former mill in squared granite with three-storey, seven-bay (each window double) face to Gordon Street and bull-faced pilasters linking first and second floors; deep, timbered eaves beneath piend roof. Converted 2000, Acanthus Douglas Forrest.

5 **Parish Church**, Church Street, 1805, Alexander Laing
Big version of that at Dysart, Fife (see *The Kingdom of Fife* in this series). On truly massive scale (seating for 1800), a huge, rough ashlar pediment-gabled rectangle with four round-arched windows and central Roman Doric pedimented doorway on each main side. West gable has deeply recessed central doorway with windows in arched recesses on either side and a tripartite lunette in the pediment. Minuscule bellcote emphasises the size of the rest of this great footprint of Presbyterianism. (Design for hall and west tower by Marshall Mackenzie but only part of hall built, 1927.)

Below *North door of Kirk*
Bottom *The gigantic Parish Kirk*

Shepherd

Shepherd

Shepherd

George Macdonald, the *fairy-tale teller, poet and preacher* was born at No 41 Duke Street on 10 December 1824. The author of *The Princess and the Goblin* and *At the Back of the North Wind* and other adult fantasies, such as *Castle Warlock, Robert Falconer and Alec Forbes of Howglen*. After reading *Phantasies,* C S Lewis claimed that *he never wrote another word without Macdonald in mind.* By the time of his death in 1905, aged 81, he had written 31 novels, six children's books and numerous poems and theological works.

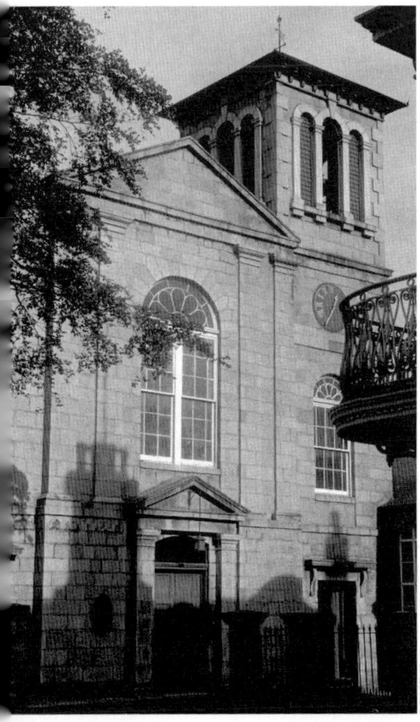
RCAHMS

6 & 8 Church Street, early 19th century
Impressively solid two-storey and basement houses in muscular ashlar with cherry-cocking on **No 6** which also has steps into arched central doorpiece, iron gate and detached coach house. **No 8** has neat door with rectangular fanlight and steps; wing *c.*1900.

Granary, Granary Street, late 18th century
Quiet two-storey, seven-bay building in grey granite rubble with pink granite dressings and quoins; openings chamfered. Altered in later 19th century for use as hall.

Sheltered Housing, Granary Street, 1977, G R M Kennedy & Partners
On either side of street, those on north particularly pleasing: low, harled, well-articulated little houses with pitched roofs and stepped fronts to courtyard. (Southern examples were refurbished, the northern ones are new build.)

1-5 Duke Street, *c.*1760
Lift the eyes above the modern shop front to see a neat echo of Nos 24, 26 The Square. Two storeys, three-window granite ashlar with semicircular wallhead gable. First-floor window recent too.

43-45 Duke Street, *c.*1840
A fine two-storey, three-window house in dark, squared local stone and droved freestone dressings. Architraved and consoled doorpiece.

6 **Strathbogie Parish Church**, 1840-1
Built as a result of the Marnoch case (see *Banff & Buchan* in this series), the precursor of the Disruption. Became Free Church on the occasion of the Disruption. Large harled rectangle with squared granite front set with paired Doric pilasters and a pediment. New front and offset Italianate tower, 1862, James Matthews; original glazing; later **hall** projects to street with plain pediment and round-headed windows echoing church. An excellent ensemble.

1 & 1A Bogie Street, 1907
Edwardian splendour for pair of shops and dwellings. Three storeys mansarded above five bays of granite ashlar. Doric columns to pair of centre doors; at first floor, deep balcony runs full length of building enclosing canted outer

bays; above, and separated by heavy eaves cornice, are two more canted outer bays flanking a centre wallhead comprising a hipped and corniched chimney with datestone. Fine cherry-cocked granite masonry laid in Aberdeen bond with shaped gable to Macdonald Street.

Shepherd

RCAHMS

Top *1 & 1A Bogie Street*
Above *The Cottage*
Left *Christ Church Episcopal*

58 Bogie Street, 1793
Dated at skew ends, but looks older, supporting title deeds of 1745/6. Two-storey, three windows in pinned roughly squared rubble. Small, widely spaced windows, coped chimneys and stone roof-ridge, the whole clinging tightly to the escarpment above the flood plain.

The Cottage, Queen Street, *c*.1835
Just what its name implies: delightfully retiring and unspoilt, harled with margins under a low-pitched, broad-eaved roof.

RCAHMS

7 **Christ Church Episcopal**, Provost Street, 1848, Thomas Mackenzie
Attractively simple nave and chancel with tall narrow lancets, porch at south-west and octagonal spirelet. Harled with fine freestone dressings including corbel course, gabled skewputs and bellcote.

8 **Scott's Hospital**, Gladstone Road, 1901, A Marshall Mackenzie
Fronts earlier symmetrical group by William Smith, 1853, 1860,1868 in harled Scots Baronial which includes pair of circular towers with conical slated roofs with pronounced bell-cast. (Built from bequest of Alexander Scott of Craibstone House for the maintenance of aged men and women.) Ambitious symmetrical design in Scots-Perpendicular. Centre block dominated

Opposite: Top *Church Street*
Bottom *Strathbogie Parish Church*

Scott's Hospital

by square crenellated *porte-cochère* tower in his Marischal College (see *Aberdeen* in this series) manner. Two-storey advanced wings. In roughly squared granite blocks of varying size with Auchindoir freestone dressings (colour page 26).

9 **Howglen**, Gladstone Road, 1898, F W Troup
Subtle Arts & Crafts villa, harled with dressings (including rugged, freestone quoins to windows) and gently rounded angles. Slates hung on upper two-thirds of gable and on gable bay cantilevered to road. Timber porch and bay, chimney diamond plan. Gently captivating.

Right *Howglen*
Below *War Memorial*

War Memorial, off West Park Street, *c.*1920, Frank Troup
Unusual, largely successful elongated octagon of square piers carrying an entablature from which rises a graceful obelisk. Screens with names between piers.

Balvenie House, 3 West Park Street, *c.*1835
Plain, harled house, two-storey, three-window with margins and skewputs, with slightly incongruous pedimented porch.

18-33 West Park Street, *c.*1930
In gritty sandstone, single-storey and tremendously sturdy council houses.

Shepherd

Left *West Park Street*
Below *St Margaret's RC Church*

RCAHMS

2-60 East Park Street, *c.*1930s
Salmon-pink sandstone, two-storey council housing formed into three-bay semi-detached houses with two cheerful pre post-modern eaves gablets to each block.

10 **St Margaret's RC Church**, 1834,
Rt Revd James Kyle
The ornate Spanish baroque tower (three stages – console scrolls at base, on portico-like ashlar front, rising through square tower to concave-sided belfry topped by console crown) throws out an exotic invitation which is not denied by the saucer-domed interior of the rubble-built octagon behind it. Beneath its lunette windows are seven contemporary Spanish religious paintings given by John Gordon of Wardhouse (qv) whose Spanish connections account for this efflorescent building. It is thought that William Robertson may have assisted with the working drawings, judging by the anta capitals of the tower; *c.*1902 altarpiece and stencilled decoration.

The original neo-Greek altarpiece is in the adjacent corbie-stepped, rough coursed granite **Presbytery House**, a solidly impressive two-storeyed rectangle. Five and four tall window pediments rise above the wallheads.

St John's Lodge, Meadow Street,
late 18th century
Former RC Chapel: very plain, low rectangle in rough granite; single round-headed window in gable (now blocked) and chamfered door jambs. Modern extension.

Top *A Huntly archetype: Mill House, 20 Deveron Street*
Above *27-31 Deveron Street*

20 Deveron Street, late 18th century
Known as the Mill House until its precipitate demolition in 1992, L-plan, in strong squared granite blocks; two windows to street, two storeys; entirely characteristic of Huntly and sadly mourned.

27-31 Deveron Street,
late 18th century / early 19th century
No 27 is late 18th century, a plain two-storey, three-window shop and house in granite ashlar with chamfered openings and a good pend arch. Note thackstanes and regrettable modern roof. **No 29**, early 19th century, in strong ashlar granite, with two storeys and attic and basement, originally had two doors to the street; steps up to surviving door. Band course between basement and ground floor. **No 31**, early 19th century, distinguished by semicircular pend arch in fine granite ashlar.

3-5 Deveron Road, 1845, J & W Smith
Former police office and prison in squared granite; cottage-style with two symmetrical gablets to front and shafted chimneys: quietly engaging.

Strathbogie Manse

Strathbogie Manse, Deveron Road, 1852
In a muscular cottage-style, rising two storeys, asymmetrical with bay window, broad eaves and shafted chimneys.

Drill Hall, Deveron Road, late 19th century
Granite ashlar with pink (Auchindoir) freestone dressings and pronounced quoins,

RCAHMS

McKean

Shepherd

RCAHMS

Shepherd

Top *The great chimneypiece, Huntly Castle*
Middle *Huntly Business Centre*
Bottom *Auchanachie*
Top right *Huntly Castle, restoration of the Renaissance Palace by Charles McKean*
Above *The great façade, Huntly Castle*

Norman

Young

Above *Forbes Lodge, Strathdon, 2004, John & Marion Donald*
Below *Mitchell-Forbes Mausoleum, Strathdon*

Top *Scott's Hospital, Huntly*
Middle *Gordon Schools, Huntly*
Bottom *Limekiln, Glenbuchat*

RCAHMS

Shepherd

Greig

Norman

Shepherd

RCAHMS

Top *Morgan McVeigh's, Culsalmond*
Left *Auchincloch, Lumsden*
Below *St Margaret's Episcopal, Forgue*

RCAHMS

Clockwise from top *Palace block, Druminnor*
Mansefield Gallery, Clatt, an excellently understated steading conversion, 2002, Gordon Gauld
Tornahaish bridge on Military Road, Corgarff
Doorway at St Mary's, Auchindoir

Norman

Norman

Shepherd

comprising two-bay gable to street with square, crenellated tower and porch bay attached. *A Company 4th VBGH* (Volunteer Battalion Gordon Highlanders) in panel with architrave topped by ogee moulding.

Shepherd

Deveron Road contains a number of late but satisfying villas, including **The Beeches**, an ample house on a granite plinth with tripartite windows; **St Anne's**, a handsome two-storey, three-window (all tripartite) stone house having central expressed gable with bays and an ox-eye over; and **Conveth**, a very neat double-gabled house with original fenestration.

Aberdeenshire Council

Top *Drill Hall*
Above *68-96 George Street*

68-96 George Street, *c.*1991, George Bennet Mitchell & Son
Cheerful group of two-storey housing alternating between large cream-harled blocks and recessed ochre-harled links. The larger blocks have splayed corners with triangular wooden oriels balanced by grander oriels with low piended roofs. Good pend arch in middle.

Huntly Station, 1854, Alexander Gibb
For Great North of Scotland Railway, an unusual carpentry forest of trusses hanging above both platforms and stretching across the tracks. Erased 2001.

Huntly Station: 21st century anonymity

Norman

Battlehill Hotel, Aberdeen Road
Substantial, in squared granite with freestone dressings in a subdued baronial which runs to corbie-stepped gables and angle turrets.

Tollhouse, Aberdeen Road, early 19th century
Two-storeyed elongated octagon with tall chimney to road, like a little boat beached on the brae.

RCAHMS

Huntly Station: 19th century confidence

STRATHBOGIE

The parishes to the north of Huntly are truly on the road to nowhere in particular (apart from Forgue, for which Banff lies far up the road). They thereby have an atmosphere at once self-contained, compact and other-worldly. *Strathbolgie lykewyse, and the Gareoth as thay baith ar copious and welthie in cornes sa ar thay verie plesant in pastural, medowis, wodis and forrest fair.* Bishop Leslie (1578)

James Stuart (1813-77), the eminent antiquary *(Sculptured Stones of Scotland,* 1856) and Secretary of the Society of Antiquaries of Scotland, 1855-77, was born in Forgue.

11 FORGUE

The parish is all curves, a *fine alternation of vales and hillocks, holms and knolls* (Groome), from whose planes the clear northern light is reflected back to the ever-changing sky. These little hills shelter a royal flush of mansions, some early and supremely Scots (Auchaber, Auchairnie, Boyne's Mill, Cobairdy, Corse, Drumblair House, Frendraught, Haddo, Mains of Bognie and Templeland). They, and the orderly farms and quiet kirks, fit well the varied contours of the place. Northern boundary is formed by winding River Deveron; much woodland.

Right *Forgue: St Margaret's Parish Kirk*
Below *St Margaret's, Forgue: 1674 monument to Alexander Garden*

Aberdeenshire Council

RCAHMS

(St Margaret's) Parish Kirk, 1819
On one of the characteristic knolls, above the road, stern Heritors' Gothic box in granite rubble enlivened by four circular windows high in south side and a projecting west gable with bellcote. Parts of the Frendraught Pew of 1638 retained inside its capacious interior: *900 sittings*. Sits in earlier kirkyard containing burial aisle of Morisons of Bognie which contains two good heraldic plaques: a re-used

Morison pediment and the remarkable be-thistled monument, 1674, to Alexander Garden (?Gordon), Professor of Philosophy in King's College, Aberdeen, and *pious, strict and blameless* minister of Forgue for 30 years, who *piously deposited his mortal remains, in the hope of happy resurrection* in this church. Interior recast 1872; organ 1872; hall 1885.

Richardson

Old Manse of Forgue

Old Manse of Forgue, 1830
At top of brae, incorporates mid-18th-century manse to north and minor alterations by J Duncan, 1887. Extensive harled double house with entry by narrow piended link at gable end. Plain U-plan steading of *c.*1825.

RCAHMS

Those [Improvement-period mansion houses] *perfectly express their time, which was comfortable, expansive, confident, a time of high prices, high rents, loyal tenants and cheap servants ... They exist in a timeless world like all good art and good workmanship. That is perhaps fair enough, for they were built for people who thought they had inherited the world and taken possession of eternity.*
J R Allan, *North-East Lowlands of Scotland,* 1952

Haddo House, *c.*1836, ?Archibald Simpson
Truly a marginal location, so close to the old county border that the walled garden, with its cracked doocot and brick walls, is in Banffshire. Set within decaying woodland, there is an air of systematic neglect about the three distinct, mostly roofless structures. A central three-storey rubble block, plain and perhaps of the 17th century, with, to the south, a T-plan Italianate mansion, harled with granite margins, deep eaves and an extravagant *porte-cochère* entrance tower, all very reminiscent of Simpson's Thainstone (see p.134). The third element, to the north, has twin curved gables and cruciform chimneys and is described as *offices,* although a grander, independent existence cannot be ruled out. The **Home Farm** of 1831 was once quadrangular but is now sadly *much altered and abused*; curved gabled entrance tower over arched pend.

Left *Haddo House*
Below *Home Farm, Haddo House*

Shepherd

St Margaret's Episcopal

Aberdeenshire Council

I am more and more astonished at the industry and skill of the Aberdeenshire people in smoothing and drying the horrible surface of their soil. It is the greatest triumph of man over nature, of obstinacy over moor and stones. Talk not of deserts, or swampe, or forests to these people.
Lord Cockburn, *Circuit Journeys*, 1888

St Margaret's Episcopal, 1856,
William Ramage
Sitting above and apart in its own beech-tree-lined graveyard, Early English nave and chancel in roughly squared granite, with fine, narrow, moulded lancets, solid buttresses and a sturdy, yet elegant, broach spire in fine ashlar rising from a tower at the north-east. Interior spare and pleasing with scissors roof truss and two-seat sedilia. Restored 1992. Attractive harled **Rectory** adjacent, a double house, with dramatic barge-boarded eaves, hood-moulded second-floor windows and a pedimented classical doorpiece between two ground-floor bay windows (colour page 27).

Parish Hall, 1884
Gifted by Walter Scott, Glendronach, a striking Tudor T-plan in squared granite, with sandstone much in evidence for the prominent stringcourse, mullions and transoms of the tall, rectangular windows, the coped chimneys and each corbie-stepped gable.

Boynsmill

Aberdeenshire Council

Boynsmill (Boyne's Mill) House,
Glendronach, 1771
Good L-plan stone house, northern portion dated from *W A (William Allardes /Allardyce)*

1771 datestone. In 1826 James Allardes founded the adjacent distillery and thereafter the house was recast in a pleasing cottage-style, dominated by gabled dormer heads and two clusters of diagonally shafted chimneys. South-east wing *c*.1835, altered internally 1964. **Glendronach Distillery**, folded into terrain, flanked by plain, low, 19th-century bonds and more recent buildings.

RCAHMS

Drumblair House, from 18th century
Unremarkable T-plan house elaborated in 1877 by the addition of pencil-thin angle towers and a crenellated central tower. An unhappy marriage of the vernacular and the Gothic. Two-storey circular **doocot** (18th century) in grounds; restored Mike Taitt, 2000.

Left *Drumblair House*
Below *Doocot, Drumblair House*
Bottom *Templeland Farmhouse*

Drumblair Lodge
(formerly Drumblair Cottage), *c*.1780
Retiring house given a radical makeover in the form of a single-storey entrance corridor between symmetrical twin advance wings with low-pitched roofs and shallow tripartite bows, all harled with freestone dressings and margins. Wings added *c*.1845, back wing 1902.

Aberdeenshire Council

Templeland Farmhouse,
from mid-18th century
Seat of the agricultural improver Lt Alexander Shand who acquired the estate in 1803 and became known as the *King of Forgue*. South part is earliest, with a later large central bow containing a staircase. The north-west wing, at right angles, is slightly later and the courtyard is completed by a single-storey laundry. All harled, forming quiet but picturesque group; walled garden. Lt Shand's father, who rose from the ranks of the Royal Artillery to become a full colonel, is commemorated on Hawk Hill by a ball-finial-topped obelisk on a tall inscribed base.

Aberdeenshire Council

Cottage Hospital, Templeland, 1875
Built by Mrs Morison of Bognie at wish of her husband, for patients resident in parishes of Forgue, Ythan-Wells, Auchterless and Inverkeithney; large cross in his memory erected by tenantry, 1876, in front.

Aberdeenshire Council

Place Mill, 1832
Just above the burn, a plain but satisfying two-storey L-plan with kiln having prominent *Aberdeenshire* vent (hexagonal with revolving cap) and neat egg-cup finials to gables; machinery removed.

RCAHMS

Top *Place Mill*
Above *Auchaber Manse*

Auchaber Manse, 1847, J & W Smith
Tall and remarkably unaltered: two storeys and attic, three-window harled house, with original glazing, railed steps to door and canted dormers. Commodious and suitably severe for a Free Kirk manse. **Church**, adjacent, very plain rectangle with round-headed windows and simple bellcote.

Auchaber House
The early 19th-century single-storey west wing with bow ends was converted into a farmhouse when most of this mansion was demolished in 1927.

Frendraught, on site of earlier castle, rebuilt 1656, recast *c*.1753, east wing *c*.1790/1800
An extended house of considerable complexity and charm. Two small chamfered windows in west gable appear to be oldest features, although cellars of this wing probably belong to the original ha'hoose, burnt in 1630. Fragments of the adjacent tower, demolished 1947, adhere to the east elevation. The 17th-century rebuild consists of an imposing seven-

Frendraught

Shepherd

window harled front with an ashlar-faced three-window centre slightly advanced and topped by a strong semicircular pediment. The porch (with 1688 datestone) was added when the angle tower was topped with battlements and bartizans, *c*.1832. Crowstepped offices to north of court, now neatly converted, 18th century or earlier. A Morison house since *c*.1690. Restoration began 1984.

Corse House, early 19th century, (?)Archibald Simpson
The symmetrical piend-roofed wings and the ashlar-fronted tripartite bays framing the wooden pedimented doorpiece on the ground floor lend an air of sophistication to this compact mansion. The earlier Corse House remains as the east wing of the **Home Farm**, rubble-built with blue ashlar dressings and corbie steps on north gable; dated 1733 from datestone.

Aberdeenshire Council

Cobairdy House, *c*.1855/60?, A & W Reid
A late Georgian Italianate survival comparable with Knockleith in Auchterless (see *Banff & Buchan* in this series), although larger and apparently somewhat earlier. Crisp two storeys harled with margins and a fine pedimented porch with broad-eaved gable.

Conzie Castle, 1699
A tall, gaunt and narrow ruin, the thinness of whose walls and the extent of whose rooms (four-window/four-storey) suggest a palace block rather than a castle.

Mains of Bognie, 17th century
A gem of restrained Scots design; a long low house foursquare in pinned boulder rubble, corbie-steps and coped chimneys. Built-up pend at north end with moulded arch; remains of oven. Large L-shaped walled garden.

James V visited Frendraught on 13 November 1535 and granted a charter to Sir James Crichton. In 1630 Crichton's grandson killed Gordon of Rothiemay and mortally wounded Gordon of Lesmore. The Marquess of Huntly arranged for him to pay a large sum to the relatives. Subsequently, one of Crichton's party seriously wounded a son of Leslie of Pitcaple in continuation of the feud. Leslie declined to accept any compensation and threatened to intercept Crichton's return from the Bog of Gycht (Gordon Castle, by Fochabers). The Marquess sent his own son, Viscount Melgund, Gordon of Rothiemay and six followers as an escort home with Frendraught in October 1630. The party reached Frendraught safely and the Gordons were invited to stay for the night; Viscount Melgund, Gordon of Rothiemay and four followers died in the fire that took hold during the night. According to the ballad, The *Fire of Frendraught*, Lady Frendraught cried:

It were great pity for good Lord John
But none for Rothiemay;
But the keys are casten in the deep draw-well,
Ye canna get away.

Crichton and his lady escaped blame, but John Meldrum, an old servant of Crichton's, was tried and executed in Edinburgh in August 1631. The *ashes and brynt bones* of the victims were gathered by the Gordons and buried at the Kirk of Gartly.

Above *Cobairdy*
Below *Mains of Bognie*

Shepherd

Battle of Slioch, 1307; sick Bruce, lying in a camp or place of *strinth* checked Comyns, thus leading to heirship [harrying] of Buchan, whose comprehensive savagery was remembered for generations:

Thafor in litter tha him lay
and till the Sleach held thar way,
And thocht that in that strinth to ly
Qhill passit war his malady
Barbour, *Brus*

12 **DRUMBLADE** is truly dispersed, having no village to provide a focus. The *extensive reclamations* to arable during the second half of the 19th century have created one of the most open, industrially farmed landscapes in the north-east. Not many semi-natural nor ancient areas survive, owing to assiduity of the improvers in removing cairns and standing stones. Happed among rolling cultivated slopes is a minuscule, dispersed kirkton, whose kirkyard stands at the edge of the drop to the burn.

Aberdeenshire Council

RCAHMS

Top *Drumblade Parish Kirk*
Above *Drumblade House*

Parish Church, 1773
Very plain harled box enlivened by cake confection of 1641 bellcote; original pulpit and gallery front retained in recast interior. Bissets of Lessendrum commemorated by mural tablets, including one to William, Lord Bishop of Raphoe, *d.*1834, whose cushion and mitre strike an exotic note. Some fine stones in kirkyard, including a winged soul of 1762 (although too many laid flat and disappearing under grass-cuttings). Renovated 1829, five rectangular windows reglazed with regrettable sub-floral glass, 1900.

Drumblade House (former manse), 1824
Among tall trees, in roughly squared granite, formerly harled, honest two-storey-and-attic, three-window house with little, piended single-storey wings. Attractive tripartite ground-floor windows, 1910; Free Church connections through one occupier, William Garden Blaikie, later Professor at New College and Moderator of Free Church, 1872. Also Robert James Brown, Professor of Greek at Marischal, 1827. Outbuildings, forming good group with the adjacent kirk, include bothy.

Lessendrum House, 1837, Archibald Simpson
Although now given up almost entirely to the

Lessendrum House

RCAHMS

ivy, the few diagonal chimneystacks that rise out of the remains of the 1928 fire, point to the vigour and wit of Simpson's *pocket Gothic ruin.* Remodelling a 17th-century house for the Bissets, *the oldest established line in all Aberdeenshire* with Norman roots, Simpson showed considerable freedom in providing a richly fenestrated two-storey house with a wealth of turrets', one ogee-capped like Newe Circular **doocot** with two rat courses; 18th or early 19th century.

Cocklarachy, mid-18th century
Good example of a large farm group showing the organic effects of Improvement. The two-storey L-plan back wing is probably mid-18th century, the three-window front, *c.*1800, and its substantial canted porch, *c.*1840. Walled garden and sizeable quadrangular steading, as well as farm chimney.

Kirkton Mill, 1792
Almost hidden against a steep slope, three solid storeys in rough granite, with small kiln attached. Iron overshot wheel and neat ball finials at gable. Conversion to dwelling 1994.

Greenhaugh Farmhouse, 1823
South front two storey with original joinery to door and three massive storeys to north.

HUNTLY PARISH

The two old parishes of Dunbennan and Kynoir (both prebends of Elgin Cathedral) were united before 1649. Both churches were used until 1725 when a central church was built in Huntly.

Dunbennan graveyard, late medieval
Peaceful site of former parish church, with some 18th- and early 19th-century gravestones.

Kirkton of Kinnoir graveyard, late medieval
On plain of Deveron; contains late 18th- and early 19th-century gravestones as well as several table tombs. Bell (1653) of former kirk moved to Kinnoir Mission Kirk.

Huntly Castle Hotel, from 1752,
back wing *c.*1832, 17th-century house within
The original part is the three-storey harled block with piend roof at the east end, formerly called Sandiestone. The *c.*1800 addition on the west in granite ashlar with four-window centre and canted bays is remarkably severe, almost

Norman
Cocklarachy farm chimney

Aberdeenshire Council
Cocklarachy

Aberdeenshire Council
Dunbennan graveyard

Top *Huntly Castle Hotel*
Middle *Castle Bridge*
Above *Avochie*

institutional, and was described as having *little regard to architectural beauty*. Archibald Simpson added the plain, harled rear wing with a simple architraved doorpiece in porch in 1832. Used by eldest son or dowager of Huntly Gordons (Lennoxes) and latterly by his factor. **Castle Bridge** over rock-cut Deveron, *c*.1800, Master Mason Elgin. Single semicircular rubble-built arch with ashlar voussoirs. Granite **icehouse**, also *c*.1800, beside large plain walled garden and, to the north, a circular **doocot** of *c*.1752, in pinned boulder rubble with red sandstone dressings, closely spaced nails bristling from joints and two tapered, sharply intaken rat courses. The conical slated roof is truncated by an oculus and there are stone and slate boxes and the remains of a possible potence within.

Binn Toll House, early 19th century
Single-storey rectangle, originally harled, with canted bay with strong coped chimney-centre; subsequently extended.

Avochie, 16th/early 17th century
Small rectangular mansion, now much depleted, with only east and west gables surviving. Had corbelled angle turret at south-east. Adjacent is **Avochie House**, pleasingly baronial, close by the river.

Right *Avochie House*
Below *Linnorie*

Linnorie, *c*.1805, additions 1856, James Matthews
Former Manse of Huntly, unusually detached from town, large L-plan single-storey-and-attic with attractive gabled dormer heads; originally harled to enhance quality of margins. Extensive offices.

13 CAIRNIE

Parish defined by rivers Deveron and Isla, bordering former Banffshire, part of lordship of

Strathbogie; it was given to Adam Gordon by Robert Bruce and is thus old Gordon holding, now dominated by great plantation forest on Bin Hill. The portrait painter William Aikman (1682-1731) was a native.

Parish church, 1803, and remains of
St Martin's Church, 1591
Simple box with bellcote and session house. An aisle of St Martin's Church survives as the Botary and Pitlurg Aisle in the kirkyard, which the Gordons of that Ilk restored as a burial enclosure in 1868. It contains effigy of Sir John Gordon of Pitlurge, Knycht, (who) *caust big this ile* 1597. (He was the father of Robert Gordon of Straloch whose atlas of Scotland was published by Blaeu of Amsterdam in 1648.) Altered 1887 and 1902.

Kirkside (formerly Cairnie Manse),
early 19th century
Severe, with central pedimented door pavilion and ashlar quoins.

St Carol's Church, Ruthven, medieval;
belfry 17th century
On a small promontory in boggy land above the Cairnie Burn, only a gable with belfry and north side wall survives of St Carol's, with recess containing effigy of Sir Thomas Gordon of Ruthven in full knight's armour. It sits in the tiny village of Ruthven which straggles along the burn bank.

Smithy and **Mill**, Ruthven, early 19th century
Mill a two-storey L-plan rubble building opposite smithy, a long low chimneyed structure; disused.

Auchanachie, 1594
All the elements of a late 16th-century Gordon house of some sophistication are still visible: the hall and offices in the two-storey main block with massive stair, turnpike and bedrooms in the tight, three-storey link block. The massive lum promises much. Inscription over door: FROM OVR ENEMIES DEFENDE VS O CHRIST 1594. 18th-century addition to north and drum-shaped 18th-century doocot in grounds. Refurbished 2004, Acanthus Douglas Forrest (colour page 25).

Davidston House, 1678, and late 18th century
Another Gordon property, of solid grace, if a trifle squat. L-plan with corbelled turrets and corbie-steps at gables. Notable for its very late

Aberdeenshire Council

Botary Aisle, Cairnie

Drumdelgie
Large holding famous in farming lore, immortalised in ballad which gives good insight into life of toil of a fee'd hand on a great improved farm:

There's a fairmer up in Cairnie,
Wha's kent baith faur and wide,
Tae be the great Drumdelgie
Upon sweet Deveronside.
The fairmer o yon muckle toon
He is baith hard and sair,
And the cauldest day that ever blaws,
His servants get their share.

At five o'clock we quickly rise
An hurry doon the stair;
It's there to corn our horses,
Likewise to straik their hair.
Syne, after working half-an-hour,
Each to the kitchen goes
It's there to get our breakfast,
Which generally is brose ...

There's sax o you'll gaun tae the ploo,
An twa will drive the neeps, ...
But when that we were gyaun furth,
An turnin out to yoke,
The snaw dank on sae thick and fast
That we were like to choke ...

O, Drumdelgie keeps a Sunday School
He says it is but richt
Tae preach unto the ignorant
An send them Gospel licht.

Auchanachie, a classic pocket laird's house

RCAHMS

Aberdeenshire Council

RCAHMS

Above *Davidston House*
Right *Turret corbel, Davidston House*

date, hence the unvaulted ground floor. (*TA* in inscription with grotesque is Abercrombie wife of Gordon laird.) Good set of offices adjoins. Refurbished 1973-4, Jack Meldrum; also 1981-2.

Pitlurg Castle, post 1539
Courtyard plan with circular tower on rock foundations, now **doocot**. Pitlurg Gordons descended from Jock o' Scudargue, near Rhynie, and held property until 1724. A descendent, General Gordon, 1815, took the name for his estate of Leask and Birness, Formartine (see p.210-211).

14 GLASS

Seclusion and a sense of age are the principal impressions to be had from a spell in this hilly, wooded area flanking the Deveron which formerly had much *heathy waste*.

Below *Glass Parish Kirk*
Middle *Glebe House*
Bottom *Blairmore*

Shepherd

Shepherd

Shepherd

Glass Parish Church, 1791
Plain harled rectangle with bellcote and recast Burgerhuys bell of 1642, with the large T-plan addition and early 20th-century internal elaboration of a quality considerably above the average. There is a Lorimer font, characteristically good glass by Douglas Strachan and an organ presented by Sir Frederick Bridge of Cairnborrow Lodge who was organist at Westminster Abbey. Renovated, 1883-4, by A & W Reid (Elgin), extended 1903, J Robertson (Inverness). Has the same feel as Fyvie Kirk.

Glebe House, 1843, Thomas Mackenzie
Built as manse incorporating parts of earlier 1772 manse in crisp cottage-style, harled with stone dressings, mullioned windows and shafted chimneys; particularly fine onion-like finial to porch angle.

Blairmore, 1884-5,
A Marshall Mackenzie
Built as Blairmore House for the Chicago grain king, Alexander Geddes, and originally heavily crenellated, the flat-roofed western part (now

mansarded), in dark rough-faced granite with light dressings, is like a half-built battleship. The overall effect of rounded angles corbelled to the square, pitched roof and crowsteps on the east and mullioned and transomed windows throughout is certainly baronial. Modern buildings of former school (1976) are wisely understated. Alterations 1986.

In 1440 Hugh Calder gained Aswanley from the Gordons; the last Calder laird died in 1768 in debt, like so many other north-east proprietors, to Duff of Braco, by then Earl of Fife and well on his way to amassing a king's ransom in land. The nearby shooting box of Innermarkie, 1705, which replaced Innermarkie Castle, was also a Duff property.

Shepherd

Aswanley House, (?)1692
Delightful, pink-harled, two-storey, L-plan mansion, most likely of the earlier 17th century, although datestones claim 1692. (GC – George Calder and IS – Isobel Skene not in original position.) The ogee-capped circular stair-tower on the north side, the coped chimneys and the archway to the courtyard are details of real quality. Slight alteration in 18th century, refurbished 1975-80. **Mains of Aswanley**, adjacent, imposing Improvement range of cartsheds, stables, chaumer, with elegant entrance tower.

Walla Kirk graveyard, 18th century
Hard-by the Deveron, on the traditional site of St Wallach's kirk and just downstream of his well and bath or baptism pool. St Wallach allegedly died in 733 and the former church may have dated from the 12th century; St Wallach's Fair was held at Haugh of Glass. Some good 18th-century stones and the burial enclosure of the Gordons of Wardhouse and Beldorney, restored by Rafael Gordon in 1913. The Beldorney Gordons, later of Wardhouse, stemmed from Adam, Dean of Caithness and third son of first Earl of Huntly.

Beldorney Castle, 1550s
Disarmingly substantial Z-plan mansion with massive circular tower (with striking rounded-

Shepherd

Shepherd

Top *Aswanley*
Middle *Aswanley, the rear*
Above *Home Farm of Aswanley*

Shepherd

Beldorney Castle

gable finish) at south-east and a square tower topped with a dog finial, at the north-west. Fine Gothic mouldings to exterior doors and panels. The ground floor is vaulted as normal; the hall at the first floor was divided into dining and drawing rooms in the late 17th century when bolection-moulded chimney pieces and coved ceilings were added. The north wing is probably 17th century, remodelled twice in 19th century (latterly by A Marshall Mackenzie); the south wing was rebuilt in later 18th century. The Renaissance gate and courtyard wall on the west are of 1673. Remodelled later 17th century, additions and repairs, 1890, A Marshall Mackenzie; restored 1982-8; Iain Begg.

Edinglassie Castle
A Gordon fortalice, burned in 1688 by General Mackay during first Jacobite troubles; recollected only by a 17th-century lectern-type doocot at the farmsteading.

Shepherd

Invermarkie Lodge

Invermarkie Lodge, from 1705
Close to the tumbling Deveron, built as shooting lodge by Duffs to replace Invermarkie Castle; an important lairdship of the Inneses, it was dismantled in the 17th century. Two-storey L-plan now in rough granite with angle quoins and pencil-thin turrets to wing and larger, fishscale-slated ones to main block, 1887.

Old Manse Inn Farm, 17th or early 18th century
Single-storey-and-attic, with one-door, one-window addition, rough crowsteps and coped chimneys. Altered late 19th century.

Mill of Invermarkie, Haugh of Glass, from 18th century
Sturdy L-plan building set against slope, with kiln as wing; 3.8m diameter iron overshot wheel.

Inscription, Edinglassie Bridge

Aberdeenshire Council

Edinglassie Bridge, River Deveron, 1855, Andrew McPherson
Original bridge built by Sir George Gordon of Edinglassie, 1655; now attractive single span in rough granite with strong rectangular voussoirs in grey granite. Two plaques record raising of public subscription, the *aid of the Heritors* and James Slorach, contractor, as well as the 1983 restoration by Grampian Regional Council.

15 **GARTLY**

Bisected by the River Bogie running northward through a moderately hilly area, making the transition to true upland. Barclays hereabouts, hereditary Sheriffs of Banff from 12th to 16th century (reflected in the barony, part of parish east of Bogie, which until 1891 was a detached part of county of Banff). They had Gartly Castle, once grand enough for Queen Mary to avoid the Gordons in, in October 1562, now gone. The influence of the railway is clear: the Great North of Scotland Railway created Gartly Station with a *post and railway telegraph office*; it is now a substantial hamlet.

Aberdeenshire Council

St Andrew's, Gartly

St Andrew's Parish Church, 1880

Plain Gothic rectangle, *cathedral glass* in windows (two of them, in east and west gables, rose), bellcote at east gable and, at session-room gable, a fragment of the previous kirk (*plain old building*), a small bellcote richly topped with finials and 1621 datestone. Mowat bell 1758; recumbent tombstones.

The previous church, 1621, was erected during the time of Mr Wm Reid who *taxed the faults of his parishioners bitterli, and not in the language of Scripture, quherby the people, insteade of being edified, wer moved to laughter and derisione* (Fasti). The victims who perished at the burning of Frendraught in 1630 were eventually buried here: *The ashes and brynt bones (were put in) sax kistes in the haill, which with gryte sorrow and cair, wer had to the kirk of Gartullie and thair bureit.*

Edinvillie, 1821

Fine two-storey, three-window, piend-roofed former manse in pinned whinstone with prominent sandstone dressings and original glazing. Single-storey-and-attic wing later.

The Mowat bell bears a Latin inscription rendered thus:

John Mowat made me,
For the use of Gartly,
To call upon the Clergy,
And mourn for the Dead.

A Jervise, *Epitaphs and Inscriptions*

RCAHMS

West Manse

West Manse, 1844

Former Free Church manse, more substantial than most; three harled storeys on north gained from fall of ground. Free Church bellcote, dated 1844, formerly with Hugh Gordon bell, in garden.

Mains of Collithie Farmhouse, late 18th/early 19th century

Another improved three-window farmhouse (coped chimneys) with sizeable wing added later. The marriage lintel of 1667, on the

Aberdeenshire Council

Above *Doocot, Mains of Gartly*
Right *Culdrain House*

Tap o' Noth
Remains of *an ancient fortress, formerly thought to have been the mouth of a volcano, but now known to be one of three forts constructed of stones vitrified by the force of fire, of which kind many have been lately discovered in Scotland.*
Francis Douglas, *A general description of the East coast of Scotland*, Paisley, 1782

single-storey back wing, not in its original position, records earlier structure.

Doocot, Mains of Gartly, 16th century
All that remains of the residence of the Barclays which accommodated Queen Mary during her enterprise in the north-east in 1562 that ended in the Battle of Corrichie. A fine pepper pot, with three rat courses. The last remains of the castle were cleared away, *c*.1975.

Aberdeenshire Council

Culdrain House, 1846-7, (?) John Smith Crisp, high gables and diagonal shafted chimneys (cf Forglen, see *Banff & Buchan* in this series). Jewel-like in rhythm of margins and treatment of glazing; a joy. Small piend-roof addition, 1900.

Coynachie Mill, mid-19th century
Two-storey rubble L-plan structure with all-iron overshot wheel which powered rope-driven threshing and sawmill.

Rhynie and Bell Knowe from Craw Stane

Shepherd

RHYNIE

Ancient parishes of Rhynie and Essie, the latter represented by little round kirkyard of considerable antiquity. Has an upland, almost alpine feel, being very self-contained, yet open and airy. The River Bogie runs past the village through a narrow valley. Formerly called Muir of Rhynie, it is characterised by a pretty green. It stands in the Aberdeenshire heartland: the progenitors of both Forbes and Gordons, the major, opposed, north-east dynasties, hail from this small upland parish. Scurdargue, on the slopes of the towering Tap o' Noth, was the seat of Jock o' Scurdargue, who, *with his brother Tam o' Ruthven, maintained the old line of the Gordons,* while Druminnor, the ancient Forbes fortress, lies but two miles apart. It was surely no accident that they are found so close to the prehistoric strength of Tap o' Noth (*sgurr dearg,* Gaelic, red pointed hill) and the Pictish complex around the Craw Stane.

RCAHMS

Rhynie Parish Church, 1823; spire and other alterations, 1889, (?)R Duncan
The octagonal tower with slated spire (detached from otherwise plain T-plan building) is the dominant feature of the village square, and of the whole, understated village. Spire, clock and bell presented by James Symon of Melbourne. Nondescript manse, 1889, in south square. 12th-century font at entry; Pictish symbol stones, very eroded, on green opposite kirk.

War Memorial, 1920, Robert Morrison
Superlative sculpted granite figure of an infantryman, the summit of craftsmanship in granite carving. On tall, square plinth.

Robert Warrack Morrison, 1890-1945, the consummate granite craftsman of this century. Son of a tailor, he worked in the granite yards of the United States both before and after the First World War, but was attracted back to his old firm, Morren & Co, Holland Street, Aberdeen, by the huge demand for memorials after the Great War. He was remembered as an extraordinarily fast yet accurate worker, who could carve the figure of a soldier in six weeks instead of the normal six or nine months. He was responsible for the obelisk at Clatt, the Celtic crosses at Lumsden and Towie, the soldier figures at New Elgin, Moray and Tarland, Kincardine and Deeside, and also executed work for Cumberland, Northumberland and parts of Wales. The great period of memorial-carving lasted from 1919 to 1926, ending with the General Strike, after which memorials became less ornate and more economical in their use of granite. Morrison became manager of Morren's in 1927; his finest work is said to be the gravestone of his wife, Anne, who died in 1930 at the age of 40, which stands in Trinity Cemetery, Aberdeen.

Left *Rhynie Parish Kirk*
Below *Morrison's superb War Memorial*

Young

Above *Free Kirk*
Right *19, 20 The Square*

Former Free Church, 1851
Plain Gothic rectangle, almost hidden from view; finial on west gable.

18 The Square, early 19th century
Moulded chimney copes and a piend-roofed porch are modest flourishes on an otherwise plain three-window, two-storey house on the south side of the square.

19, 20 The Square, early 19th century
Set back in one long, five-window, two-storey frontage of squared rubble. **No 20** is slightly earlier, with moulded chimney copes and forestair at back. **No 19** was the birthplace of Mackay of Uganda (1849-90) and bears commemorative plaque.

23 Main Street, early 19th century
A strong, flat-shouldered pend arch is the main feature of this substantial squared-granite rubble house.

The Rhynie Man

Rhynie Man
In 1978 a large slab bearing the carving of a fierce male figure, was ploughed up on the farm of Barflat, beside the old kirkyard. It is a rare example of a small series of Pictish stones with figures and may date from the sixth or seventh century ad. A cast can be seen in the vestibule of the school; original in Woodhill House, Aberdeen.

St Luag's Church, medieval (site)
A gabled and moulded Gothic recess containing a slab to Alexander Gordon, 1668, and an adjoining medieval stone coffin are the only survivals from this early foundation. Two early Pictish symbol stones (one with otter head) at the entrance were found in the kirkyard and may have come from the adjacent field which also produced the Rhynie Man (and Craw Stane; still there). Eighteenth-century graveslabs along kirkyard walls.

Daluaine, mid-18th century
Tall, imposing former manse, L-plan with coped chimneys and high gables, one with

finial and heavy skews. The walled garden, with small drum-shaped fruit houses at southern angles, coped rubble walls and (later) wrought-iron gates, is a delight.

At the beginning of the last century the men of Rhynie formed a society for mutual improvement through the discussion of scientific ideas and philosophical notions. The members ... got adventures among words and ideas while they composed papers with their legs writhed round the kitchen table.
J R Allan, *North-East Lowlands of Scotland*, 1952

RCAHMS

Mill of Noth

Mill of Noth, late 18th/early 19th century (1835) On Burn of Eassaiche, a harled rubble group, two-storey-and-attic with an 11ft 8in diameter start-and-awe wheel and kiln with small revolving ventilator. Later additions.

Castle of Lesmoir, from 13th century Represented by circular earthwork of a medieval homestead moat, possibly of the Frendraught family, holders of lands of Essie before the third quarter of the 13th century and fragments of a late medieval fortalice, all largely hidden by farmyard rubbish. However, the great Gordon fireplace from this latter strength was found recently in a cottage nearby and now graces the restored Terpersie (qv). Demolished by General David Leslie in 1647, when 27 royalist *Highlanders* were hanged.

AUCHINDOIR AND KEARN

An area of deeply incised burns and steep hill slopes. The village of Lumsden was founded, *c*.1825, by Mr Leith Lumsden of Clova (see p.79), a new town on *barren moor*. Like Rhynie nearby,

Auchindoir, *field of the chase*, refers traditionally to the flight through the parish of Lulach, stepson of Macbeth, to Essie, where he was slain on 17 March 1058.

The Craig Burn, whose *horrible rocks and precipices, the caves and dens* are described in Johnston's *Parerga* (Aberdeen, 1632).

it is graced by a village green. The plain **Free Church**, 1843, became parish kirk; also **UP Church**, 1803. **War Memorial**.

Southern entrance to village is dominated by a giant steel-plate bacon slicer at roadside and a jolly Witches' Hunt and Sculpture Walk, all the products of the dynamic Scottish Sculpture Workshop, now well established in the village.

Lumsden Well, 1814
Ashlar, with gable top and metal lion's-head spout.

Auchincloch, probably 1937, Roy Meldrum
Pine-begirt and pleasing, an almost perfect Modern Movement cube, flat-roofed and stuccoed with spare, functional outshots. (colour page 27)

Young

Shepherd

RCAHMS

Top *Witches' Hunt, Lumsden*
Above *Auchincloch*
Right *St Mary's Episcopal Church, Auchindoir*

The Mary Fair was held at Newton of Auchindoir twice a year – in spring and autumn – until about 1822 when it was moved to Lumsden village, the tenant farmer making a gift to induce the move *in consequence of the annoyance to which he was subjected at the time of the market*. It was a long-standing practice to award a prize to the best-looking servant girl that attended the *feeing market*. The judges were the neighbouring proprietors who happened to be at the fair. The gift was a flower — said to have been a lily with a pound note tied round its stalk. The winner was dubbed *The Flower of Mary Fair*, possibly a distant echo of the dedication of the medieval parish church.
A Jervise, *Epitaphs and Inscriptions*

Auchindoir kirkyard includes tombstone to James Gordon Esq of Littlefolla who died, 1823, aged 72 years:
For long factor for Dukes of Gordon, and being anxious on all occasions to save the purse of his chief, he is said to have demolished the grand staircase of the old castle of Strathbogie, and had the materials stored for building purposes.
A Jervise, *Epitaphs and Inscriptions*

St Mary's Episcopal Church, 1859
Early English, roof steeply pitched, ending in very plain entrance gable; two very slim lancets on flanks and gabled bellcote astride the roof ridge. **Auchindoir Church**, 1811, shell only.

16 **St Mary's Church**, 13th century
This serene country kirkyard forms an important early group with the adjacent earthen castle motte, similar to the juxtaposition of Cunninghar motte and the old kirk of Midmar (qv). Early 16th-century remodelling, 17th-century details. Unroofed 1810-11, the kirk is a long pink rectangle with, on south side, a fine Transitional Norman doorway with a chevron-moulded hood and nook shafts with bell capitals. A striking 16th-

Shepherd

St Mary's, Auchindoir

Concerning one of the lairds of Newmill it was said:

Here lies the Great Newmill,
Wha likit aye the ither gill;
Aye ready wi his aith and curse,
But never cared to draw his purse.

A I McConnochie, *Donside*, 1901

century sacrament house, shaped like a monstrance, is inserted into a lancet window in the north wall; also a Gordon of Craig armorial plaque of 1557 and a good grave slab of 1580. Ball-capped gatepiers; kirkyard walls 18th century (colour page 28). *Historic Scotland; open to the public*

Lodge of Auchindoir, *c*.1845
Hefty two-storey, three-window ashlar former manse; 1765 lintel on single-storey rear wing.

Aberdeenshire Council

Lodge of Auchindoir

Craig Castle, (?)1548
At the head of the magical Den of Craig, one of the most magnificent castellated mansions in Scotland. Quite French in its towering expanse of smooth, pinkly harled, blank wall, pierced by extravagant gunloops, and its closed wallhead walk. If the mass of the great L-plan chateau astonishes, the detail delights. Coped crowsteps on the wing gables, corbelled parapet and turret on the east side, the surviving yett, the ebullient heraldry (lovingly regilded by the late Mrs Barlas: most notably the two Gordon panels flanking the royal arms above the severe,

***The first Gordon of Craig** was a grandson of the famous Jock o' Scurdargue [who] died at Flodden, 1513. His grandson was slain at Pinkie, and the next laird was involved in the murder of the bonnie Earl of Moray at Donibristle in 1592. And so it went on.*
N Tranter, *The Eastern Counties*, London, 1972

Craig was the unlikely victim of a Zeppelin raid during the First World War; it is thought to have attracted attention owing to its being all lit up from the precocious installation of electricity.

Shepherd

Craig, vaulting of entrance

Shepherd

Craig, the château par excellence

segmental-headed doorway), the rib and groin vault to the entrance, and, finally, wall chambers and mural gallery to the great hall (remodelled (?)1726). (The plan and the rib vaulting link Craig to a small group of north-east castles: Towie Barclay, Delgaty and Gight; select indeed.)

It is fortunate that the family contrived to expand beside the great château, rather than to alter it overmuch. The **east wing**, 1767, John Adam, is a three-storey, three-window, ashlar-fronted plain block whose wallhead was raised in 1942 after a fire. The flamboyant rusticated **gateway** with reinserted coats of arms of 1667 also belongs to 1767. The single-storey Jacobean **central wing** of *c*.1832 is by Archibald Simpson. Its plasterwork is similar to that at the now-demolished Newe (qv) (wing also cf Old Balmoral). The **west wing**, 1908, is plain and flat roofed.

The **walled garden** dates from the (?)18th century and contains a baluster table sundial of 1821.

***The* Forbes house**, the original Castle Forbes until the name passed to the new castle on the Don at Putachie (qv Keig), Druminnor was the scene of an infamous dinner during the Troubles of the mid-17th century at which 20 Gordons were murdered by their hosts. That a similar story is attached to Castle Fraser – *Hospitality or no said Lord Fraser, if I smell treachery I'll touch my beard. Then stab every man!* Inadvertently he did and 20 dead Gordons lay stretched on the floor – rises from the general tenor of the times and the fact that many people thought that there were at least 20 Gordons who would be the better for the letting of a little life out of them! Harry Gordon Slade, *Proc Soc Antiq* Scot, 1977-8

Glenbogie, Brux, 1845, James Henderson
Single-storey farmhouse with attic and basement. Sophistication in projecting pedimented centre with door, narrow side panes to main windows and canted dormers. Substantial rubble-built steading.

RCAHMS

Right *Druminnor prior to demolition of Simpson's wing*
Below *Druminnor, on its slope*

Aberdeenshire Council

17 **Druminnor**, 1440, 1577
The present palace-block originally had an L-plan tower-house to the north-west. The main entrance is, Huntly-like, in stair-tower at north-east, adorned with three armorial panels over the door. From the courtyard the main block appears subdued but rears up four storeys on the dramatic south front, owing to the fall in the ground. Tiny dormers pierce the wallhead. Nothing now remains of Archibald

Simpson's wing of 1815 which had dramatic pointed gables and three good dormer-heads; house guests in the 1950s were each invited to remove a stone by the Hon Margaret Forbes Sempill who restored the castle with advice from Ian G Lindsay (colour page 28).

Druminnor entrance with armorial panels

Garden Cottage, ?17th/early 18th century
Intriguing single-storey-and-attic rectangle in split boulder rubble with pinnings, straight skews and skewputts; *not originally domestic*.

18 **CLATT**

From *cleith*, Gaelic for concealed, an apt name for an organic little sprawl of a kirkton which nestles beside the Gadie Burn. It retains the feel of the burgh of barony in which it was created in 1501. A weekly fair on Tuesdays, and the yearly fairs, which lasted eight days, bore the name of Moloch, the patron saint of the parish.

William Gordon, fourth son of the third Earl of Huntly, who became Bishop of Aberdeen about 1546 and died in 1577, was previously minister of Clatt. Spottiswood describes him as a *very epicure* who squandered the revenues of the See *upon his base children and their mothers*, and adds that he was *a man not worthy to be placed in this catalogue of bishops*.
A Jervise, *Epitaphs and Inscriptions*

Parish Church, 1799
A harled rectangle on medieval site (with *carved tabernacle and piscina*), crowning a knoll, lightened at the east gable by corbie-steps ascending to an angular 17th-century bellcote. Reseated, 1828. Refurbished as community facility, 2004, Morrison Ptnrs.

Left *Clatt Parish Kirk*
Below *Knockespock House, restored*

Knockespock House, from late 16th century
Demolition of the extensive 1889 western quarters has restored some semblance of order to the ensemble. From the north and south the nucleus of two round towers of the original Bishop's residence peep forth while from the north the ordered two storeys over basement of a plain 18th-century house are clear. *An ongoing puzzle* (IBD Bryce). (Colour page 93)

Tower Lodge, Knockespock

Aberdeenshire Council

Norman

a *Mansefield Gallery; a thoughtful steading conversion, 2002, Gordon Gauld (colour page 28)*

Tower Lodge, Knockespock, 19th century
A baronial surprise on a narrow back road, its height on so narrow a base being rather improbable. Two lower of three storeys are circular, corbelled to square for a tall, gabled (with crowstepping) third floor, the whole flanked by tall, rocket-like stair-tower. A small, rustic version of William Kelly's gates at Dunecht. Restored and extended sensitively with small single-storey wing, also corbie-stepped, in 1992, by James Masson and Robert Crabbe; Geraldine Scott Design Award.

Mill of Clatt, early 19th century
Pleasing group, in granite rubble, of an L-plan mill and kiln, miller's cottage (low, with piended dormers), lean-to dairy and byre. Plaque to Revd Andrew Murray (1794-1866) on front wall of cottage; born here, he was, for 44 years, minister of the Dutch Reformed Church at Graaf-Reinet, Cape Colony (1822-66), and an important figure in church and Afrikaner affairs.

Kennethmont Parish Kirk

Aberdeenshire Council

19 KENNETHMONT

From *ceann* and *moine* meaning head of moor or moss, it incorporates the ancient parishes of Kennethmont and Christ's Kirk.

Parish Kirk, 1812
As spare and simple a Gothic rectangle as could be conceived. Blind north wall in coursed rubble; four elegantly pointed windows with original

glazing and plain glass in south wall. East gable shows a fine ascent from pointed door and light, to matching window to a delicate little bellcote containing a Mears and Stainbank bell of 1910. The interior, with Leith-Hay pew and wall tablets, originally contained a horseshoe gallery. Interior recast, 1910, by G Bennet Mitchell.

RCAHMS

Manse, 1794
Tall, three-window, L-plan house, harled with margins, flying stair to door, and vulture-like, 19th-century eaved dormers. Offices include a neat circular henhouse with conical roof.

The Lodge of Kennethmont Farm, ?1822
Former Masonic Lodge (1822-45), with plain two storeys, three-window harled front and coped chimneys; modern porch.

Shepherd

Top *Manse, Kennethmont.*
Above *Rannes Public Hall*

Rannes Public Hall, 1909
An elaborated version of a village hall, with twin conical-roofed drum towers aping Leith Hall.

Ardmore Distillery, late 19th century
Good group of one- and two-storey rubble buildings, a fine pyramidal-roofed kiln and circular brick chimney, with its typical separate village, set back from the main road.

Old Kirkyard (St Rule's or St Regulas's), medieval
Attractively set amidst fields, now dominated by the square harled Leith-Hay burial vault in ultra-plain Gothic; some good stones from 17th century onwards.

Leith Hall, from 1650
The complete château effect came late, the quadrangular plan being finally achieved only in 1868 with the building of the west wing,

Leith Hall, from south-east

Shepherd

which visitors see on their approach. The main elements are the north wing, a severe rectangular block of 1650; the east wing of 1756 and, containing the fine principal rooms, the south wing, built around 1797 by General Alexander Leith-Hay. These apartments, as normal, on the first floor, are lit by flush-pedimented Venetian windows. Drum towers date from 1868. *National Trust for Scotland: open to the public*. (Colour page 93)

The crisply harled semicircular offices, 1754 (extended 1901), are half of an intended round square. The walled garden, recast 1900, contains two important Pictish symbol stones in a shelter, and a Chinese Moon Gate opening on to the old turnpike road. **Home Farm**, early 19th-century fort-like steading, rubble-built, harl-pointed quadrangle with entrance tower. Very plain.

Railway bridge, Leith Hall east drive, 1852-4, Alexander Gibb
Distinguished by battered, rusticated buttresses and balustraded parapets; detailing possibly by William Smith who was Gibb's brother-in-law. **Howets of Kennethmont Bridge**, 1852-4, also Alexander Gibb: solid double bridge in coursed rubble carrying main road over railway and Water of Bogie.

20 **Wardhouse**, (?)from 1757
Grand Palladian mansion, spectacularly sited and perhaps created to rival Haddo, which it readily surpasses. Small datestone high on centre front states: (A)RTHUR'S SEAT BUILT IN THE YEAR 1757-17..., a reference to the instigator, Arthur Gordon, and to John Hardyng's verse on his map of *c*.1465 which describes King Arthur having held his court at *Donydoure* (Dunnideer).

Shepherd

Aberdeenshire Council

Top *Offices, Leith Hall*
Above *Railway bridge, Leith Hall*

The house has always reflected the more exotic aspects of the Gordon family. In 1763 it passed to Arthur Gordon's nephew, Alexander Gordon, who was unable long to enjoy it owing to his beheading in 1769 after arrest in Brest as a spy. His younger brother, Charles Edward, who was Captain and Paymaster of the sixth Regiment of Scotch Fencible men (1750-1832), completed the building, and passed it to his eldest son who had spent most of his adult life in Spain. Thereafter the lairds were Spanish Scots, most notable Charles Edward's grandson, Pedor Carlos, *The Mad Laird*, who was responsible for the Home Farm. The Ring of Spain spent part of his honeymoon at Wardhouse in 1906, but the family fortunes waned after the fall of the Spanish monarchy in 1931, Rafael Carlos Gordon arriving at Wardhouse destitute. The estate was sold in 1952 and the house gutted shortly after.

Wardhouse in happier times, c.1907

RCAHMS

This date has led to suggestions that John Douglas may have been the architect, although the building's form and energy suggest earlier, (?)John Adam, times. Locally pronounced *Wardis*, this is symmetrical about a stylish two-storey and full basement centre block with a pedimented centre raised above the wallhead, in a curious slatey ashlar. Grand central first-floor window with Gibbsian surround; staircase in half-hexagon bow to rear; single-storey quadrants link to square, two-storey wings, the east one much extended. Restoration scheme, Acanthus Douglas Forrest, began 2005.

Home Farm, *c*.1835/1842,
(?)Archibald Simpson
Much Spanish influence evident in the great bullyard, set within a quadrangular courtyard, entered through an impressive pedimented gateway and with a large square doocot tower at the rear. *Granary used for entertainment: at New Year 1873, 90 sat to dinner and 190 couples came to the subsequent ball.*

Aberdeenshire Council

Shepherd

Top *Wardhouse Home Farm*
Above *Bellcote, Old Parish Church (restored 2004: Aberdeenshire Historic Kirkyards Project)*

INSCH

A burgh of barony lying within a *diversity of hill and dale*. Very much a local centre; in the 19th century it had monthly cattle fairs, and hiring fairs every May and November. The street pattern is almost random. Principally Insch is endowed with a delightful series of good, late 19th-century cottages, most single-storey-and-attic with consoled doorpieces, hood-moulds to windows, skewputs, canted dormers and ridge tiles – often excellently done.

Old Parish Church (St Drostan's),
renovated late 18th century
Only dark gable survives of kirk, but with fine bellcote of 1613, richly carved with tiny spiky finials. Medieval graveslab (13th century?) at base of gable, inscribed: ORATE PRO ANIMA RADULFI SACERDOTIS (Pray for the soul of the priest Radulfus). Originally recorded as having *contained some interesting carvings in wood*.

Lloyds TSB

Aberdeenshire Council

Lloyds TSB, High Street, 1867,
William Smith
Originally the Town and County Bank; very deep, almost double block of two storeys and attic, with windows outlined in granite ashlar. Flashy Renaissance front to entice the new farmers' wealth, dominated by Doric porch with

balustraded top, a segmentally pedimented tripartite window, quoins, and cornice and parapet. Shallow, two-window, chimneys projection in gable. But overall, spare in comparison to its neighbour.

Shepherd

Clydesdale Bank

Clydesdale Bank, High Street, 1883, A Marshall Mackenzie
Former North of Scotland Bank (over door), two storeys and attic, four-bay asymmetrical block in grey granite; polished and rusticated ground floor with pilasters between bays and columns at windows. Door at end, slightly advanced with fluted cornice. Above, granite ashlar rising to three stone dormer-heads with fleur-de-lis finials; the slightly advanced door bay is topped by a broken curvilinear moulding. Characteristic Mackenzie vigour.

Parish Kirk

Shepherd

The opposite side of the High Street is marked by a saw-toothed skyline of good skewed dormer-heads, nine in all, above a range of granite shops and houses. The shops are also cottage-style, eg Stephen/Milne, Commerce Street, latter low, with gable to road and solid chimneyhead; former asymmetrical, with good moulded gable for shop and neat cottage adjacent, having one hooded and one canted dormer.

Parish Church, 1883, Matthews & Mackenzie
Five-window Gothic rectangle in squared granite with sandstone dressings. Door at base of detached octagonal spirelet with clock, balanced by single finialed buttress. Church **hall** opposite with sympathetic, well-wrought extension, 1993.

Community Centre, Commerce Street, mid-19th century
Five-bay rectangle in Corennie granite with heavy pedimented ashlar doorpiece in gable.

Shepherd
Community Centre

41 Commerce Street, late 19th century
Triple ground-floor windows and doorpiece, all in squared grey granite; portly dormer-heads above with moulded skewputs and ridging.

St Drostan's Episcopal, Commerce Street, 1894, Alexander Ross
Agreeable rustic Gothic, in red granite with sandstone dressings, pairs of simple lancets in nave and small chancel. Red-tiled roof ridden by broach-spired wooden bellcote and two solid crosses. Strong porch and muscular gatepiers.

RCAHMS

Left *St Drostan's Episcopal*
Below *Old Rectory*

Shepherd

Old Rectory
Crisp, bright asymmetrical front; gable with gentle bow window at ground floor, deep eaves to gable and dormer head. Tiny double cottage opposite with heavy, advanced porches with gables and skewputs; formerly police station.

In the Gareoth (Garioch) is ane montane, quhilke goldne thay cal, the vulgar and commone stile of this montane is Dunedere, because it is said to abund in golde. This thay collecte of the scheip, quhilkes ar fed in this montane, quhais teeth and flesh in lyke maner ar yallow, as with the cullour of golde thay had bene littid.
Bishop Leslie, *Historie of Scotland*, 1578

More prosaically, the deposit on the sheep's gold teeth was found to be an incrustation of lime, phosphoric oxide and organic matter.
Proc Soc Antiq Scot, 1934-5

Husk Mill, Commerce Street, mid-19th century
Two-storey-and-attic, L-plan survivor of large milling complex. In coursed pink-grey granite rubble with pinnings; four-bay sunken ground floor, ground banked for loading husked grain for despatch to main mill across the road (now gone).

Station Hotel, mid-19th century
Previously harled with dressings, three window, two storeys and attic, consoled doorpiece, splayed corner with good curved return to square over.

Insch Station, 1854, Great North of Scotland Railway
Two-platform through station with, on up platform, a low stuccoed conceit, dated 1880, with two narrow wings to rear (U-plan), and a heavily consoled doorpiece flanked by triple windows with wooden mullions and transoms; prominent skewputs. Wooden signal box at level-crossing and good wooden footbridge.

Shepherd

Right *Insch Station*
Below *Detail, Drumrossie House*

Aberdeenshire Council

Drumrossie House [Rothie], rebuilt *c*.1840, (?)John Smith
Rebuilding in Smith's Tudor style of an attractive low, long single-storey, five-bay, probably 18th-century, house in pinned boulder rubble with elaborately gabled wings ending in bays. Porch in angle, fine octagonal hall within; 1687 panel incorporated; two-storey offices to rear. Contemporary **coach-house and stables**, Tudor, two storeys harled with margins, openings chamfered, main front five-bay with slightly advanced central gable containing carriage arch with stepped, three-light window over with hood-mould and shield above. Coped skews with deep end skewputs on corbels. Also doocot.

Castle of Dunnideer, *c.*1260
Weather-beaten rectangular tower, partly built from the remains of the prehistoric vitrified fort in which it stands. Possibly the earliest tower-house on the Scottish mainland, its masonry is close-packed and striated; it is gathered to a rough course every 6ft or so in a manner seen at other early castles such as that other Balliol property, Red Castle, Angus, or at Boharm, Moray (qv). Single great shattered lancet of the first-floor great hall pierces the west gable.

Aberdeenshire Council

Above *Castle of Dunnideer*
Left *Bridge, Shevock Burn*

Aberdeenshire Council

Bridge over Shevock Burn, near Castle of Wardhouse, (?)17th century
This simple parapet-less neatly wrought arch carried the road over the Shevock Burn and up to the castle, now flattened by agriculture, whose earthworks remain.

In 1260 the lord of Dunnideer Castle, Sir Josceline de Balliol ... *granted to Abbey of Lindores an annual sum and wayleave for a mill-lade from the Shevock Burn to the Mill of Insch, upon condition that the abbot should pay to Sir Josceline and his heirs a pair of white kid gloves every Whitsunday at his Castle of Dunnideer.*
W D Simpson, *Earldom of Mar*

Connected, in popular tradition, with King Arthur, *At Donydoure, also ... he is said to have held court* (John Hardyng, *c.*1465), and even with Giric, King of Alba, 878-889, although he appears to have died at Dundurn, Strathearn.

Opposite Dunnideer is the gently rounded Hill of Christ's Kirk, crowned by a small prehistoric fort, which name refers to the pre-Reformation Christ's Kirk on the Green, reputedly the scene of King James I's poem of that name. (The parish also bore the evocative name Rathmuriel or the Haugh of Moreal.) The nearby farm of Sleepytown commemorates the annual market, held on a night in May, called Christ's Fair or Sleepy Market.

21 CULSALMOND
Part within the safety and warmth of the Garioch, the rest shading into the fastness of the Glens of Foudland, round Hill of Tillymorgan.

Glens of Foudland slate quarries, early/mid-19th century
Clay slate, of excellent roofing quality, was at one time quarried on Foudland (Groome): These quarries afford employment to many industrious workmen and keep within the county a large sum of money which used to be sent out of it, for this very useful and now indispensible article (James Blaikie, *On the Slate Quarries of Aberdeenshire*, 1847). Now represented by giant, mute pockmarks, high above the A96; during the 1830s some 800,000 to 900,000 slates were produced each year. In the 1860s, 65 men were employed.

St Serf's (called St Sare's) Fair used to be held on last Tuesday of June on a hill to the north-west of the kirk.

Aberdeenshire Council

Shepherd

Top *Old Parish Kirk, Culsalmond*
Above *Culsalmond Parish Kirk*

Old Parish Church, 1791
Agricultural Improvement kirk, now roofless. Typically rectangular with four round-headed windows, re-using a pretty 17th-century bellcote similar to that at Insch. Good stones in kirkyard, which is said to have been built on the site of a stone circle. *Scene of one of those conflicts that led to the Disruption.* **Mort House**, a square, harled single-storey, early 19th-century structure over a subterranean basement. Pyramidal roof and large window from which to survey the kirkyard. Sizeable **manse** to rear of kirkyard; originally smart and laird's house-like with crow-stepped and quoined pavilions; now disfigured by central front projection of two storeys – a surfeit of children?

Parish Church, 1866
Former Free Kirk, an early English surprise, with striking spire rising above a battlemented entrance set within one angle of the kirk's T-plan. Harled, with sandstone dressings and buttresses, it stands alone at the roadside but for an enormous **manse**; (**Culsalmond House** qv).

Newton House, (?)1692
A Gordon house of immense serenity and dignity, on site of earlier castle. Exceptionally tall and narrow, harled, three storeys, attic and full basement, with four widely set windows and a pedimented doorpiece reached up railed

Newton House

RCAHMS

b *Morgan McVeigh's Tillymorgan, 2000, Acanthus Douglas Forrest (colour page 27)*

Norman

steps. The curved bays on the gables are 19th century. Kitchen court at rear. Very spare, like the original Esslemont and Ardmeallie.

Important garden divided into four (now three) by stone-coped brick walls, designed by the late Theodore Haughton of Williamston, and executed by the late owner, A Parkin-Moore.

Aberdeenshire Council

Mill House of Williamston

Mill House of Williamston, early 19th century
Two storeys, three windows, plain and functional in rough dark whinstone. Renovated 1977.

Aberdeenshire Council

Left *Williamston House*
Below *Home Farm, Williamston*

Aberdeenshire Council

Williamston House, Colpy, 1825, Alexander Fraser
Smart classical laird's house, harled with pronounced granite dressings (including two bands) and piended roof; two storeys, five bays with porch of granite columns. Two, two-window, single-storey wings with conspicuous gables added. A modified Grecian surprise within a renowned garden (which was destroyed by the great gale of 1953 and triumphantly rebuilt). Wings 1850.
Contemporary **Home Farm** is a quadrangular harled courtyard with subdued doocot tower.

Culsalmond House, *c*.1870
Tall L-plan former manse, front dominated by twin steeply raked gables, the advanced one with flat-bay projection, the other with tower-like bay stack running up to hooded eaves.

How Highland in an Aberdeenshire way ... less obvious than Deeside: *It seems proper to mention here that so recently as 1766 school-masters were required to teach Erse as well as English in the Highland parishes of the presbytery (of Alford), Strathdon, etc.*
A I McConnochie, *Donside*, 1901

STRATHDON

The steep-sided glens and open, domed hills have confined settlement over the millennia to a comparatively narrow zone on the mid-slopes above the rivers and burns. *The arable land, which lies all in the glens, most of it in that of the Don, consists of considerable haughs, belts of hanging plain, and skirts of pastoral heights; and it possesses in general a light, sharp, and somewhat fertile soil* (Groome). The water sources were themselves of great importance to the scattered farms and kirktons, for there is no area of Aberdeenshire so well provided with traces of the self-sufficiency granted to earlier people by the efficient management of water power. Truly upland now, following indentation of *the troutful Don* (Groome) which controls settlement; survives on sheep, game and forestry.

RCAHMS

Above *Interior, Invernochty Kirk*
Right *Kirk of Invernochty*

Kirk of Invernochty, 1853, James Matthews
Retaining ancient name for parish, the kirk and manse form a pleasing group, the former rubble-built but with precise Gothic windows to nave and transept and a tower at the south-east with a short broach spire. Within are wooden heraldic panels of Elphinstone of Bellabeg, and the Forbes and Skellater families, dated 1597, 1636 and 1688, and many marble monuments. The kirkyard contains a Tardis-like red granite ashlar Egyptian mausoleum of two storeys built for Mary Forbes, wife of Daniel Mitchell, 1829: the spare elegance suggests Archibald Simpson's hand,

RCAHMS

Mr Gordon, the writer of the Old Statistical Account of the parish, says that, according to tradition, the inhabitants of Strathdon were *rough and uncivilized in their manners*, that hostile lairds would have rushed upon one another in the churchyard on Sundays with their dirks and shabbies, and that, on one occasion, a laird cut off the head of Mr Baxter, a minister [in the 17th century], at the manse door, with a Lochaber axe ... Luckily the people have changed with the times, for even on the occasion of the Lonach annual gatherings, it is but rare that impropriety of conduct is to be seen; while their courtesy and hospitality are worthy of ambition in many parts of the Lowlands.
A Jervise, *Epitaphs and Inscriptions*

There is an **ambitious mausoleum** at the principal entrance, the lower part of which served on our last visit as a board for advertising sales of turnips etc.
A I McConnochie, *Donside*, 1901

designer of nearby Castle Newe for Forbeses, 1831. Other stones of interest include a winged soul (Donald McSween, on wall of kirk) and a primitive grim reaper in relief (colour page 26).

Manse, 1791
Simple Tudor frontage with projecting harled gabled bays; remodelled 1831, (?)Archibald Simpson.

RCAHMS

Ralston

Above *Manse of Invernochty*
Left *Doune of Invernochty from the air*

The footings of the original kirk are still visible on the crown of the great earthen castle mound opposite; the **Doune of Invernochty**, 12th century (60ft high, 250ft x 129ft). Gigantic motte or castle mound, surrounded by a rare system of dams and sluices. Water, from *River* Bardoch, remained in system as late as 1823.

The Lonach Highland and Friendly Society, established 1825, *for the preservation of Highland garb and language*, now oversees the annual Lonach Highland Gathering and Games, the quintessential Highland games.

Sheltered Housing, Bellabeg, *c*.1990, Gordon District Council
Low cluster near base of motte, rubble angles and pleasing massing.

Bellabeg House, 1765, overlooks the Lonach field, just beside the little hamlet of Bellabeg. Fine two-storey-and-attic, five-window building in red granite ashlar with cherry-cocking. Central bay crowned by agreeable semicircular wallhead. Plain L-plan mid-18th-century **mill** with ball finials to the gables. Original stream wheel was replaced by a small overshot wheel when the mill was converted to a joiner's shop early this century. **Bellabeg Bank** and **Lonach Hall**, contrasting statements in granite and timber.

Old Forbestown Female Public School, 1838
Imposing single-storey schoolroom with tall Gothic, wood-mullioned windows, and adjacent schoolhouse. Also in Forbestown is the single-

Below *Sheltered Housing, Bellabeg*
Bottom *Bellabeg House*

Shepherd

Aberdeenshire Council

RCAHMS
White House

storey-and-attic **White House**, in Newe Estate Tudor, *c.*1830; substantial, with deep eaves and two-bay windows.

Colquhonnie Castle, early 16th century
Beside the Colquhonnie Hotel is a fragment of Colquhonnie Castle, an L-plan tower which Forbes of Towie is said never to have finished.

RCAHMS

Right *Castle Newe*
Below *New Castle of Newe*

Aberdeenshire Council

Castle Newe, from 1604, 1831, Archibald Simpson
Pronounced *Neyouw. Handsome castellated edifice* with central tower 85ft high; demolished, *c.*1950, and stones used to build Elphinstone Hall at Aberdeen University.

New Castle of Newe, 1992, O R Humphries
Boxy and a little stolid; two harled storeys and attic with baronialising touches in angle tower, heavy sills and coped chimney head; rather large conservatory wrapped round angle. For Lonach Chief, Sir Hamish Forbes.

Mill of Newe, from 18th century
Large L-plan structure, internal workings removed and the fabric restored. The kiln vent has an ostrich vane in Aberdeenshire style.

In 1829 three miles of turnpike road were destroyed near Inverernan and the bridge of Nochty was swept away; two bridges survived: at Castleton of Corgarff (built 1749) and at Poolduilie (built 1715). *Indeed the numbers of auld briggs which have stood, while new erections have been swept away, is rather a reproach to the boasted superiority of modern masons.*
Sir Thomas Dick Lauder

Mill of Newe House, *c.*1830
A long, low structure in Newe Estate Tudor: finialed dormers and hood-mouldings above ground-floor windows.

Bridge of Newe, 1858, John Willet engineer, James Abernethy & Co, contractors
Sophisticated central section, consisting of three longitudinal brick barrel-vaults carried on four cast-iron arches, has been supplanted

RCAHMS

Bridge of Newe: Victorian sophistication, now destroyed

by a concrete pastiche, faced by two of the original iron arches (1993, Grampian Regional Council). Bull-faced masonry on two small segmental stone-built arches flanking main span. Built by Sir Charles Forbes, Bt, when the main road was diverted in 1856 in order to enlarge the policies of Castle Newe; plaques on cast-iron railings. Likewise **Bridge of Buchaam**, *c.*1856, John Willet: two wide semi-elliptical arches with red sandstone voussoirs, the rest good bull-faced masonry. Parapets replaced in chunky masonry, 1999. Second World War pillbox lurking in the trees on north side of bridge.

The prospect here is luxuriantly grand, wild, picturesque and sublime. The current glides in a gentle motion until it nears the arch, where it forces a passage among shaggy rocks and falls under the bridge with impetuosity and noise, clothed in white spume.
A Laing, *The Donean Tourist*, 1828

Deskry Bridge, 1858, John Willet
Spans the Deskry Water just south of its confluence with the Don, a low, strong structure with three segmental arches in bull-faced granite, probably built when the main road was diverted south of the river to increase the privacy of Castle Newe.

Poldullie Bridge

RCAHMS

Poldullie Bridge, 1715
Crosses the dark, winding Don by a single 70ft rubble span of considerable grace. Over the southern keystone is a tablet inscribed *John Forbes / of /Inverernan /1715*. Long approach on west side.

Aberdeenshire Council

Poldullie Tollhouse

Forbes family fortunes were founded by Bombay Jock, John Forbes of Newe, 1743-1821, after whom Forbes Street in Bombay is named. Another grand Strathdon family, the Wallaces of Candacraig, are also commemorated in a Bombay street name.

Poldullie Toll House, 1800
Typical bow-fronted, single-storey harled cottage; restored *c*.1990.

22 **Auchernach Bridge and House**, 1832; (?)1809
Engaging complex, consisting of the remains of Auchernach House, *long reputed the best in the district*, and a double-arched bridge over the Nochty whose parapets terminate in curves with piers. On the west face is the inscription: ERECTED/BY/GEN. N. FORBES/1832. House demolished 1945.

Garden, *c*.1809, where the wall is alleged to have been modelled on an Indian fort. The centres of east and west walls bear circular crenellated towers, while there is a tall, slim square granite ashlar-fronted tower with crenellated parapet and, formerly, a weathervane in the centre of the north wall. Circular rubble **doocot** with conical roof and weathercock flanked by single-storey pyramid-roofed symmetrical wings. Converted to silo.

Charles Forbes of Auchernach (*d*.1794) was master of the barracks at Corgarff Castle; his son rose to a Lieutenant-Generalship in India, hence the garden (and perhaps the house itself).

Auchernach Cottages, Firs Cottage, 1809 or earlier
Elongated single-storey-and-attic range, harled, no margins, with outside stair at gable. Elaborate log-work additions create an asymmetrical pair. Alterations 1980.

Auchernach Lodges, 1809 (northern), 1858 (southern)
The northern one is single storey in pinned rubble with broad eaves and piend roof plus chimney with three crisp diagonal shafts; the southern one is single-storey-and-attic, harled, also with Tudor chimneys; rises at rear.

Norman

Above *Auchernach tower in garden*
Right *Auchernach north Lodge*

RCAHMS

Aberdeenshire Council

Edinglassie House

Edinglassie House, 18th century
Long, low, formless sprawl grown from a two-storey red granite rubble U-plan house with its three-window centre, and one-window gabled advance wings. It is a reduced version of Skellater House (*c.*1700). Remodelled early 19th century, extended to the east in the later 18th century and again in the mid-19th. The west addition has a bay window, *c.*1850. **Lodges** and **gates**, late 18th/early 19th century, are moderately imposing: the gates have square granite piers with harled panels; the lodges are single storey with harled margins and one-window gable elevations with segmental heads rising into roof.

Shepherd

Left *Candacraig House*
Above *East Lodge, Candacraig House*

Candacraig House, 1835, John Smith
The house itself is much remodelled. The present two-storey asymmetrical harled structure is a delightful reconstruction by A G R Mackenzie of Smith's Jacobean house (which had itself incorporated a house of earlier date). The west wing was added, 1900, by George Gordon and partly remodelled, 1956, after a fire. It has an angular and all too obtrusive bay rising above the wallhead. The east **lodge** is a single-storey red granite ashlar Jacobean joy by John Smith with elaborately

Aberdeenshire Council

Above *East Gates, Candacraig House*
Right *Inverernan House*

pedimented windows and captivating miniature Dutch gable. The **offices** are a single-storey-and-attic harled court of *c.*1835 and later; good stone dormer heads in coach-house.

The long, walled **garden** has a simple single-storey Gothick summer house, a striking Tempietta, and elaborate gates with wrought-iron ball finials to piers. The 17th-century **doocot** is a square plan with rat course and crowstepped gables on all four elevations and a room with hearth below the doocot proper. The west **gates** are square rubble piers with broken pediment tops by A G R Mackenzie, *c.*1956, an amusing caprice.

The first Forbes of Inverernan was *Black Jock*, Bailie to the Earl of Mar in 1715. Urged by Mar to take part in the Rising, he was taken prisoner and died in Carlisle the night before the day fixed for his execution.

Inverernan House, from 1764
The east elevation is, thanks to G Bennet Mitchell, 1935, a near reproduction of Bellabeg, dated 1765, with a red granite ashlar front with cherry-cocking. (Formerly had a four-column Roman Doric porch.) The gatepiers of *c.*1828 are dwarf square piers with low wing walls. Good original timber and iron gates survive. The **offices** to the north of the house are two-storey, U-plan, harled with margins and with a low pitched broad-eaved roof and an iron-columned verandah between advance wings, *c.*1830. (Reconstructed *c.*1828, and 1935, G Bennet Mitchell.)

Mill of Glenconrie House

Mill of Glenconrie House, 1768
A two-storey, three-window harled house of singular split-level design, dated at skew, and with original glazing. The west end is lower at ground-floor level yet higher at the first floor; mill demolished.

Skellater House, *c*.1690/1700
A crisply harled T-plan laird's house with a three-window centre and stone-gabled dormers of 1845 above, flanked by gabled advanced wings. The centre doorway is moulded with an oval window and armorial panel, dated 1770, above. Inside, good central wooden staircase with double-arched treatment at ground floor. Severe yet stylish, restored 1975-6.

Aberdeenshire Council

Above *Skellater House, panel above the door moulding*
Left *St Mary's RC Chapel and Chapel House*

Colnbaichin Toll House, *c*.1825
Subdued beneath its beetling eaves, distinguished by its semi-octagonal bay and mixed granite walls. Additions at rear, 1965.

Aberdeenshire Council

St Mary's RC Chapel and **Chapel House**, (?)early 19th century
Chapel a simple rubble-built rustic rectangle with west porch and round-headed windows; small harled cottage attached at right angles.

John Forbes of Skellater married a Portuguese princess and became a Field Marshal in the Portuguese army; he died in Brazil in 1809.

1727 motto over door erected by Lachlan Forbes to show intention of his family to be *alone amongst many* in the staunchness of their adherence to the Jacobite cause. George Forbes of Skellater fought at Culloden and died at Boulogne in October 1767.
R Winram, *The Land o' Lonach,* 1986

23 **Bridge over Burn of Tornahaish**, mid-18th century
Part of the old military road crossing from Deeside to upper Donside, and heading for Corgarff; very evocative single rubble arch without parapets, which swells up gracefully from the moor (colour page 28). Repaired 2000.

RCAHMS

Burn of Tornahaish military bridge and road

Edom o' Gordon

'Gi up your house, ye fair lady,
Gi up your house to me,
Or I will burn yoursel therein,
Bot and your babies three.'

'I winnae gie up, you fals Gordon,
To nae sik traitor as thee,
Tho you should burn myself therein,
Bot and my babies three'...

O then bespake her youngest son,
Sat on the nurse's knee:
'Dear mother gie owre your house, he says,
For the reek it worries me.'

'I winnae gie up my house, my dear,
To nae sik traitor as he;
Cum weil, cum wae, my jewels fair,
Ye maun tak share wi me'...

Church of Scotland, Corgarff, 1834, *Mr Daniel*
Rewarding Gothic rectangle in squared rubble with four, fine, pointed windows with original glazing on east side (cf Smith's Keig), the west side blind and, inside, horseshoe gallery carried on Doric columns.

Luib Bridge, 1830
Chunky rubble-built to cross the Don by way of two semicircular arches, one smaller as flood relief. Panel on parapet inscribed LUIB BRIDGE/ BUILT BY SIR CHARLES FORBES/OF NEWE AND EDINGLASSIE MDCCCXXX.

RCAHMS

Right *Corgarff and Cock Bridge, as idealised 1786/95 (Cordiner)*
Below *Corgarff*

Shepherd

24 **Corgarff Castle**, 1537; fire-damaged 1571, 1607, 1689 and 1746
Tall and gaunt on the brae above the (sacrilegious) new Cock Bridge, this began life as a plain three-storey, basement and attic hunting lodge of the Earl of Mar. Acquired by Forbes of Towie, it was burnt, along with 26 of the residents including Mistress Forbes and her children, in 1571, by Captain Ker, on behalf of Adam Gordon of Auchindoun (*Moray*, qv). This savage deed, but one episode in the abiding enmity between Gordons and Forbeses, is commemorated in the ballad *Edom o' Gordon*. Occupied by Montrose, 1645, converted to Hanoverian garrison, 1748, by adding single-storey *pavilions* to east and west of the tower and enclosing all within an elongated eight-point curtain wall, in plan a star-shape, for musketry defence (cf Braemar).
Garrisoned until 1831 in attempt to control whisky smuggling out of Moray. Within is an effective Historic Scotland evocation of Hanoverian barrack-life.

Posts *(such as Corgarff or Braemar) to be occupied by the regular troops in the Highlands to put the laws in execution for disarming the Highlanders, suppressing their dress and for preventing Depredations ... all regiments of foot would be employed in carrying out the new roads.*
War Office paper, 1748

Auchmore, *c*.1650
Formerly the dower-house of Allargue, a two-storey, three-window front with small piended dormer heads to left and right like eyebrows. Bar and barhole behind door. 18th century in present form.

Rippachie (east bridge),
probably 18th century
Plain, slightly hump-backed, with single rubble-built segmented arch over Don.

Keeper's House, Allargue, 1960s
Successful implant to stark, exposed location: plain harled block with strong stair-tower. Rectangular grey-stained timber **chalet**, 1992, by steading by re-aligned Cock Bridge with small thistle finial above porch, for the Duke of Rothesay.

Delnadamph Lodge, 19th century
Large upland hunting lodge whose *sheltering plantations* (were) *the uppermost in the valley*; short-lived testament to Highland deer-stalking; demolished 1988; offices remain.

Top *Auchmore*
Above *Cockbridge chalet*

Cock Bridge, made famous by so many winter weather reports, was named after the inn which stood nearby, whose sign was a red muircock. Demolished to create new bridge, 1989.

25 GLENBUCHAT

Upper Donside at its most typically rural; evidence of depopulated farms all around.

Parish Kirk, 17th century
Reposing in its own kirkton, this harled rectangle has an urn-crowned bellcote on the east gable and a panel inscribed *M.A.K. [Minister Andrew Kerr]* 1629 high on the west gable. Simple square-headed windows with clear lights suggest another plain Scots kirk, but the orthodox interior (pulpit with sounding board on south wall, box pews) is enlivened by

Bishop of Aberdeen, Thomas Spens, an *active courtier and statesman erected a chapel at Glenbuchat in consequence of six of the parishioners there having been drowned in crossing the Don while on the long journey to their church of Logie-Mar at Eastertide.*

Glenbuchat Parish Kirk

John Gordon, *Old Glenbucket* (1676-1750), was the last Gordon laird, who fought not only in the 1715 and 1745 Risings but also at Killiecrankie (1686); died in Boulogne at an advanced age. *From place to place he was hunted, til, letting his beard grow and assuming the garb of a beggar, he at length effected his escape to Norway* (Groome). It is said that during the Jacobite advance to Derby, George II would awake from nightmares screaming *De great Glenbogget is coming.*

an eastern gallery with square marbled centre column and the arms of the Duff family. Pleasing clutter of stones from 1686 in the kirkyard, adjacent to the solid manse of *c.*1785 and later.

Shepherd

Right and below *Glenbucket*

Shepherd

Glenbucket, 1590
Commanding, if such a quietly understated mock-military country house can be so peremptory, the confluence of the Buchat and the Don. Built by John Gordon, for his wife, in rubble, but with long fancy quoins, squinch arches carrying turnpike stairs in re-entrant angles of its Z-plan and crisp corbelling of the angle turrets all hinting at a sophisticated chateau. Good heraldry, a marriage-lintel and a variety of cupboards, one with a stone shelf, still survive. Elaborate ashlar entrance to garderobe on first floor; fine kitchen arch (also ashlar): in all, quality of facing masonry to cupboards, doors, stairs and garderobes breathes expense. Needs re-roofing, re-harling and community use. NOCHT ON EARTH REMAINS BOT FAME over doorway an appropriate Gordon epitaph? (Colour page 95) *Historic Scotland; open to the public*

Adjacent to the castle, the large, rubble-walled garden of **Glenbuchat House**, with piended sheds, is probably part of the castle garden. Glenbuchat House itself (1826) with double-bow front, broad eaves and square-shafted chimneys has been altered subsequently but remains striking.

Aberdeenshire Council

Mill of Glenbuchat

Numerous disused limekilns in Strathdon are evidence that the quarrying and burning of limestone to produce lime was a small-scale but widespread local industry in the 18th and 19th centuries. More details of these workings can be found in '*The Limekilns of Upper Donside – a forgotten heritage*' by Ken Cruickshank, John Nisbet & Moira Greig. (Colour page 26)

Mill of Glenbuchat, 1829
Rectangular rubble building, one storey and attic, containing an 18th-century central kiln and an iron wheel of *c*.1900, wheel gable in ashlar; the whole set into hillside. The millhouse, simple, with steep roof, and the outbuildings, one with ball-finial gable, form a pleasing group.

Badenyon and Netherton
Limekilns, early 19th century, by roadside; of drystone construction, circular and tapering kilns with corbelled draw holes.

Aberdeenshire Council

Badenyon

Badenyon, the head of the glen, is a classic Donside farm, solid single-storey-and-attic farmhouse of *c*.1800 with two half-dormers emerging at the wallhead and a U-plan, single-storey, with lofts steading, (?) *c*.1830, adjoining. Nearby is site of **Badenyon Castle**, long gone. A door-hinge in steading is said to come from the castle.

Glenbuchat Lodge, 1840, by Earl of Fife
Built as *shooting box*, on or near site of dwelling of John o' Badenyon (hero of song by Revd John Skinner); enlarged and remodelled, William Kelly.

26 TOWIE

The hills are undulating, smooth and heathy; and the arable lands are partly haugh, partly the steep declivities of the hills (Groome). Formerly Kilbartha, indicating an early ecclesiastical focus, it became Towie-Kinbattoch *(the north-lying land at the head of the fair hill)*. Classic tiny kirkton remains.

Parish Kirk

Aberdeenshire Council

Parish Kirk, 1803
On the Don's southern bank, at a sharp bend, the kirkton of Towie is distinguished by the

honest rectangle of its parish kirk. Round-headed windows retaining the original glazing bars and a bellcote capped by a ball finial convey a sense of simple grace. Inside are the original pulpit with sounding board and a U-plan gallery. A fine example of an Aberdeenshire mortsafe lies inverted in the kirkyard whose wall contains a medieval graveslab with calvary cross and chalice. Altered 1894.

Aberdeenshire Council

Above *Old Manse of Towie*
Right *Towie Castle*

Old Manse of Towie, early 19th century
Tall former manse, with three-window frontage and steps up to door and the *manse offices*, U-plan and harled. The early 19th-century **old schoolhouse** has an eccentrically placed door and a single-storey schoolroom extension with large windows raised above the wallhead.

RCAHMS

War Memorial

Young

Parish Hall, 1845-50
Sizeable hall, which began life as Oddfellows Hall, has square windows and wooden mullions. It occupies part of the site of **Towie Castle**, a ruined three-storey, L-plan Forbes mansion of the early 17th century, which had prettily corbelled angle turrets on its tall walls. Demolished 1968; plaque by Alford Academy pupils (Sandy Braso, art teacher) on small cairn beyond hall.

War Memorial, *c.*1919
Wonderfully understated; a Celtic cross bearing, in relief, sheathed sword and wreath.

Kinbattock Farmhouse, *c.*18th century
A tall, solid block with evenly coursed three-window front. The substantial early 19th-century quadrangular steading of squared red granite rubble with, on the front, a central

projection containing three segmental arches and pediment gable shows a determined effort at Improvement. *Kinbattock* records an early name of the parish; reflects nearby moated site?

Waterside, Glenkindie, later 18th century
Plain two-storey rubble house with piend roof and wing, formerly the factor's house of Glenkindie.

Glenkindie Arms Hotel, 1820
Masonic hall. Its length is striking – five two-storey bays, the central bay having an architraved door with large heraldic panel over.

Glenkindie House, from 16th century
A snug château, amidst ancestral trees, and partly clad with ivy (Jervise). A confection of towers of different dates. U-plan, open to the south, the oldest surviving part is the east wing, two storeys and attic, probably 16th century recast in 1741 – judging by date on door. Quoined surrounds to windows and an elaborate scale-and-platt stone stair with squat Ionic columns inside. The balancing west wing may date from 1787 or earlier. The north wing, which comprises the present main house, is 1900, by Sydney Mitchell, a two-storey house with nicely off-centre three-storey and cap-house tower oversailing all. Also fine gable with oriels, similar to those of the hall at Mitchell's Well Court in Edinburgh. This replaced the central house of 1785 which in turn had been built over the site of the house built in 1595 and destroyed in 1644. Dr Douglas Simpson postulated a frontal range with gatehouse like Tolquhon.

Below *Glenkindie House, first-floor landing*
Bottom *Glenkindie House from old postcard*

RCAHMS

Shepherd

A clutch of comfortable lairds' houses scattered along the flanks of Strathdon span the years. The progenitor is glorious Glenbucket, but they encompass those with equally early beginnings, subsequently aggrandised – Glenkindie and Candacraig; the austere but refined breath of the early 18th century – Bellabeg or Skellater; and the melodrama of the 19th century – Newe and Auchernach.

The **gardens** are extensive: largely 18th century, with the coped sections, 17th century or earlier – much topiary, including teddy bears, toy soldiers and egg-cups. The fluted gatepiers with wrought-iron work on the axis of the house are mid-18th century. Two sundials, one of 1722. The **east gates** have four piers capped with urns, 1900; the **west gates** a former bow-fronted tollhouse, rebuilt from old materials early this century. Rectangular, 17th-century **doocot** with double rat courses and crowsteps.

Granite obelisk erected on Dalrossach Hill, 1908, to General Sir Alexander Leith KCB of Freefield and Glenkindie, *d.*1859, aged 84. Fought in Peninsular War etc. Knighted 1815; known by soldiers as *Cauld Steel.*

Mill of Glenkindie, from 18th century
Rubble, with a brick-built kiln and a large overshot wheel with segmental gearing which drove the millstones and adjoining sawmill. The mill was rebuilt early this century after a fire.

Glenkindie Bridges
Two-span lattice girder with masonry abutments and central pier; nearby, small concrete-arch bridge, 1884, one of earliest of its type.

A variety of oat called the Kildrummy oat, with a thin light character and abundance of straw, ripens about a week earlier than other approved varieties of oat, and is very suitable to high situations, having long been diffused and appreciated throughout many parts of Scotland.

27 KILDRUMMY

The close-set, rounded hills of upper Strathdon begin to open out, still moulding themselves around the winding Don and still with a sternness befitting this power centre of the ancient earldom of Mar, which was also an important point in the route to Moray.

There is some debate whether the calm green mound on which the old **kirk** of Kildrummy sits is a Norman motte or castle mound, the precursor of Kildrummy Castle. Its elevated site at the end of a ridge is a natural feature

Kildrummy Kirk

Shepherd

and the mounding is not inconsistent with the development of an ancient graveyard. Dedicated to **St Bride** and once called the *chapel of the lochs* from the encircling marsh, the upstanding walls are mostly those of relatively recent burial enclosures, making the plan of the old kirk difficult to discern. However, there is a wealth of tombstones from the 16th century onwards, including some fine armorial stones. Original archway survives as a tomb recess behind wooden doors; excellent stone with three praying figures in half relief.

Parish Kirk, 1805
Striking rectangular block with high piend roof and a bow end containing a staircase and a horseshoe-shaped gallery, the end topped by a ball-finialed bellcote of some solidity. Rubble-built with pinnings and cherry-cocking and ashlar for the bellcote. Inside all is light and seemly, lit by two huge south-facing Gothic windows with astragals and clear glass which flank the pulpit. Plain, painted wooden pews and gallery, *c*.1845/50.

The pine-capped mound along the road to the kirk is a Bronze Age burial mound which may have later seen service as a bell knowe, cf the Bell Knowe at Rhynie.

RCAHMS

Bear Lodge

Bear Lodge, 1850, Thomas Mackenzie and James Matthews
Former manse of Kildrummy: imposing neo-Jacobean, two-storey-and-attic with twin Dutch gables. Large back wing of 1865.

Quarryfield, 1840
Modest single-storey house and steading, the former having a pedimented porch in ashlar.

Shepherd

Early tombstone, old kirk

The embalmed body of a lady was found in 1746 in a perfect state of preservation beneath the aisle of Kildrummy church where the Mar Family were said to have been laid. It was believed to be that of Isobel, Countess of Mar, who married Alexander Stewart in 1404 and who took part in a bizarre ceremony at Kildrummy.

Also stone erected by **Revd Dr James Sherriffs** of Aberdeen to memory of William Sheriff, farmer, and his son Alexander Sheriff Esq, who died, 1801, in the island of Jamaica. Dr Sherriffs was minister of St Nicholas, 1778-1814, and having been made residuary legatee to his kinsman *of Jamaica*, Dr Sherriffs was, in consequence, proprietor of 163 negro slaves at the time he was moderator of the Kirk of Scotland (Jervise). Several great north-east houses relied, at critical periods in their development, on West Indian slave estates, eg Leith Hall (Leith Hays), Craigston (Urquharts) and Cairness (Gordon of Buthlaw).

Dr Douglas Simpson used to relate a local tradition that plans for a mill were used for the kirk by a local mason, whence the phrase: *Mak a kirk or a mill o it.*

Shepherd

Above *Kildrummy Castle, the Chapel*
Below *Kildrummy Castle Hotel from castle*

Kildrummy Castle, from 13th century
The great castle of enclosure broods on the edge of the hole from which its stones were gouged. Although now shattered and broken, the smooth ashlar faces of its curving towers still gleam in the light. It was begun by Alexander II as a plain polygonal enclosure. The chapel was soon built, protruding, strangely, from the curtain wall. Possibly following a visit from Edward I of England in 1296, the towers, ashlar plinth and gatehouse were added, thereby creating a high medieval stone castle with donjon, archers' slits and portcullis, which was – Bothwell excepted – without rival in 13th-century Scotland. Pit for counter-balanced drawbridge inserted (?15th-century) into Edwardian gatehouse front. The Elphinstone Tower, a tower-house, was built at the west end of the hall in the 16th century (colour page 93). *Historic Scotland; open to the public*

Historic Scotland

Opposite: Left *Clova House*
Right *Tullynessle House*

Burnt in 1306 after Nigel Bruce had held it against the young Prince Edward of Caernarvon and repaired in time to be besieged by Balliol's men. It was burnt in 1530, captured by Cromwell in 1654 and finally destroyed after being the centre, *the hatching place*, of the Earl of Mar's Jacobite Rising of 1715.

Kildrummy Castle Hotel, 1900, A Marshall Mackenzie
Lovely two-storey Jacobean pile in ashlar with good interior work, wooden ceilings. The celebrated garden, which has been terraced into the quarry hole of the castle opposite, includes an elaborated version of the medieval Brig o' Balgownie in Aberdeen, also by Mackenzie.

Kildrummy Mill, 18th and 19th century
One-storey-and-attic rubble with kiln at end of wing; large 3.76m diameter paddlewheel.

Aberdeenshire Council

Clova House, 1760
The original house at the centre stands to attention with an almost military bearing, its harled gable and quoins imparting a sense of discipline rather than warmth. Columned porched garden on the south wing. Stables are much-altered confection of 1819. South wing *c.*1850; north-east wing *c.*1880.

Clova RC chapel, designed by Hugh G Lumsden of Clova, 1880, dedicated to Our Lady and St Moluog. Now removed.

TULLYNESSLE AND FORBES

Parishes united 1808; the bare boundary with the Garioch, rising to the now afforested rolling crests of Suie Hill.

28 **Parish Church**, 1876
Plain Gothic, of *finely dressed Sylavethy granite;* bellcote of old parish church, 1604, set up in kirkyard, like a petrified cake decoration. Moulded aperture with finialed gablet over. Classical monument to Andrew Marshall, *d.*1812, with urns. In the old kirk in the early 19th century *the seats were mere boards placed on turf-piles* (McConnochie).

Tullynessle House (former manse), (?)1804
Sizeable, two-storey, attic and basement, three-window, L-plan house in a muscular ashlar cherry-cocked with slate. A fine example of the prosperity of the rural clergy of old.

Manse Cottage (Beadle's House), 18th century
Small, severe but, for its function, a remarkably solid two-storey house, harled with margins and quoins, with curious oblong windows to first floor. Extended 1973.

In 1402 Sir Malcolm Drummond of Kindrochit, Braemar, was *so mishandled* that he died, and shortly after, in 1404, the supposed instigator, Alexander Stewart, son of the notorious Wolf of Badenoch, seized Kildrummy Castle and married his victim's wife, the Countess Isabella, partaking in a bizarre ceremony.

On 9 September 1404 Countess Isabella herself, accompanied by the Bishop of Ross, *Red* Sir Andrew Leslie, Sir Walter Ogilvy, and other magnates ... and tenants assembled outside the great gate of the castle ... Suddenly Stewart appeared and, coming forward, solemnly renounced everything he had taken, including the Castle of Kildrummy with all the furniture, precious metals and charters. He then gave the keys into the Countess's hands in token of this grand and high-minded deed of renunciation ... The Countess, handing back the keys to the usurper, with equal solemnity, *before all our tenants,* declared that of her own free will ... *outside our Castle of Kildrummy, not shut up or detained in the same* she chose Alexander Stewart to be her husband, conferring on him the Earldom of Mar and Lordship of the Garioch ...

Let us try to picture this extraordinary scene. In the background the frowning Edwardian gatehouse, streaming with banners. Between its massive towers the deep-recessed portal, in front the drawbridge and the long trestled gangway spanning the wide, palisaded ditch. Beyond in the field is a little group of brilliant figures, with the Countess herself in the middle; the grave faces of the ecclesiastics, the busy clerks, peasants and retainers ... Dominating everything and everybody is the haughty figure of Sir Alexander Stewart himself, as, clad in shining mail, he crosses the bridge, superbly confident, and bends the knee in solemn mockery as he delivers over to his unhappy victim the keys of her castle.
W D Simpson, *The Earldom of Mar*

Aberdeenshire Council

Forbes Arms, Bridge of Alford, early 19th century
Welcoming athwart the river and the bridge, a sturdy two-storey, three-window L-plan in robust ashlar, part pinned, with later crenellated porch to river. Large mansard added to back wing, 1980.

Bridge of Alford, 1811, William Minto
At Boat of Forbes, an important ferry point on the north/south route, built by Parliamentary Commissioners for a not inconsiderable £2000. Graced by three segmental arches in ashlar, the central one the largest, with cutwaters topped by pedestrian refuges; approaches splayed.

RCAHMS

Aberdeenshire Council

Top *Montgarrie Meal Mill*
Above *Portico, Whitehaugh House*
Right *Whitehaugh House*

Montgarrie Meal Mill, probably 1886
Tree-girt but on an industrial scale, as befits its date, four storeys with colossal wheel, 23ft 6in. in diameter and 4ft 6in. broad, by James Abernethy, 1886, driving five pairs of stones in line. Lade in reinforced concrete, 1947. Aberdeenshire vent to kiln. Still produces excellent oatmeal.

Whitehaugh House, 1745, 1838-40, W & J Smith additions and reconstruction
The Smiths did their best for Col J J F Leith but the articulation of their wings and heavy-columned porch with the earlier spare Georgian box is achieved with some grinding of the gears, despite the strict adherence to symmetry. The original two-storey-and-basement, seven-window ashlar block with advanced and pedimented central part rather lurks behind the Smiths' over-large Doric portico. Their wings are one-window, single-storey-and-basement, with neat pediments echoing the central block. The single-storey

Aberdeenshire Council

north wing has columned and glazed square bay. Nevertheless an honourable endeavour. Neo-Tudor chapel nearby.

Walled Garden and **gazebo**, 1831/8, probably John Smith. Within an almost circular walled garden, an engaging ashlar octagonal two-storey gazebo with deep ledge (for plants?) above the lintelled ground floor and 17th- and 18th-century skew and datestones built into rear.

Mausoleum, *c*.1838, (?)John Smith. For a military man, Lt Col Forbes-Leith, which perhaps explains the almost forbidding, bunker-like appearance of the square plan, sturdy granite walls and slack roof pitch. Yet all uplifted by fine tracery in east gable window, gable bellcote and urns (now fallen) at angles. 1588 and 1597 slabs within.

Forsyth

Terpersie Castle, 1561

Miniature Z-plan mansion with all the presumption of a spaniel. Really only one room on each floor in main block and service rooms in generous towers. A Gordon house, proclaimed by *G* in lowest corbel of stair-tower and boar's-head top to chamfered opening. Burned 1665/restored; ruinous post-1885. Pleasing, no frills restoration, William Cowie Partnership, for Lachlan Rhodes, 1983-9, and an appropriately warm harl for these latitudes (colour page 95).

Muckletown Steading, 19th century; part perhaps earlier

Elemental in its low, ground-hugging profile and rubble build. Quadrangular plan incorporating threshing mill with large start-and-awe wheel. Ball finials at gable tops; the mid-19th-century farmhouse, like so many in

A Mr Little came from England to settle on his estate, *c*.1735, which he found in a ruinous state: *A most uncomfortable scene for an Oxonian to enter upon! What was he to do? Was he to return to England, and say that he found nothing upon his estate but a parcel of beggars? In that case what could he hope to draw from them?... He took his resolution, put his hand to the plough, and his labours have met with the success which persevering diligence rarely fails of. His rent-roll is improved, his tenants thrive... and he has the pleasure of seeing many hundreds of acres of thriving wood where not a shrub grew when he commenced farmer.*
Francis Douglas, *A General Description of the East Coast of Scotland from Edinburgh to Cullen Paisley*, 1782.
A characteristic Improver's mixture of condescension, congratulation and avarice.

Above *Terpersie*
Below *Muckletown Steading*

RCAHMS

The Church of Alford was given, *c*.1199-1207, by Gillechrist, Earl of Mar, to the Priory of Monymusk; this gift was confirmed by Pope Innocent and some of his successors. Original Alford lay to the west of the present village which owes its origins to the railway. The earlier village may take its name from ford over Leochel Burn by the kirk.

Kirkyard walls internally embanked; relief carvings of open books (?judgement symbol) flank gates, (?)1694. Some 17th- and 18th-century stones, most 19th; includes graves of early botanist John Duncan and poet Charles Murray:

He cut a sappy sucker from the muckle rodden-tree,
He trimmed it, an he wet it, an he thumped it on his knee;
He never heard the teuchat when the harrow broke her eggs,
He missed the craggit heron nabbin puddocks in the seggs,
He forgot to hound the collie at the cattle when they strayed,
But you should hae seen the whistle that the wee herd made!
Charles Murray, *The Whistle*

Below *Melville slab*
Right *West Parish Kirk*

Aberdeenshire Council

Aberdeenshire, shows that the money went into the steading. A good survival, in granite ashlar with pinnings, straight skews and canted dormers; very plain, very characteristic.

Forbes Church, 17th century, perhaps incorporating earlier work
Roofless, rubble-built rectangle with crisp corbie-steps to gables and simple chamfered south doorway. Aumbry in north wall. Stands above great elbow of the Don in a little circular kirkyard.

ALFORD

Pronounced *aaaford*, this is the epitome of rural Aberdeenshire, less well celebrated than the Garioch, served in the 19th century, for reasons of geography, only by a branch line, a landscape wrought largely by generations of farmers. The Howe of Alford is now a fertile basin bisected by the River Don; settlement in earlier times avoided the heavier soils of the Howe, focusing on the well-drained slopes instead. Ringed with hills, some domed and inhospitable, one feels one is entering a separate, inviolate country. The village grew up at terminus of the Vale of Alford railway, opened 1859. The single main street is almost unchanged from the 19th century. There can be bustle but no rush, interspersed with periods of extreme, joyful silence. Not an obvious place, through which the road hastens, yet it merits more than a pause.

West (old, St Andrew's) Parish Kirk, 1804 and 1826
Began as a version of Kildrummy, a square with bow staircase to rear; third window added to south to create an imposing, spare rectangle with three fine round-headed windows. Harled with margins and bellcote on west gable.

Aberdeenshire Council

Inside, gallery is carried on Doric columns; outside several good wall monuments including a flamboyant armorial to George Melville, 1678, and a primitive extravaganza, the Balfluig Monument (1725, Mary Forbes), with squat supporting figures, winged *putto* and *memento mori* skeleton below (cf Cuminestown, *Banff & Buchan* in this series).

Mansefield (former manse), 1718 (central part), 1832 north addition; matching south wing later
Original house a neat, harled two-storey affair, now represented by the two-window gable on the present west front. North and south wings are successive, plain, additions in large-coursed granite blocks.

Aberdeenshire Council

Faber Lodge, West Church, 1992/3, Ian J Duncan
Slightly stolid, single-storey-and-attic house with asymmetrical gabled front in recycled granite.

Bridge over Leochel (at Mansefield), *c.*1820
Well-built semicircular arch with slightly curved parapet, all in granite set in large courses.

Annfield, *c.*1800
Solid, rubble-built two-storey, three-window farmhouse with low extension. **Annfield Mill**, *c.*1800, tall (partly from fall of land), two storeys and loft in pinned, squared rubble set in big courses. Wheel and kiln gone.

Gallowhill Farmhouse, *c.*1800
Rather gaunt, former inn (*Headhoose*), comprising two-storey, three-window, piend-roofed house in squared rubble, pinned with cherry-cocking, with centre chimney and

***Within this isle** interr'd behind these stones,*
Are pious, wise, good Mary Forbes' bones;
To Balfluig daughter, and of blameless life,
To Mr Gordon, Pastor here, the wife.
Espiravit Apr27 AD 1728 Aet. Suus 46.
A I McConnochie, *Donside*, 1901

An inscription in the west kirkyard reads: *Here lys jean aitken, lawfull daughter to George Aitken in Hoodhouse of Alford, aged three years, dyed May 17, 1724.* The *Hoodhouse* or Headhouse is an old name for an inn or hostelry. The Headhouse was generally situated near the parish kirk, as were those ofAlford and Clatt.
A Jervise, *Epitaphs and Inscriptions*

Left *Faber Lodge*
Below *Annfield*
Middle *Annfield Mill*
Bottom *Gallowhill Farmhouse*

Aberdeenshire Council

RCAHMS

Aberdeenshire Council

Battle of Alford, 2 July 1645, between Montrose and Covenanters under Baillie. Montrose cleverly lured the Covenanters into the boggy ground beside the Don at Bridge of Alford, where they became easy prey. However, Lord George Gordon, eldest son of Marquis of Huntly was mortally wounded. The Gordon Stone, which marked where he fell, was buried beneath the town dump; a replacement stone can be seen at the entrance to the cemetery. In *c*.1744 horse and *armour-clad* rider found in moss by peat-diggers. Groome

Alford Valley Railway, a railway of south central Aberdeenshire, deflects from the Great North of Scotland at Kintore, and runs 16? miles westward, by the stations of Kemnay, Monymusk, Tillyfourie and Whitehouse, to Alford village. Authorised in 1856, and amalgamated with the Great North of Scotland in 1866. Its gradients are steep, the summit level on Tillyfourie Hill being 636 feet; and the journey occupies 65 minutes.
Groome

Below *St Andrew's Episcopal*
Right *Correen*

RCAHMS

single-storey wing. Tripartite window to ground-floor centre.

East Gallowhill Steading, *c*.1800
Typical single-storey, quadrangular Aberdeenshire steading in roughly squared granite; additional close to rear.

Fountain, 1891
A ponderous pink and grey granite erection in memory of Robert Farquharson of Haughton whose family arms are on the wall of the adjacent (once Station) hotel.

Grampian Transport Museum/ Railway Museum
In restored station, built for Alford Valley Railway, 1859 (closed 1950). Single-platform station with seven-bay, single-storey, rubble building on terminal platform. Carriage and engine sheds beyond, latter three-bay with round-headed rail accesses and windows. (Alford Valley Railway now only 2ft-gauge passenger line in Scotland.)
Conveys something of the optimistic spirit of the Railway Age coupled with the rustic scale of rural Aberdeenshire.

St Andrew's Episcopal Church, 1869
Granite, early English rectangle, rather lurking behind squat detached entrance tower at south-west, fronting road, angle-buttressed and topped by spire which flows down between the elevated corners.

Aberdeenshire Council

Correen, Bank Brae, 1859, William Smith
Formerly a bank, whence solid Tudor display most evident in three-window granite front with parapeted centre porch,

tripartite end windows and central gablet flanked by two large gables, all with traceried bargeboards. Heavy eaves carried all round; the coped chimneystacks and good iron railings complete the confident display. Alterations 1985; separate house created from laundry in 1986.

Medical Centre, 1988, Ron Gauld
Square-plan, with tall, pyramidal roof. Glazed, cut-away corners add excitement externally; light and airy public spaces inside contrast with clever gallery for staff.

Alford & Donside Heritage Centre, Mart Road
Created from former cattle mart (in late 19th century grain and cattle markets were held every week throughout the year).

Aberdeenshire Council

Aberdeenshire Council

Above *Medical Centre*
Left *Haughton House*

Haughton House, *c.*1800 or slightly earlier
Spare but not unimpressive earlier work is rather over-shadowed by wider rear addition: former tall and restrained, three storeys and basement in quoined ashlar with slightly projecting centre bay, on three-window front, a cornice and gabled ends. Porch and centre gable added at same time, 1860, as the ponderous rear wing. **Icehouse**, *c.*1800, barrel-vaulted with boulder rubble front.

Haughton House Cottages, 18th century
Very trig, L-plan group in granite ashlar with cherry-cocking and chamfered openings. Ogee-moulded coping to chimney. (Converted, 1980, into **interpretive centre** for Country Park.)

Charles Murray (1864-1941), author of the perennially popular *Hamewith*, was born in Alford; he emigrated to South Africa in 1888 where he rose to become Secretary for Public Works; he retired to Banchory. He is commemorated in the birch-filled Murray Park, which he presented to the town, and his ashes are buried at the West Church. His poetry is essentially that of the exile:

There's braver mountains owre the sea,
An fairer haughs I've kent, but still
The Vale o Alford! Bennachie!
Yon is the Howe, and this the Hill!
from *Bennachie*

Shepherd

Above *Balfluig*
Right *Breda*

29 **Balfluig Castle**, 1556
Dated on voussiors of doorway and formerly marsh-girt, this medium-sized Forbes place is more than moderately competent. Link-plan, with three-storey main block and tall, five-storey tower on south-east. Two cells in thickness of staircase-wall linked by circular stair-tower. Of pinned boulder rubble with mix of sandstone and granite dressings: nicely knobbly rounded angles, corbels for brattice at second floor on east side. (One corner turret not replaced: see Giles's painting, Leith Hay, 1849.) White harl a bit stark for these climes. Lay unoccupied from 1753, when it was sold to the Farquharsons, until restored in 1966.

Balfluig Castle Cottage, 18th century
Substantial L-plan group with skews and chamfered jambs of openings. Altered 1968.

In 1720 the laird of Balfluig left £2 sterling annually for the benefit of the parish schoolmaster. In 1854 the Revd Mr McConnochie, the late incumbent, had a portrait of Balfluig painted by John Phillip, the Aberdeen artist who was then painting studies in Alford for his picture *The Collecting of the Offering*. This Mr McConnochie was parish schoolmaster at Alford for nearly 50 years. His favourite dog died in 1870 at Crobhar where a brass plate bore his epitaph:

To my favourite Dog, Forres.
Almost imbued with human mind,
Throughout life faithful, true and kind;
Beneath this verdant fir-tree's shade,
My good dog, Forres, now is laid.
16th May 1870

A I McConnochie, *Donside*, 1901

Aberdeenshire Council

30 **Breda**, 1894, A Marshall Mackenzie (Mackenzie & Matthews)
The rather sawn-off appearance of this baronial edifice derives from the demolition, in 1963, of the original house of Broadhaugh, which lay immediately to the west. Coursed red granite gives gritty texture to front which is dominated by three-storey main block with circular conical-roofed entrance tower, balanced, just, by diagonally set angle-tower corbelled to square at end of single-storey-and-attic, four-bay wing. Upper windows pedimented above wallhead throughout; all in slightly heavy Scots style. **Mausoleum**, 1831, for Andrew Farquharson of Breda, within a circular rubble-built enclosure, with arched ashlar granite gateway, a single-storey mausoleum with very plain two-storey façade (with inscriptions) at front; all rather forlorn. **East Lodge** (gatepiers), 17th century; neat corbie-stepped lodge in granite ashlar with tripartite windows and tall chimneys, behind gate with squat ashlar piers with pyramidal coping and ball finials. **Breda Park**, 2005, Lorimer Homes. Enabling development of 13 widely-scattered pink villas of varying plans and pretensions.

Breda enabling development, 2005, Lorimer Homes.

Norman

Fairlea Farmhouse, late 18th century
Retiring two-storey, three-window, harled with margins; in gables, squared, harl-pointed rubble with attic windows and coped chimneys.

Aberdeenshire Council

Aberdeenshire Council

Above *Fairlea*
Left *Castleton of Asloun*

Castleton of Asloun, *c.*1830
Spare but substantial two-storey-and-basement house in granite ashlar with cherry-cocking. Three-window front beneath broad-eaved roof with marked bellcast; windows divided by central transom. Remodelled 1964/5; extended 1984; 1988. **Castle of Asloun**: *We lay at Leslie all night, they (Montrose) camped at Asloun: 2 July 1645*. A Calder then Forbes Z-plan castle now reduced to the remains of a single tower, guarding entrance to large modern farm.

***A mile of Don's worth** two of Dee,*
Except for salmon, stone and tree.
or
The river Dee for fish and tree,
The river Don for horn and corn.
while
Bloodthirsty Dee
Each year needs three;
But bonny Don,
She needs none.

Kingsford House, 1849, (?)J F Beattie
Curious conjunction of standard two-storey-and-attic, three-window granite ashlar house, albeit substantial and well-endowed with a Doric porch with red granite shafts, and a square, four-storey crenellated tower added on the north-west.

Mill of Bandley, from 18th century
Attractive, subdued T-plan complex of differing dates, all rubble-built; block with skewputs and apex finial the earliest; kiln in piend-roofed part. Start-and-awe wheel. **Mill of Bandley House,** (?)19th century or earlier, very plain, rubble-built.

Lintmill
Lofty timber and stone house, recalls flax mill which stood here (followed by woollen mill producing renowned blankets).

Kingsford House

Aberdeenshire Council

Climate *necessarily severe* in this high parish (Cushnie kirk at *c*.1000ft):
Cushnie for cauld,
Culblene for heat,
Clashanreach for heather.
or:
The Nor'lan' win is blawin snell,
And Cushnie hills are cauld...

LEOCHEL-CUSHNIE

United with Cushnie in 1795 (previously united temporarily 1618), this hilly parish forms part of the southern and western rim of the Howe of Alford, dominated by drainage pattern of Leochel Burn, running almost due north to Don.

New **church**, 1797, plain and harled with porch, stands on a mound between the remains of the two old kirks, in Little Howe of Cushnie.

Aberdeenshire Council

Above *Old Manse of Leochel-Cushnie*
Right *Mains of Hallhead*

Manse, 1797
Modest two-storey, three-window house, with additions possibly by J & W Smith, *c*.1845.

Shepherd

31 **Mains of Hallhead**, 1688
A classic laird's house of the Gordons of Esslemont, set high and remote; T-plan, two-storey and attic with crisp corbiesteps. Moulded door in south re-entrant angle bore date, now indistinct (?1668 or 1688); converted to farmhouse in 19th century. The steading has acquired a splendid, finely moulded arch with 1703 panel and initials (IGMR) over. Attic dormers, 19th century or possibly earlier. Refurbished *c*.2002.

Arch, Hallhead steading

Shepherd

St Bride's Church, 1637
Ruins only, reduced to rectangular footings. Cushnie Church was thatched with heather until *c*.1792. 1637 on skewput. Bell of time of Mr Patrick Copland (or Kepland), minister from 1672 to 1710: *P.K. 1686* on it (Jervise). Now represented by wall footings. Some good 18th-century tombstones.

Kirkton of Cushnie House, (?)1724
Date from panel over door. Former Manse of Cushnie, with low first-floor windows now blocked up: effect now of a building more severely plain than it once was.

Aberdeenshire Council

Cushnie Lodge

Cushnie Lodge (old Place of Cushnie), 1707
In the wooded narrows of the Howe, a fine two-storey, L-plan, harl-pointed and corbie-stepped laird's house with centre wallhead gable to five-bay south front and (earlier) roll-moulded doorway in re-entrant. Altered, 19th century; garage/doocot added deftly, 1990.

Old Mains of Cushnie, 18th century
Three fine stone dormer heads, dripping eaves and graduated slates distinguish this two-storey, harl-pointed rubble house, which is augmented by the coat of arms of Alexander Lumsden of Cushnie (1645-1714), whose family owned Cushnie from 1470 to 1876. Altered 1973-5.

Forsyth

Forsyth

Above and Left *Coach-house*

32 **Coach-house**, (?)18th century
In harmony with rolling upland landscape, a strong low L-plan in rough, squared granite with dressings (including skews). Converted to house, 1988, John Scott, eschewing any new openings, giving great authenticity and a very pleasing scale. All slated, as is new detached garage block nearby.

Leochel-Cushnie Old School and **Schoolhouse**, early 19th century and later
House single-storey-and-attic with heavy porch; schoolroom harled, with large windows and a stone dormer head.

Leochel Church (St Marnan's)
The isolated little kirkton contains an excellent group of 18th-century tombstones including two with cheerful grim reapers nestling within a fragment of the old kirk. Burial vault below north aisle.

Forbeses of Craigievar have burial aisle, known as *The Howff* at Leochel. John Forbes, Commissary and son of Bishop of Caithness, was buried here in 1688 *at nycht with torches in the Laird of Craigievar his yle and burying place.*
A Jervise, *Epitaphs and Inscriptions*

Kirkton of Leochel Farmhouse, rebuilt 1767
From its situation, this was probably the manse: now a plain, but sunny, two-storey, three-window rubble house with skewputs and a later back wing.

RCAHMS

Right *Craigievar, the great hall (Billings)*
Below *Craigievar*
Bottom *Mains of Craigievar House*

RCAHMS

Aberdeenshire Council

33 **Craigievar**, 1610, I (John) Bell, re-roofed 1826, J Smith
The consummation of Scottish châteaux: perfect both in mass and detail. The ascent of its creamy, battered walls in a plain, stepped L-plan to an assemblage of corbel-table, corbie-steps, turrets and flats is utterly satisfying.

In 1610 *Danzig Willie*, William Forbes, who found wealth in the Baltic trade, bought the partially completed chateau from the Mortimers and, with the help of one of the Bells, master masons, completed it in the spirit of the Scots Renaissance (colour page 95).

The perfection continues internally, with a great hall whose groined vault (medieval in inspiration) is plastered with a profusion of relief work and pendants of high fashion, similar to the designs in Glamis, Angus, and Muchalls, Kincardine. Baltic connections seen in Memel pine panelling in withdrawing room (Queen Margaret theme on ceiling). Long gallery on fifth floor and stair to balustraded flat, set high and exhilarating over all. A rare fragment of barmkin wall survives. *Open to the public; guidebook available*

Mains of Craigievar House, 1776
Long comfortable block with four finialed stone dormer heads and lintel with 17 *WsF 76* to door; this and other openings are dressed.

Mains of Craigievar Coach-house, late 18th century
Transformed into a single-storey cottage suntrap on L-plan with triple window and loft door on wing; converted 1964.

Aberdeenshire Council

Mains of Craigievar Coach-house

Ladymill, Muir of Fowlis, early 19th century
Substantial, two-storey mill on L-plan in coursed red granite. Prominent kiln vent with saw-wheel vane; wheel inside and below ground level; low wooden sawmill extension.

Wester Ininteer, early 19th century
Dark coursed rubble with red stone dressings and a lofty situation lend tone to this two-storey-and-attic farmhouse.

Lynturk Church, 1866
Former United Presbyterian church with archaic feel from three great pointed windows with basket-work glazing on both sides. Remarkably tall and strong in coursed rubble; coped bellcote on south gable.

Aberdeenshire Council

Manse of Lynturk

Manse of Lynturk, 1866
Well-finished two-storey-and-attic house in coursed rubble with three-window front, the first floor having good 12-pane windows. Chimneys elaborately coped.

Castleknowe of Lynturk, (?)1816
Gaunt two-storey, three-window house within the earthwork of much earlier (?15th century) Lynturk Castle, one of whose gunloops survives in the steading. The castle was held by the Strachans, one of whose sons, John, was renowned in mid-16th-century Scotland for *every sort of villainy*.

In 1526 Alexander Seton of Meldrum was slain by Master of Forbes and John Strachan of Lynturk: in 1531 Strachan beseiged and plundered Kildrummy Castle; in 1537 he plotted to implicate Forbes in an assassination attempt on King James V, resulting in execution of Forbes. Lynturk was thus *the cradle of so much dastardly plotting*.
W D Simpson, *Earldom of Mar*

Lynturk Farmhouse, early 19th century
Tall two-storey, three-window house with rough ashlar granite front and projecting eaves course. Narrowness of gables suggests earlier work. Probably the manse of 1774 for the Burgher congregation of Lynturk, whose church, 1762, was absorbed into buildings of farm when new church built at Buffle in 1791, itself replaced by present Lynturk church.

Aberdeenshire Council

Milton of Cairncoullie School

Milton of Cairncoullie School, early 19th century
Single-storey-and-attic harled house of some grace, won from stone dormer heads and consoled doorpiece (single-storey wing is earlier). Schoolroom at back, also with consoled doorpiece.

TOUGH

A semi-secret area of hill country, includes former great marsh, west of Bents Burn, which was drained and reclaimed over the last 300 years.

34 **Tough Parish Church**, 1838, John Smith
Very simple but effective treatment of rough granite rectangle, dignified particularly by four slender round-arched windows on east flank and a north gable gently elaborated by projecting centre and spiky bellcote. Interior largely original with marble tablets to Farquharsons of Whitehouse from 1838 onwards. Simple iron and granite **mortsafe** in kirkyard.

Below *Tough Parish Church*
Bottom *Fairholme*

Aberdeenshire Council

Aberdeenshire Council

Fairholme (former manse), 1835, John Smith
Substantial, very plain harled L-plan enlivened by porch, good windows with mullions and transoms, splayed angles to front gable and moulded skews to dormer heads and gables. Extensive rubble-built offices. New porch, 1978.

Kirkton Cottage (now Craig Pot), *c.*1800
Possibly built as a girls' school, a sturdy single-storey, two-window cottage in large red granite blocks with grey dressings. Very broad in plan with a tall roof and tripartite windows; curious arcade feature on one gable.

Tonley House, 18th and 19th century
Also known as Kincraigie, Old Tonley survives as a precarious narrow rectangle in boulder rubble; chamfered lower jambs of doorway

Shepherd

RCAHMS

Above *Knockespock House and the Tap o' Noth*
Left *Kildrummy Castle*
Below *Kildrummy Castle across den*
Bottom *Leith Hall*

RCAHMS

Shepherd

Below *Persephone, Chapel of Garioch*
Bottom *Leslie, restored*
Right *Maiden Stone*

Opposite:
Top *Glenbucket restoration by Charles McKean*
Middle *Terpersie restored*
Bottom *Fraser Mausoleum, Cluny*
Right *Craigievar*

Shepherd

RCAHMS

Shepherd

McKean

Shepherd

Shepherd

RCAHMS

McKean

Top *Harthill restoration by Charles McKean*
Below *Castle Forbes Perfumery*
Bottom *Railway carriage summer house, 2000, Mike Taitt, Oyne*
Right *Kirkyard monument, Cluny*

Shepherd

Shepherd

Norman

Shepherd

James Byers of Tonley, the noted antiquary, spent much of his life in Rome, following his father's exile in 1747. He returned to Tonley in 1790 and maintained a close friendship with Miss Elyza Fraser, of Castle Fraser, whose mausoleum he designed.

Left *Tonley House today, with its railway carriage*

Norman

Statue of Aberdeen Angus Bull, Alford, 2002, commemorating the development of the breed (see page 98)

visible beside a pocket baronial mansion of two storeys in squared grey granite; main front five bays dominated by central, projecting half-round entrance tower corbelled to square and gabled with corbiesteps. Angle turret leads round to gabled west front with prominent stone dormer heads. 1829 additions, John Smith; 1890s, A Marshall Mackenzie rebuilding. Estate was sold in 1947 and the house went in the spate of country house destruction in the early 1950s. Mackenzie's baronial hall survives only in McConnochie's description: The ceiling (by Hay & Lyall, Aberdeen) is *panelled, each panel being highly enriched with pendant centres; on the middle panel are the full arms, with motto, of the family (the Moir Byres), while the family crests are placed in each of the four corner panels. All round there is a deep festoon frieze in high relief with centres about four feet apart, on which are emblazoned coats of arms of the various families connected with Moir Byres.*

Walled Garden, Tillymair, (?)18th century
Irregular in plan, following bank of Lyne Burn and defined on the north by a coped wall of pinned coursed rubble with a wide segmental arch at centre; now much overgrown.

Gardener's Cottage, early 19th century, (?)John Smith
Apparently ordinary single-storey cottage in squared granite rubble, but with intriguing bowed north end and circular ashlar chimney. Improvements, 1983.

Kincraigie, 18th century
Supremely plain two-storey, three-window house in coursed rubble (described as *mansionhouse* in *Statistical Account*).

Aberdeenshire Council

Tillyfour Steading

Tillyfour Steading, *c.*1840
Cattle courts on a majestic scale, behind an elongated symmetrical frontage, harled with margins (with cartshed openings filled in), the pride of William McCombie MP (1805-80), *the king of graziers*, whose principal claim to fame (besides being the first tenant farmer to become a Member of Parliament – 1868, Liberal) is that he perfected the Aberdeen Angus breed of cattle. Queen Victoria visited his herd in 1866.

Tullochvenus House, 18th century
Although much altered, the origins of this two-storey (harled) house with small south-west angle tower are clear.

Below *Keig Parish Church*
Middle *Malahat*
Bottom *Old Church of Keig*

Aberdeenshire Council

Aberdeenshire Council

Shepherd

KEIG

Set back from the main road on the ample hilly flanks of the Howe of Alford.

35 **Keig Parish Church**, 1834-5, John Smith
Excellent Gothic rectangle in vigorous, squared granite, whose crisp details are perfectly judged and never overstated. The west porch and pinnacled bellcote, the angle buttresses, also deftly pointed, and the (wooden) perpendicular tracery in the windows have, particularly on a sunny day, a faceted, scintillating appearance which lifts the spirits. Internally, the gallery was originally U-plan; much remains including the brass lamp standard and other oil fittings. Interior re-arranged, 1891, William L Henderson; further alterations, 1902, A Marshall Mackenzie.

Malahat (formerly Manse of Keig), 1834, John Smith
Another quiet Smith triumph, imparting grace to an otherwise simple two-storey, three-window squared granite house by subtle details such as the Tudor hood-mould over the door, fanlight, chamfered openings and corbie-steps. Alterations and repairs, 1866, J Russell Mackenzie; garage added, 1977.

Old Church of Keig, 17th century
On a grassy shelf above the Don, set within traces of an earlier enclosure, a roofless rubble-built rectangle, lacking bellcote as the bell was hung from a nearby tree. West window unusual in being narrower above the transom; south flank has three windows with doors between. James, 16th Lord Forbes, commemorated on

east wall – church now used for Forbes family burials; 18th-century stones in kirkyard.

Oakbank (old Manse of Keig), 1774
Prior to 1771 the manse stood by the kirk; this was replaced by a severely plain two-storey, three-window house, harled with chamfered margins. Rather spoiled by modern renovations, 1974, 1983; garage added 1986.

Aberdeenshire Council

Above *Oakbank*. Left *Bridge of Keig*

RCAHMS

Bridge of Keig, 1817, Thomas Telford
Brilliantly spare treatment: the Don is crossed by a single segmental arch of 101ft span in sharply squared granite. Above, the road is carried on a slight hump.

36 **Castle Forbes**, 1815-21, Archibald Simpson, completed John Smith
Originally called *Putachie*; an impression of going through the motions pervades this large

Lord Forbes *... has lately built a new house, in as bad taste as possible. It seemed to me like a copy of the house at Johnstone, near Paisley; only what may be excusable in one place may be inexcusable in the other. Castle Forbes is on the Don, and in Aberdeenshire! I wonder that the builder did not tremble lest the true old castles of this most architectural shire should step out and tread his base tower and contemptible bright freestone under their feet.*
Lord Cockburn, *Circuit Journeys*

Forsyth

Castle Forbes

Forsyth

baronial block. Smith took over after trouble over the north staircase. In squared granite with simple detail, it is dominated by a four-storey circular battlemented tower at the south-west angle.

Perfumery (formerly dairy then game larder), *c.*1815-20; converted 1998, (?)Archibald Simpson, intriguing single-storey squared granite Y-plan with two-storey central battlemented rotunda and quadrant colonnade of Batty Langley pattern and crowstepped gables (colour page 96).

Above *Castle Forbes. The entrance porch has been sensitively added, 1992 (in stone salvaged from the old kitchen),* Douglas T Forrest
Right *Perfumery (former dairy then game larder), Castle Forbes*

Aberdeenshire Council

Mill of Keig, mid-19th century
Two parallel blocks in partly pinned dressed granite. Kiln roof still pyramidal; conversion to house, 1975, seriously marred by window surrounds of (acceptable) swept dormers and eyeless window glazing throughout.

Auchnagathie, *c.*1800 rear wing; 1870 front house
The single-storey-and-attic rear wing with tall stacks came first, probably with a front range which was replaced with the existing rather florid, two-storey-and-attic, three-bay house. The canted, Gothick porch may have been re-used or else imported. All in squared rubble with polished dressings. Stable block, *c.*1850, includes carriage house with loft above.

Craigpot suspension bridge

Shepherd

Airlie, *c.*1845
Aggrandised farmhouse, single storey, attic and basement, with consoled centre doorpiece, railed steps and large wooden bays and canted dormers.

Craigpot (pedestrian) suspension bridge, late 19th century
Rare Donside example of Victorian high-tech; the two single wire cables are slung over severely classical pairs of hollow cast-iron columns and the decking is of wooden slats, laid diagonally across the supporting struts.

THE GARIOCH

A name redolent of ancient mystery, pronounced *Geerie* possibly from the Gaelic *garbhthach*, meaning *rough ground*, it extends *c*.20 miles westward from Oldmeldrum. *It comprises fertile, warm, well-sheltered valleys, notable for the salubrity of their climate; it used, on account of its fertility, to be called the granary of Aberdeenshire; it has long been famed as a summer resort of invalids; it experienced great development of its resources from the opening of the Inverurie Canal, and now enjoys better advantages from the superseding of that canal by the Great North of Scotland Railway ...* (Groome, 1897).

***The Gareoth** situat in a certane plesand and plane valey, betuene four gret and hich montanis, is sa fertil a ground that yeirlie sik a birth [harvest] it beiris, as for quhilke cause it has obtained this name, ... Barn or garnel [granary] of Aberdine. Heir ar many baith Barounis and Gentle men up sprung and flurised of that able and ancient stock of the Laeslies [the house of which Leslie was an illegitimate descendant], thair haue evir and ay flurised.*
Bishop Leslie, 1578

37 LESLIE

Backed against wooded slopes and bisected by the Gadie Burn, the name *Leslie* comes from Lesselyn, a Garioch landholding ancient in the 12th century when it was adopted by Bertolf, a Fleming, who had been granted it.

Parish Church, 1815
A tall, plain kirk, rubble built, with two rectangular windows in south wall and a 17th-century bellcote in the west gable (bell 1642). Uncompromising, but light inside.

Aberdeenshire Council

Gadie House (former manse), 1794
A high, harled, L-plan house, two storeys and attic, with a three-window front. Ground-floor windows tripartite; pretty, 19th-century railed steps to door and canted dormers with heavy eaves.

Aberdeenshire Council

Top *Leslie Parish Church*
Above *Gadie House (Leslie Manse)*
Left *Leslie*

Leslie, 1661
Built for William Forbes of Monymusk (whose father had acquired barony through marriage to widow of his debtor, the last of Leslies) on site of

RCAHMS

In 1198-9, **David Earl of Garioch** granted all eight of the parish churches in the Garioch to the Tironensian Abbey of Lindores, in Fife, his new foundation, in grateful thanks for his deliverance from tempest on return from the Third Crusade and capture. Inverurie, Montkegie (Keith Hall), Logie-Durno, Premnay, Rathmuriel (Christ's Kirk in Kennethmont), Insch, Cusalmond and Kennethmont ... *Indeed, save for the one fact that it was situated beyond the bounds of the Earldom, Lindores Abbey was as completely the monastery of the Garioch as Deer was the monastery of Buchan or Monymusk of Mar. The whole vast holding in Aberdeenshire was sometimes referred to as* the North Abbacy of Lindores.
W D Simpson, *Earldom of Mar*

RCAHMS

RCAHMS

Top *Duncanstone Congregational Church*
Above *Former Premnay Parish Church, now house*
Right *Lickleyhead*

castle of Leslies of Leslie (the surrounding ditch of this earlier castle is visible from the air). Although in conventional L-plan, with the entrance in a square tower in the re-entrant, this was built for comfort and display. Three substantial storeys rise to turreted angles. Ruinous until 1981... *might yet be saved by a determined restorer* (Tranter), it has been ambitiously restored by David Leslie of Leslie, 1981-9, and now stands as a white-harled surprise soaring up from the level plain. Marred by green slates (although fish-scale turrets do appear on Giles – problem of deciding to what date one is restoring) and vast fire stair, for which there was no evidence at all. (Colour page 94)

Duncanstone Congregational Church, 1818
Severely plain rubble rectangle graced by three broad pointed windows on flanks and two narrow lancets in gable. Tiny pyramidal-topped bellcote and rolled skews.

PREMNAY

A small, intensely rural parish at the back *o'Bennachie,* in which little Auchleven, formerly with a woollen factory, is the only large settlement.

Parish Church, 1792
In a little kirkton detached from Auchleven, a simple rectangular preaching kirk in squared granite with bellcote; enlarged 1828. Kirkyard and manse on opposite side of road. Now house.

Lickleyhead, late 16th century (conventionally 1629)

Shepherd

For William Forbes of Leslie, the seat of the lairds of Premnay. A tall link-plan; in form really 16th century in date, dominated by distinctive, two-storey turrets with occuli, very like Craigievar, another Forbes seat. It does not, quite, possess the *esprit* of Craigievar, being altogether more firmly rooted to the Aberdeenshire soil, but there are several pretty features like the turrets and the small, pedimented dormers (?influenced Mackintosh). A roomy, two-storeyed, L-plan wing was added to the east in the 18th century; restored *c.*1876.

Towmill, early to mid-19th century
Water-powered threshing mill in rubble with strong quoins and a single ring start-and-awe wheel.

OYNE

Encompasses much of the great ridge of Bennachie, whose vast, ship-like profile so dominates eastern Gordon and southern Buchan.

***Bennachie** is a very respectable range of mountains, with one towering summit, and one or two of lesser pretensions, – no rocky accompaniments that are apparent, and no ravines or corries, but a very acceptable long line of hill.*
Lord Cockburn at Westhall, *Circuit Journeys*, 10 April 1852

Aberdeenshire Council

Left *Harthill*
Below *New garages in coach-house style, Harthill*

Aberdeenshire Council

39 **Harthill**, *c.*1600
Chunky Z-plan chateau with small spiky turrets, four storeys containing 19 rooms below a small wallhead walkway, with bedroom stack in round tower, as usual. The original gateway retained in the rebuilt barmkin wall and crisp new garages (1983) in the style of a coach-house. Internally, cool white and charming; 1975-8, William Cowie (colour page 96).

Kirkton of Oyne has traces of several kirks, the ancient is one of two Oynes; the later, railway one, was a station on the GNSR, 1/2 mile to west.

Former **Parish Church** (St Ninian's), 1807, on prominent hill, roofless; farm store now but little bellcote still proclaims its origins. Graveyard, down by road owing to rocky site.

Shepherd

c *Archaeolink Prehistory Park, 1997, Edward Cullinan Associates*

Westhall has a small place in railway history, being the point where work began on the Great North of Scotland Railway in 1852. The estate owner, Sir James Elphinstone, had formerly been active in the Aberdeen Canal Company.

Below *Westhall old tower*
Bottom *Westhall*

RCAHMS

Oyne House, early 19th century
Former manse, by little kirkyard, detached from hilltop kirk owing to latter's rocky terrain. A substantial T-plan house (two periods); to road, a two-storey, two-window block with pitched roof and coped chimney; to rear, two-storey, four-window wing with stepped and consoled door at angle and coped chimney. All in light grey harl.

Benna-Gaudie, Kirkton of Oyne, 19th century
Converted steading, 1991, low, random granite, roughly squared, with pleasing mass of pitched roofs to road.

Former Free Kirk, 1860s
Converted to house with two large garage openings on west side, 1994; gable to road, finialed buttresses. Three lancets on sides, two on gable, restored with basket tracery.

Kirklea, Old Westhall, 1860s
Former Free Kirk manse, plain but broad (three-window gable), two storeys in pleasing off-white harl; retains original glazing and consoled doorpiece. Very neat and surprisingly lavish for Free Kirk.

40 **Westhall**, 16th century with 17th- and 19th-century additions
Estate the property of Bishops of Aberdeen; at Reformation to branch of the Gordons, then purchased by Revd James Horne, vicar of Elgin in 1681. Complex house, Z-plan with 17th-century round tower with conical roof at south-east angle. Tall crenellated parapet to the original, strong, south-west tower, is carried on chunky corbels. Squinch arch in re-entrant for stair-tower. A large, sprawling three-bay house was added at the east and rear in the 19th century.

RCAHMS

Aberdeenshire Council

Norman

Top *Railway carriage summer house, 2000, Mike Taitt (colour page 96)*
Left *Pitmachie Farmhouse*

Pitmachie Farmhouse, *c.*1710
Formerly Pitmachie Inn, now a secluded country farm by a busy main road, formerly buzzing with horses, coaches and travellers. Fourteen horses could be accommodated in the stables (and three coaches in the coach-house), while the human travellers were refreshed in the inn. Honest in squared diorite, it has skewputs and coped chimneys. The stables are tall, two storeys and loft in granite rubble with a lean-to coach house on the east wall. The chaumer (accommodation for hired help) above the stables has now gone.

Corbrigdale

Aberdeenshire Council

Corbrigdale, Oyne, 19th century
Single-storey steading converted to dwelling, 1992/3, Ian J Duncan. Most successful at front with square windows and strong projecting porch.

41 **RAYNE**
Formerly Rane, Raine, Rain and Rayn, from the Gaelic *Raon*, meaning a field of good ground; once seat of Archdeacon of Diocese of Aberdeen (which office once held by John Barbour, author of *The Brus*). The Bishops of Aberdeen had a residence at Rayne, in an earthwork castle (the school, 1880, sits in the middle of it), and held their barony courts - *apud stantes lapides* – at the Standing Stones of Rayne, the stone circle still visible on the ridge above the village. Old Rayne was known as the girnal (grainstore) of the Garioch, from its central position in the fertile area, and prospered from passing cattle drovers until they were supplanted by the railway, which avoided the village.

Lowrin Fair, or the fair of St Lawrence, which dates from at least medieval times, was held at Lammas:

I never had but twa lads,
Twa lads, twa lads;
I never had but twa lads,
At the back o Bennachie.
The taen was killed in Lowran fair
In Lowran fair, in Lowran fair.
The taen was killed in Lowran fair,
And the ither drowned in Dee.
from *Oh gin I were whaur Gaudie rins*

Market Cross, Old Rayne, 17th century
Although the small village of Old Rayne is now off the main road, it was once an important

Aberdeenshire Council

Old Rayne Market Cross

Nothing, however, was done until 1686, when the (Aberdeen Town) Council had before them, from that great seminary of masons, Old Rayne, *ane modell and frame of timber and paseboard* by John Montgomery of a design for a new Market Cross ...
A Keith, *A Thousand Years of Aberdeen*

First four lairds of Warthill were commemorated for their longevity in a tablet in the kirkyard, having attained respectively 72, 90, 80 and 102 years. The inscription ends thus:

Lege Viator, qui fuit, quod es; qui est quod eris.
Vade, vale, festina lente.
(Read, Traveller – What you are, he was;
what he is, you will be. Go, farewell, hasten slowly.)

Right *Warthill House*
Below *Mill of Bonnyton*

Aberdeenshire Council

market centre, having been created a burgh of barony in 1492. The mercat cross is well preserved, with an octagonal granite shaft and a wrought-iron saltire finial, the whole standing on five circular steps.

Parish Church, 1789, aisle 1754
Detached from village, in prominent position *on table land*, T-plan, main part a pleasing harled rectangle with plain round-headed windows and florid bellcote sitting on a little balustrade. On north, an earlier aisle of Leslies of Warthill and the vestry, boasting beetle-browed faces at the skewputs. Interior recast 1930.

Warthill House, 17th century, altered 1801, 1850s Mackenzie & Matthews
Began as a low, L-plan harled block with square corbie-stepped angle turret carried on deep corbel table. Sympathetic 1801 mansion with pedimented dormers forms courtyard; large bays on original block presumably part of extensive 1891 *Elizabethan* additions, most of which have been demolished. Offices continue early theme. 1681 panel. Of Leslies of Warthill; passed to Arbuthnot-Leslies.

Aberdeenshire Council

Freefield House, mid-18th century
A two-and-a-half-storey mansion with two advanced wings, linked by quadrants; Ionic porch and extensive internal alterations, 1885, Marshall & Mackenzie.

Mill of Bonnyton, early 19th century
Practically sited, scarped into slope, an L-plan building in which nothing is superfluous. A plain two-storey-and-attic meal mill in squared and pinned whinstone rubble with gabled loft opening to bank at north. Iron, six-spoke, mid-breast wheel: *1833 Grandholm Foundry.*

The Ploughman's Society Hall, Rayne

The Ploughman's Society Hall, *c.*1830
Marking almost the high point of agricultural improvements in Aberdeenshire, it reflects in its quiet sophistication (squared diorite, tooled dressings) both confidence and vigour. Set foursquare on rising ground, two storeys, four bays, two middle doors and an external stair on west gable. A round-headed panel on the upper centre front contains a plaque of 1778, a (?)plough symbol and a coat of arms with initials AL, JG, MR (Leiths of Freefield who helped to defray some of costs of building). Restored, *c.*1980, Douglas T Forrest Architects.

William Leslie, second son of the fifth laird, who was born in 1657, was schoolmaster at Chapel of Garioch, became a Roman Catholic and at the age of 33 was appointed Professor of Theology in the University of Padua. He was afterwards created Bishop of Laibach and Metropolitan of Carniola and a prince of the Holy Roman Empire.
A Jervise, *Epitaphs and Inscriptions*

42 DAVIOT

From *davoch*, a medieval portion of land producing 48 bolls of grain. The ridge-top village commands long views to Bennachie and north to bleaker lands, giving the feel of a boundary zone. The compelling place that Bennachie, with its craggy tors, occupies in many north-east hearts (*the Mount Fujiyama of Aberdeenshire* – Marquess of Aberdeen) can be readily appreciated from Daviot.

Parish Church (St Colm), 1798
Three large round-headed windows dominate the south wall of this dark granite rectangle; ball-capped birdcage bellcote with, 1752, John Mowat (of Old Aberdeen), bell (recast 1923). Bright remodelled interior. Late 18th-century stones in graveyard; good Greek-revival pedimented burial enclosures of Setons of Mounie (?1828) and Mackenzies of Glack.

Bell given by George Paul, hence the rhyme:

For Paul's name
And Paul's bairns
And a' that lie
In Paul's airms

Two silver communion cups, gifted by the last Episcopal incumbent, are inscribed:

For Daviot
Mr Alexander Lunan Minister
For the use only of Episcopal ministers
1705

Mr Lunan succeeded his father at Daviot 1672 and was deposed 1716 for his part in the rebellion of previous years.
A Jervise, *Epitaphs and Inscriptions*

Old House of Glack, 1723
Rather barrack-like, three-storey-and-attic, five-window house originally built for John Elphinstone, with chamfered openings, skewputs and capacious chimneys at gables with deep moulded copes. Altered 1889,

Old House of Glack

Mackenzie of Glack, who built the New House, spent one night in it then returned to the familiarity of the Old House.

Aberdeenshire Council

RCAHMS

Top *House of Daviot*
Above *Loanhead of Daviot, the great recumbent stone circle*

Matthews & Mackenzie to form nurses' home for adjacent asylum. Rear wing, 1934, G Bennet Mitchell.

House of Daviot (formerly New House of Glack), 1876, James Matthews for J Mackenzie
On an elevated site, commanding the Garioch and now signalling *institution* from its many-gabled skyline, it occupies an important place in the history of the humanising of the care of the mentally ill. Rather municipal baronial, part ashlar, part squared granite rubble, rest harled. Oriel window over door in south; corbel course at top of second-floor level; corbiesteps and central, battlemented tower with weakly expressed turrets (*a conspicuous object* – Groome). The grounds are now the site of a fascinating exercise in competitive architectural grandiosity, but the view is spectacular.

Loanhead of Daviot, 3rd millennium BC
One of the earliest structures in Gordon, a stone circle erected nearly 5000 years ago, of unique north-east type, with a massive slab laid recumbent between two flanking pillars.

Gordon District Council

Right *Mounie Castle*
Below *Garden House, Mounie Castle*

Aberdeenshire Council

Mounie Castle, 1641
Built by Robert Farquhar, Provost of Aberdeen (and passed in 1701-2 to Alexander Hay of Arnbath and in 1714 to George Seton, hence the last Seton castle). Plain harled three-storey rectangle with fine details such as the circular stair-tower very elegantly corbelled to square to form little cap-house-like top, the crowsteps and the coped chimney. The neat one-and-a-half-storeyed block at the north-east is late 18th century.

The **Garden House** of 1694 (with an incised date 1735 IG) was delightfully restored by Robert Lorimer in 1898. Lorimer was also responsible for the wrought-iron gates between the alternately fluted and rusticated gatepiers of (?)1694 (and had other, more elaborate plans which were never realised).

Seton of Mounie commanded the Birkenhead, as in *women and children first.*

Aberdeenshire Council

Fingask House

Fingask House, 1834
For Thomas Elmslie, woollen manufacturer, close by his carding and spinning works (now long gone, but for area of dam), a quietly dignified merger of the vernacular and the classical. Two white-harled storeys, three widely set windows and a slightly projecting pedimented centre bay with Ionic-columned porch in wood make a statement both calm and precise. Back wing of 1923 represents the rebuilding of earlier (?1821 from datestone) house.

The public front was more ponderous, as seen in the four heavy rusticated gatepiers (1824-7) topped with urns and ball finials. The Gothic, piend-roofed **lodge** is contemporary. Further indications of refinement lie in the garden whose rubble wall includes the shell of a former **bath house** with brick Gothic arches. Baluster **sundial** of 1851.

Norman

e *Field Assembly Unit, 2002, Michael Gilmour Associates (colour page 131)*

Lethenty Castle, later 16th century
Of the tower house *soundly plundered* on 27 June 1640 by 200 Covenanters, and again in 1645, nothing now remains, but the ground floor of an angle tower with chamfered slit windows, and gunports of a miniature wide-mouthed type were recorded in 1982.

Shepherd

Lethenty Castle

Lethenty Mill, mid-19th century
Typical nucleated complex; largest building is three-storey-and-attic; circular brick chimney rose above all; greatly missed.

43 CHAPEL OF GARIOCH
High on a ridge which forms the skirts of Bennachie, with a bird's-eye view of the

Parish Church

Garioch, the tiny hamlet once held the Capella Beatae Maria Virginis de Garryoch, one of three chapels in the parish, which was formerly called Logie Durno.

Parish Church, 1813
Large pleasing kirk in rough local red granite ashlar, with cherry cocking. Interior lit by four strong pointed windows with original wood-traceried Gothic glazing. Slightly undersized bellcote on west gable. Originally rectangular, A M Mackenzie added a north chancel with good furnishings, 1923; further additions, 1968, Albert McCombie. These, and the war memorial stained-glass windows and an extraordinary mosaic memorial, make the interior more than usually interesting.

Traces of lintels and sill quarries can still be found on the northern and eastern slopes of Bennachie, eg at Little Oxen Craig.

Kirkyard Gateway (Pittodrie's yate), 1626
Across the road, a rather grand, if solid, roll-moulded archway pierces a gabled wall topped with three ball finials.

Maiden Stone

44 **Maiden Stone** and **Persephone**,
8th century AD, and 1961, Shaun Crampton
The salmon-pink granite monolith known as the Maiden Stone was erected by the Picts in the eighth century AD at the time when Christianity was filtering into the north-east. It bears, Janus-like, a series of vivid symbols, carved in relief, and, on the other face, a round-headed cross, set between a possible calvary scene and a great roundel filled with interlace. The symbols, which are vigorously carved in relief and include a beast or dolphin, mirror and comb, look back to the powerful range of animal and object symbols used as a kind of heraldry on memorial stones in the two previous centuries. The cross side indicates its use as a preaching site during the conversion of the Picts (colour page 94).

The notch out of the northern edge of the stone has fed a legend concerning the daughter of the laird of Balquhain who was baking bannocks on her wedding day and bet a stranger that she could finish her task before he had built a road to the top of Bennachie, *ere she would become his own.* Being the Devil, he won: she took to her heels and, in answer to her prayers, was turned to stone as he caught her, the notch being the spot where he grasped her.
Historic Scotland; open to the public

The wonderfully monumental statue of Persephone, carved from 8½ tons of millstone grit, which stands in a glade 100m to the west of the Maiden Stone, is a distant echo of the legend; in Greek mythology, Persephone was the daughter of Ceres, the goddess of corn and harvest. She was carried off to the underworld by Pluto, the god of death, to be his wife, but Jupiter, king of the gods, decreed that she should return on condition that she had eaten no food in the underworld. Because she had eaten the seeds of a pomegranate, she was allowed to spend only six months of each year with her mother. Her time in the underworld stands for the grain which for half the year is below the ground, but on her return the corn springs up and grows. The splendidly sensual statue is carrying a mirror in reference to the Maiden Stone (colour page 94).

Bennachie Centre, 1994,
Dodd Jamieson & Partners
Simple vernacular feel of materials belie the elegant simplicity of the courtyard design of this visitor centre.

Castle of Balquhain, 15th century; rebuilt 1530
A grand Leslie seat, somewhat reduced but impressive in the scale of enclosure and the height of its brooding tower. Queen Mary stayed here in 1562 during her pursuit of the Gordons. The castle had been rebuilt a generation before for Sir William Leslie, although the blank lower walls (6ft thick) and the vaults of the great keep are clearly early. This is now split in two, although still standing to four storeys.

Of the *200 feet of frontage* of outbuildings, only part of a round tower and overgrown foundations survive.

Shepherd

Persephone

The Colony, Bennachie
Between 1801 and 1850 several people displaced from their previous landholdings by the agricultural improvements colonised the common land below the Mither Tap. About 60 people lived and worked there, in quarrying, dyking and crofting. In 1859 nine lairds persuaded the Court of Session to divide the common land between them and boundary stones were erected to mark these divisions. The colonists became tenants, suffered steeply rising rents and many were evicted. The last, George Esson, died on his croft in 1939. Many traces of the colony remain in the woods above Esson's carpark.

Sir Andrew Leslie of Balquhain
is said to have left six of his sons on the field of Harlaw (1411). It is also said that *he had Seventy Children.* But most of them were unlawfully begotten. It is reported *That in One Night, he begot Seven Children in sundry Places, and that all their Mothers lay in Child Bed at One Time, and that his Lady sent to every One of them in Charity Half a Boll of Meal, Half a Boll of Malt, a Wedder, and Five Shillings of Money. Macfarlane's Genealogical Collections.* Little wonder his widow founded both a chapel and a chantry on his violent death so that there might be prayers of his soul in both places.

RCAHMS

Castle of Balquhain, c.1900

Aberdeenshire Council

Inveramsay Bridge

Inveramsay Bridge (over Urie), 1845/55
A notable survival of early Victorian high-tech, showing a strict functionality worthy of the Modern Movement. The main span has three perforated arched girders cast in two pieces and bolted in the middle, springing from granite ashlar abutments. Plain girder flood-span on west side and cast-iron plate parapets to both spans. A gem.

The Battle of Harlaw

As I cam in by Dunidier,
And down by Netherha,
There were fifty thousand
Hielanmen
A marching to Harlaw.

... The Heilanmen wi their lang swords,
They laid on us fu sair;
And they drave back our merrymen
Three acres breadth or mair.

... The first ae stroke that Forbes struck,
Made the great Macdonell reel;
The second stroke that Forbes struck,
The great Macdonell fell.

And siccan a pilleurichie,
The like ye never saw,
As was amang the Heilanmen
When they saw Macdonell fa.

... And sic a weary burying,
The like ye never saw,
As there was the Sunday after that
On the muirs down by Harlaw.

And gin Heilan lasses speer at you,
For them that gaed awa,
Ye may tell them plain and plain enough,
They're sleeping at Harlaw!

Harlaw House, *c.*1843, (?)William Henderson; 1883 additions
Built close to the spot where the highland host camped before the Battle of Harlaw (1411), an eccentric group, born not of whimsy but rather a perfervid north-eastern world view. The earliest part, the harled cottage-style house with gablets over the first-floor windows, was originally a Free Church manse (the bay windows are an addition). The church was then near the railway line but in 1853 was taken down and rebuilt at Pittodrie where a new manse was built. That church is now demolished but the manse survives (qv).

The narrow, four-storeyed tower with full baronial parapet in rough red granite ashlar (and the thin angle turret on the original house) was built by Alexander Collie, Slate Merchant of Aberdeen ... *as a tribute to the memory of those brave citizens of Bon Accord who along with their noble Provost Sir Robert Davidson fell fighting for their country's rights against the usurper Donald of the Isles on Friday 24 July 1411. George Fordyce & Co. Builders, Aberdeen* (plaque over door).

Harlaw House

RCAHMS

Harlaw Monument, 1914, William Kelly
Has the strength necessary for this windswept

site, previously a *desolate, blood-boltered moor* (W D Simpson). A battered hexagon of dark granite rubble, 40ft tall, built by the successors of Provost Davidson, Aberdeen Town Council.

RCAHMS
Harlaw Monument

East Balhalgardy, late 18th century
Cottar houses, part of complex and extensive improved farm.

45 **Pittodrie**, 1490, early/mid-17th century
On the north-eastern slopes of Bennachie, almost hard by the craggy Mither Tap itself, a wonderfully matured house, grown from the stepped rubble L-plan block to the west. This is most likely of the early 17th century, although a date as early as 1490 has been suggested for the wheel stair in the south-east re-entrant angle. The north-west re-entrant angle was infilled in 1675, when a north-east wing was also added.

In 1841, to the east of this conglomeration, and to some extent wrapped round it, Archibald Simpson built a comfortable neo-Jacobean mansion complete with three-storey balustraded entrance tower to east and an ogee-capped (very like Newe, qv) tower on the south. (The 1605 armorial panel came from Balhalgardy, just west of Inverurie.)

A billiard room was added 1900-3 and a canted bay window to Simpson's drawing room in 1926. Now run as a hotel, it was greatly extended in 1990 by the addition, on the south, of a magnificent pastiche of the 17th-century part of Drum Castle by Mike Rasmussen: interiors, Amanda Rose & Sylvia Lawson Johnstone.

Some early interior details survive (eg water chute and shot hole), while the grounds contain surprises, most notably the detached **gunroom** – 18th century in present form but the two transverse vaults in the lower part may indicate 16th-century work. Also plain, 17th-century sundial with cube dial and ball finial.

Pittodrie
Left *Simpson's side*
Below *Front*
Bottom *Rear*

Shepherd

Aberdeenshire Council

Aberdeenshire Council

Logie House

Gadie wi its waters fleet,
Ury wi its murmurs sweet,
They hae trysted aye tae meet
Amang the woods o Logie.
Like bride and bridegroom happy they,
Wooing smiles frae bank and brae,
Their wedded waters wind and play
Round leafy bowers at Logie.

The Wedded Water by Wm Thorn, quoted in A I McConnochie, *Donside*, 1901

Logie House, 1680 (ruined)
A neat little house in 1732, a fire in 1974 has left but little of this most complex building. It began as a five-window, three-storey block with circular angle towers. Around 1740 a two-storey block was created, on the east side of the courtyard (whose gate arch survived). A two-storey wing was also added to the north side of the court and, *c*.1760, the original block was extended south. A drawing-room wing with excellent plasterwork was added at the south-west between 1770 and 1780 and, *c*.1785, a matching dining-room wing was created.

Unusually, diagonally set game larders were built flanking the gate, *c*.1800, the whole originally harled with margins; chimneys coped. Now a melancholy sight. (Wing at back habitable.) Good **lodge**, *c*.1790, T-plan, distinguished by a centre pediment.

Lodge, Logie House

Logie Durno Churchyard, late medieval
Foundations of rectangular church abandoned 1599; 1720 granite tablet on north wall. Marvellously Gothick Dalrymple Horn Elphinstone burial enclosure of shortly after 1798; west front has pointed moulded archway with a concavely skewed gable above, all flanked by pointed niches.

Above f *Barn o' Braco, 2002, Andy McAvoy, BL@ST (colour page 130)*
Right *Logie Durno Churchyard*

Mill of Durno, *c*.1800
Monumental grain mill: a high rectangular block with double-framed, start-and-awe wheel on west flank. Kiln vent retained. Conversion to house, 1979, marred by modern extension to north. (New house in recycled granite beside mill is better.)

Aberdeenshire Council
Arcot

Arcot, Pitcaple, 1853
Intriguingly pretty cottage-style, former Free Church manse, harled, with symmetrical three-window front with two advanced gables; central gablet with quatrefoils (kirk now gone).

46 **Pitcaple**, from late 15th century
Core, a Leslie tower (Leslies were granted lands in 1457) with open parapet; reconstructed early 17th century as a substantial Z-plan chateau of four storeys, five for the round angle towers, all harled, crowstepped and very select. William Burn added a two-storey extension to the south-west with a new entrance porch and turret in the angle in 1830. Service court and other additions including red granite Corinthian columns of 1870 in hall by Duncan MacMillan. Burn also redid concave tower and delightfully spiky turret roofs.

Aberdeenshire Council

BOURTIE

Calm, gently undulating, rising to green ramparts of the fort on the Hill of Barra with the widest prospects of the Garioch, whose great plain is set with blue distant hills.

Left *Pitcaple*
Below *Bourtie Parish Church in 1910*

RCAHMS

47 **Parish Church**, 1806,
probably by W & A Clerk (on early site)
Tranquil amongst tall cypresses on a sunlit slope, at the eastern end of the Garioch. Deceptively simple on a near-square plan, in boulder rubble with a tall piend roof. Two large

A large boulder to the east of the kirk, known as the *Piper's Stane,* was said to have been the spot where *bagpipers waited for marriage parties on their return from church, when their services were required to convey them home...*
A Jervise, *Epitaphs and Inscriptions*

RCAHMS

Aberdeenshire Council

Top *Early Christian cross slab in Manse offices – a testament to the antiquity of worship at Bourtie*
Above *Mains of Thornton*

Gothic windows with original glazing pierce the south wall and are echoed by two pointed doorways in the north wall. Gablets to east and west, the latter with plain bellcote and ball finial. The interior is a wood-lined delight, with coved ceiling, horseshoe gallery and original ogee-canopied pulpit with precentor's box. Door furniture also original, and bell, 1760, by John Mowat.

(High on south wall, near south end, is a Pictish symbol-stone fragment; 19th-century sundial also.) In the quiet kirkyard lies A G R Mackenzie ARSA PPRIAS (1879-1963).

Old Manse of Bourtie, mid-18th century
Perched above the kirk, possibly built, 1744, for settlement of Revd Thomas Shepherd. Very similar to Cromlet House in Oldmeldrum, although in unharled, pinned rubble. T-plan, originally two-storey, three windows with chamfered openings, skewputs and largely original glazing. Sizeable addition; garden wall coped.

Mains of Thornton, shortly after 1744
A substantial, five-bay building, impressive in its height (although formally of two storeys and attic, there is a high expanse of blind wall above the first-floor windows). Harled, with chamfered margins, battered walls. Plan rectangular, with a later single-storey piended back wing. Original woodwork throughout.

Bourtie House, 1754, extended 1884, 2002
Composed yet refined, it must have turned many Aberdeenshire lairds' heads when first erected by Patrick Anderson and Elizabeth Ogilvie (the PA and EO in the pediment). On south front texture (pinned, rough ashlar with cherry-cocking) and form (three storeys – with

RCAHMS

Bourtie House

laigh ground floor - five windows, projecting pedimented centre bay) meet in almost perfect union. The interior is remarkably unaltered, with fine panelling in the drawing and dining rooms; house extended tactfully to H-plan in 1884. The tiny **Garden Cottage**, *c*.1800, has a piend roof with a mast-like central chimney. Bourtie House was home of A G R Mackenzie.

Bourtie House Garden Room created sympathetically, 2002, Leslie Hunter Architects

48 **Barra**, from 15th century
Pleasing early 20th-century restoration of building whose history is complex and whose ambience is captivating. The structure forms three sides of a cobbled courtyard, the fourth being occupied by a screen wall, pierced by a doorway. The earliest part, the vaulted kitchen and adjacent hall on the ground floor of the west range, and the chamber above, may survive from a tower or keep associated with *the Goodman*, a Blackhall, an hereditary *Forester and Coroner of the Garioch*, recorded in the second half of the 15th century. An L-plan tower appears to have been built to the south-east by 1592, when the Blackhalls forfeited the castle.

The main phase of surviving building was the responsibility of the new owner, George Seton, Tutor and Vicar of Meldrum and Chancellor of the Diocese of Aberdeen, who heightened the south wing and erected conical-roofed towers at either end of the south façade and a stair-tower and caphouse in the centre, 1614-18. Decoration in the form of 1614 and 1618 datestones, an MGS monogram and three interlocked crescents testify to Seton's work. The castle was sold in 1658 to James Reid, an Aberdeen advocate, whose son, a Nova Scotia baronet, was responsible for inserting wooden panelling and creating the formal garden, of which the terrace and summer house with forestair survive.

In 1750 Barra was sold to John Ramsay, a *Russian* merchant (ie he traded in Russia), who added the north wing in 1753, thus changing the alignment and requiring the creation of two piended pavilions in the outer court. From 1766, on the purchase of the adjoining estate of Straloch, to 1909, the castle was used as a farmhouse. It was restored 1910/11, in conjunction with George Bennet Mitchell, by Ramsay's great grand-daughter, Mary, who married Alexander Irvine of Drum and, herself, rebuilt all the farmhouses on Barra and Straloch.

Shepherd

Barra

***A prehistoric fort** on Barra Hill ... is traditionally connected with the victory of Barra ... by King Robert Bruce over Comyn Earl of Buchan ... 22 May 1308 ... his force of 700 men soon routed the enemy, 1000 strong, chasing them far and wide ...*
Groome

Arthur Johnston (1587-1641) was an eminent poet in Latin; his ancestors held Caskieben.

Here Urie with her silver waves
Her banks in verdure smiling laves,
And winding wimples by.

Here Bennachie high towering spreads
Around on all his evening shades,
When twilight grey comes on.

With sparkling gems the river glows;
As precious stones the mountain shows
As in the east are known.

The bare, weathered masonry of Seton's south front is set in a perfect succession of curves and angles, conveying a sense of immense age and tranquillity; charmingly French (colour page 129).

KEITHHALL AND KINKELL

Monkegy prior to 1700, Kinkell added 1754, both predictated on the wide, slack Don which crooks and curves to the south.

Parish Church, 1772 (on south-west skewput)
Very plain: squared granite rectangle with simple bellcote; internally recast, *c*.1920.

Aberdeenshire Council

Aberdeenshire Council

Keith Hall
Above *Main door*
Right *Front*

49 **Keith Hall**, 16th century;
late 17th-century south front
Formerly *Caskieben* (name of original earthwork castle, still visible to the north).
Began as Z-plan house to which a four-storey south front (whose *masterly* fenestration was subsequently disturbed by the *extrusion* of two large oriels) with ogee-roofed pavilions was added in the late 17th century, creating thereby *a large and stately mansion* of the later Scots Renaissance.
This was the result of the purchase of the estate, in 1662, from Johnstons by Sir John Keith, third son of Earl Marischal, who was created Earl of Kintore in 1677 after gaining the credit for saving the Honours of Scotland. His initials, those of his Countess and the prayer MAY TRUTH AND GRACE REST HERE IN PEACE are over the door and comprise the lowest part of an heraldic echo, 95 years on, of the great Huntly doorpiece. Revivified by sensitive restoration and conversion, 1984, to 14 **houses** and **flats**, Douglas T Forrest Architects. 19th-century **offices** to north.

Keith Hall: George Bennet Mitchell's exemplary draughtsmanship

RCAHMS

South Lodge, Keith Hall, probably 1810
Captivating central octagon of two storeys, with small turret over and little projections linked by colonnade, the whole crisply rendered in white; layout of extension, 1986, brilliantly achieved, William Lippe.

Shepherd

Kinkell Church, early 16th century
Battered but tranquil ruin on its haugh by the Don, probably built by Alexander Galloway, Parson of Kinkell (*d.*1552) and architect of the Bridge of Dee in Aberdeen. Sacrament house of 1525 on south wall and excellent early stone of an armoured Gilbert de Greenlaw, who fell at the Battle of Harlaw in 1411; *the only authentic, contemporary memorial of the battle of Harlaw* (Simpson). It was re-used in 1592, including a Greek New Testament text which is the earliest in Scotland. Baptismal font now in St John's Episcopal Church, Aberdeen. *Open to the public*

RCAHMS

50 **Balbithan House**, 17th century
Extensive three-storey, harled, L-plan house with corbelled stair-tower in angle and turrets at corners. Owned by the Chalmers family until 1690, the south wing and the stair-tower are a good deal older than the rest. Important garden re-created by Mrs Mary McMurtrie.

Aberdeenshire Council

Top *South Lodge, Keith Hall*
Above *Greenlaw Stone, Kinkell Church*
Left *Balbithan House*

The largest community of Friends in Scotland was once that at Kinmuck, based on land given by Jaffray of Kingswells. The Kinmuck meeting was founded by Patrick Livingstone from Montrose; the first Quaker school in the country opened here in 1681, in the cottage beside the Meeting House, teaching *the Latin toung and other commendable learning*. The community flourished, with cobblers, tailors, blacksmiths and a wool mill. The school closed in 1807, but annual meetings were held until the Second World War.

Friends' Meeting House, Kinmuck

Aberdeenshire Council

Friends' Meeting House, Kinmuck, 1680
On a back road through open country, a modest yet compelling complex complete with simple burial ground. Meeting House a plain harled rectangle with spur stones and skews. Single-storey harled cottage with wing on north. Mounting step at gateway. Completely reconstructed, 1832; saved from ruin, 1967.

The spelling of Inverurie ... was adopted in 1866. The reason for the change from *Inverury* was recorded in the Burgh Minutes as being due to *the many annoyances and delays caused to the Merchants, Traders and Inhabitants generally by the name of the Town not appearing in the list of the General Post Office as a Post Town, and their correspondence being thus frequently sent to Inverary.*
S Wood, *The Shaping of 19th-century Aberdeenshire*, 1985

It took nearly 30 years, from 1867 to 1895, for Inverurie Town Council (sitting as Police Commissioners) to tackle the problems of water supply and sewage disposal which made the town notorious, and which were greatly exacerbated by the large number of private slaughterhouses within the town's streets. The Board of Supervision maintained strong pressure on the Commissioners, pointing out, in 1874, that *the Police Commissioners of this rich Burgh of Inverurie have been so appalled by the prospect of a (rate) assessment of four pence (compared to Huntly's ninepence or Fraserburgh's shilling) as to condemn the inhabitants for years past to the use of water in some parts so polluted as to be unfit to give an animal to drink.*
S Wood, *The Shaping of 19th-century Aberdeenshire*, 1985

So straggling is its alignment, that it looks more like a village, yet it possesses far greater importance than many a place of more pretentious appearance, and it dates from remote antiquity.
Groome

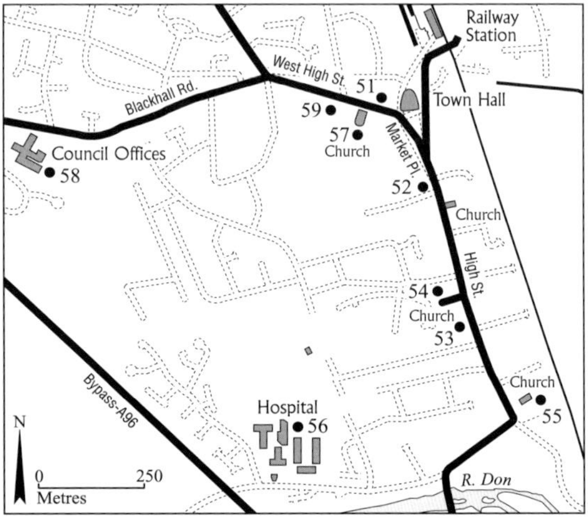

Reproduced from Ordnance Survey based mapping on behalf of HMSO. © Crown copyright 2006. All rights reserved. Ordnance Survey Licence number GD03127G/01/06.

INVERURIE

A lang toon squeezed between the meanders of the Urie as it nears its confluence with the Don and the low, rolling hills of the Garioch (in the words of the *Inverurie Poet*, William Thom, ... *whaur creepin Ury greets its mountain cousin Don*). It began as a swampy medieval caput, its motte-and-bailey castle now split and tonsured in the cemetery. Across the Don, Port Elphinstone (named after Robert Elphinstone of Logie) was the terminus of the Aberdeen Canal (1807-54) and saw the real lift-off of Inverurie. Entrepot and banking centre for the agricultural expansion of the Garioch, the grain girnal of Aberdeenshire, an important stop on the new turnpike, communications became enshrined in its now defunct railway works, which are still visible (Harlaw Road). Now a thriving, bustling market town of some 19th-century grace at its centre and considerable oil-related expansion to the north. Farming, industry, oil – a blend which epitomises eastern Aberdeenshire life at the beginning of the 21st century.

Town Hall in the 1950s

RCAHMS

Town Hall, Market Place, 1862,
J Russell Mackenzie
Replaced a townhouse of 1807, of similar grace to those at Old Aberdeen and Oldmeldrum. The triangular Market Place is dominated by the present baroque, granite ashlar town hall, of two storeys with projecting end bays topped with handsome lions. Its centrepiece has giant Doric pilasters, and a balustraded parapet from which rises a fanciful, diagonally set cupola of Spanish baroque inspiration in painted wood.

On a sunny day the whole has a pleasing Empire look, but has been unbalanced by the addition of the plain **Library** and **Museum**, 1911, H MacLennan of Jenkins & Marr.

1-12 Crosslet Court, late 18th century
Forms the east side of the Market Place and consists of two substantial and attractive blocks: the larger, two storeys and symmetrical about a central pend, the smaller, plain, three bays and with original glazing. Both were once harled but now stripped, their stonework is honest and strong enough to grace this central space.

Royal Bank of Scotland, 21 Market Square, late 19th century
Four extravagantly gabled dormers lurk like startled rabbits behind the modern polished bankers' granite facade.

War Memorial, *c.*1921
Slightly over-wrought granite infantryman, on a bull-faced granite plinth; very like Ellon's.

56 Market Place, late 19th century
Five bold round-headed windows in granite rubble; no glazing bars and poor pointing; very similar to **4 High Street**, granite rubble, two storeys and attic, with six round-headed windows to street; honest trade. Refurbished 1991, subdued glass porch added.

51 **Edwards**, formerly Gordon Arms Hotel, *c.*1900
Has most of the elements of a solid sub-baronial pile: granite ashlar plinth, harled above, stringcourse, crenellated turrets and thistle finials; yet over-fenestrated and rather top heavy. Extended to rear 2003: an almost resolute finish to Market Place.

52 **1 High Street**, *c.*1845
Formerly North of Scotland Bank, its heavy cornice, Doric porch and fine granite ashlar quoins impart the required tone of solidity. A line of three pedimented dormers distinguishes it from **80 High Street**, 1857, William Henderson, formerly Union Bank, remarkably similar in proportions and details to 1 High Street. Good original woodwork. Its south gable is of rougher ashlar with three blind first-floor windows.

Redhythe, 1905, High Street, George Gray
Built from stones removed from (New) Slains

Shepherd

Aberdeenshire Council

Shepherd

Top *Crosslet Court*
Middle *4 High Street*
Above *Gordon Arms Hotel, now Edwards*

80 High Street

Shepherd

William Thorn (1798-1848) was born in Aberdeen, worked as a weaver in Inverurie, knew great poverty, but, thanks to his poetry, achieved a brief fame. He was patronised by J A Gordon of Knockespock who took him to London in 1841. He supported the Chartists and presented a table cover which he himself had woven for the committee room of the Anti-Corn Law Bazaar, inscribed:

If Heaven intended corn to be the property of one class only, corn would never have been permitted to grow but in one land only. Corn is the child of every soil; its grains, its stalks are numberless as are the tears of the hungry or the curses that follow oppression.

Most of his verse, in contrast, is firmly rooted in the kailyard and hovers on the wrong side of sentimentality:

Oh! speak him nae harshly - he trembles the while -
He bends to your bidding, and blesses your smile!
In their dark hour o' anguish, the heartless shall learn
That God deals the blow for the mitherless bairn!
(last stanza of *The Mitherless Bairn*)

Right *Kintore Arms Hotel*
Below *St Andrew's Parish Church*
Bottom *St Andrew's Manse*

RCAHMS

Aberdeenshire Council

Castle (see *Banff & Buchan* in this series), notably the bow windows and ogee gables.

53 **Kintore Arms Hotel**, 83 High Street, 1854, William Ramage
A long, lean surprise, set back to waylay the trade, its two storeys and attic stretch to seven windows and sit on rising ground. Harled with granite margins and a line of wary, canted dormers. The glazing is original apart from the *c*.1920 bays. The central Doric porch is topped by a magnificent achievement, the Kintore arms with spear-carrying supporters, fresh from Harlaw. It was equipped for the new Railway Age with hot and cold water, shower baths and a library.

Aberdeenshire Council

Earlsmhor, *c*.1905, George Gray
A grey granite battlemented blockhouse relieved by Arts & Crafts mullions.

54 **St Andrew's Parish Church**, High Street, 1841-2, John Smith
The style is gothic moderately ornamented (NSA): a plain neo-Perpendicular rectangular box, barely enlivened at its three-bay eastern front by a clock, a spired bellcote and square and octagonal pinnacles. It is in rough granite ashlar with polished dressings – in all nothing to frighten the burghers. Interior altered, 1876 (sanctuary added), and refurbished, 1965, with good new woodwork and mosaics.

St Andrew's Manse and **St Andrew's Cottage**, Glebe Road, 1854, Mackenzie & Matthews
Here is the grandeur and style not found in the parish kirk: a severe late-Georgian throwback in granite rubble, a type specimen of two-storey-and-attic with original canted dormers (corners angled), a solid back wing with pedimented dormers and extensive offices for the servants kept on the minister's stipend of £322.

100 High Street, *c*.1770
A reserved, two-storey, three-window rubble granite house with good details such as corniced doorpiece and coped chimneys.

106 High Street, *c*.1800
Harled, with a segmentally arched tripartite doorpiece, fanlight and original woodwork.

55 **St Mary's Episcopal**, High Street, nave 1841, James Ross
Curiously insubstantial west end owing to tall, narrow windows (the side ones are dummies) set in a gable front crowned by overgrown pinnacled bellcote. East end much better with three tall, spaced lancets and enclosing hood-mould. The bishop turned down a design by a local builder, suggesting the church at Portsoy as a model. Chancel, 1857, William White of London. The glass dates from 1858 to 1945 and is very variable in quality; the Mitchell window of 1908, by the pulpit, with bold blues is excellent. The hall housed St Mary's Episcopal school, with 64 children in 1892.

Shepherd

Shepherd

Top *St Mary's Episcopal*
Above *The Bass and Pictish horse*

Old Kirkyard, Keithhall Road
The walls of the old kirk were demolished about the beginning of the 19th century and the kirkyard dykes built with the stones. The Bass (motte) and Little Bass (bailey) surgically separated in 19th century. Robert Bruce lay sick in Inverurie on the eve of his victory of Barra at Yule, 1308. Four Pictish stones (including unique single horse), 17th-century stones (eg Walter Innes of Ardtannes, 1616) and ball-capped gatepiers. Mortsafe tackle now in Inverurie Museum (above Library). On grave of Helen Bruce who died in her 28th year:

O, painted piece of living clay;
Man be not proud of thy short day;
For like a lily fresh and green
She was cut down, and no more seen.

Urie Bridge, Keithhall Road, 1809
Well executed: strong segmental arch and massive spandrels with some nicely understated detailing. Built during the same burst of Improvement that saw the first Don bridge (1791), the turnpike (1800) and the canal (1805) and which provided the conditions for Inverurie's rapid growth (from 450 to 3058 inhabitants between 1801 and 1901).

On 23 December 1745, Lord Lewis Gordon, with 1000 Jacobites, surprised and defeated *c*.700 loyalists under the Laird of Macleod. These comprised three of the *Independent Companies of Militia*, Highlanders mobilised against the Rising, who, discouraged by poor leadership and a proper *delicacy in fighting their friends and relations*, departed for home, making excellent, not to say remarkable progress, some of them winning Skye by 2 January 1746.
Alasdair Maclean in *The 45*, L Scott-Moncrieff (ed), 1988

Aberdeenshire Council

Aberdeenshire Canal

Aberdeenshire Canal, Canal Road, 1796/1805, John Rennie
Bridges over the intake sluices for the Aberdeenshire Canal: the larger segmental arch has the remains of sluices, another has iron-plated voussoirs.

Duncairn, St James's Place, *c*.1900
Double-fronted Arts & Crafts house with splayed front angles and expressed, angular bays and heavy porch.

4 St James Place, William Lippe, 1992
Largely successful rendering of a contemporary timber-framed architect's office into a more enduring form, with plinth, granite quoins and central doorpiece; upper windows rather weak.

As well as conveying a wide range of essential supplies for the farming hinterland, the canal also supported a passenger service to and from Kittybrewster. The horse-drawn boat took four hours and, *being licensed for the sale of porter and ales was frequently tenanted by parties making a day's outing who spent the hours chiefly in playing whist.*
S Wood, *The Shaping of 19th-century Aberdeenshire*

56 **Inverurie Hospital**, St James's Place, 1936, R Leslie Rollo
Splendid complex embodying most of the elements of the Modern Movement, from the open porch on the gatehouse, to the semi-round bays on the main block and the glazed corners on the casualty wing. Even the ancillary buildings are right, with an atrium to the boiler house and stucco on all, including the entrance walls. The Ashcroft Wing (1980s) with slated eaves and flat roof is a suitably sympathetic extension. Well-planned and exemplary. (Colour page 129)

Inverurie Hospital

Shepherd

57 **West Parish Church**, West High Street, 1876
Former Free Kirk, Early English substantial rectangle, with addition of broach spire in north-east corner which energises the streetscape.

17-25 West High Street, *c*.1870
Above modern shop frontages, two subdued Dutch dormers each surmounted by a single diamond chimney-shaft: the whole in coursed

granite with the Aberdeen Bond in black whinstone.

Clydesdale Bank, 26 West High Street and 1 Constitution Street, 1840-50
Former Aberdeen Town and County Bank whose harling and pedimented gables lighten the massive effect of two blocks with deep eaves meeting at right angles.

Aberdeenshire Council

30 West High Street, late 19th century
The substantial turret with fish-scale slates and thistle finial turns the corner with panache. Two storeys of ashlar granite to West High Street, more guileless squared granite round corner; careful, substantial, extension in recycled granite, *c.*1988, by William Lippe, matches mood perfectly.

RCAHMS

Former Great North of Scotland Railway Works, Harlaw Road, 1898-1905, William Pickersgill
Created by the GNSR Company engineer as a replacement for their cramped site at Kittybrewster, Aberdeen. The single-storey, steel-framed, granite-clad works buildings covered an area of $4^1/2$ acres; powered by the company's own generator; closed 31 December 1969. The surrounding railway housing, six blocks of two-storey granite houses, 1898-1905, and recreation facilities, developed a character so distinct from the burgh that it was known as *The Colony*.

RCAHMS

Top *Clydesdale Bank*
Middle *Former Great North of Scotland Railway Works*
Above *'The Colony' railway housing*

Inverurie Station, Station Road, 1902
A three-platform through station of the Great North of Scotland Railway replacing the small, cramped station of 1852, which lay half a mile to the south, and emphasising Inverurie's key position at the heart of the new communications system in central Aberdeenshire. On down-platform is a long single-storey office building in coursed rubble with cupola and wind vane which doubles as a ventilator. Good cast-iron piers for awning; was also junction for Oldmeldrum railway. Station refurbished 1989.

RC Church of the Immaculate Conception

Aberdeenshire Council

RC Church of the Immaculate Conception, 116 North Street, 1852, (?)Rt Revd James Kyle
... *in strict medieval style, as far as circumstances permit*, according to the *Catholic Directory* of 1852. And the grouping of church, porch, Presbytery House and outhouse, each

Shepherd

Aberdeenshire Council

Top *Gordon House*
Above *1-11 Wallace Road*

with steep slated roof and pinned granite walls, is simple and distinctive.

58 **Gordon House**, Blackhall Road, 1982, Aberdeen Construction Group
Restrained Skye marble cladding above rubble plinth: formerly headquarters of Gordon District Council. Extended with nuclear bunker 1991.

Tulloch Mhor, 1993, Ian J Duncan
Post-colonial single-storey-and-attic house with deeply overhanging bellcast roof carried on colonnade and neat, all glass, triangular dormers. Crisp and fresh as a lettuce.

1-11 Wallace Road, 1993, Grampian Regional Council Dept of Property
Quiet, well-articulated cluster of two-storey sheltered / special needs housing with good woodwork to windows and door canopies.

Shepherd

Aquhorthies Circle, off Blackhall Road, 2005, Michael & Sue Thornley Architects for Castlehill Housing Association: aesthetic sustainability

Garioch Court Housing, 1991
Unquiet three-storey block, harled, with flat wooden window bays, depressed centre and plain porch.

Garioch Nursing Home, 1991
Exotic two-storey piend-roofed block encompassed at first floor by lean-to roof of wider ground floor, creating, with their oversailing eaves, a nested effect; low wing at right angles; all dry-harled.

Shepherd

Right *Royal Mail Letter-delivery Office.*
Below *Ghillie and Glen*

59 **Royal Mail Letter-delivery Office**, 1987, Grampian Design Associates
Adroit treatment of large rectangular shed by expressing structural steelwork of oversized roof and carrying it on thin perimeter columns, all painted Royal-Mail red. Lighthearted yet functional.

Aberdeenshire Council

Ghillie and Glen, Blackhall Road Industrial Estate, 1993, Mercer Blaikie
Low-pitched roof carried on expressed, red-painted metal frame; timber and glass frontage; very energetic and effective.

1 & 3 Business Park, Oldmeldrum Road, 1993, William Lippe Architects
Offices and workshop for and by Scotframe Timber Engineering, the former almost domestic in scale, a retiring single-storey, harled L-plan with pyramidal roof brightened by louvred top-piece, triangular lights and deep eaves.

Aberdeenshire Council

7-29, 22-30 Blackhall Road, 1930s
Wonderfully strong and spare council houses in muscular, pinky granite; each square, piend-roofed block contains three houses.

RCAHMS

Top *1 & 3 Business Park (Scotframe)*
Above *House of Aquhorthies*

INVERURIE PARISH

House of Aquhorthies, 18th century
From 1799 to 1829 this was the Roman Catholic seminary, following the reappearance of Catholics from their hill-fastness of Scalan (*Moray*). A very substantial, if plain, three-storey-and-attic, seven-window front in rosy granite ashlar, with a piended slated roof, neat, piended dormers and two massive lums.

Aquhorthies Steading, early 19th century, classic improved farm complex grouped very pleasingly on slope; includes lofty granary and neat stables.

Easter Aquhorthies, 3rd millennium BC
Excellent example of a recumbent stone circle, showing clearly an interest in differing types of stone on the part of the early farmers. Now on The Stone Circle, Aberdeenshire Council's archaeological trail.

60 **Manar House**, 1811 (at rear), John Smith
Empire link in name, after Manner in Ceylon; a no-nonsense Smith house, two storeys high, five windows broad, the elaborations are confined to a Doric portico, ashlar panels to ground floor and a small cornice. Graceful, full-height bow to side. Alterations 1981. A solid, 18th-century **doocot** in policies, on circular plan with high rat-course (just below the pigeon-holes) and conical slated roof with cupola.

Below *Manar House*
Bottom *East Gate Lodge, Manar Home Farm*

RCAHMS

Manar Home Farm, late 18th-century quadrangle having a rather grand harled west frontage with central ashlar tower and belfry over the pend arch as well as piended dormers (colour page 132). Dressed stone runnel to carry water between two (now gone) water-wheels. **East Gate Lodge**, *c.*1800, delightful, diminutive, circular, harled lodge with conical slated roof and central round chimney.

RCAHMS

Arthur Johnston of Caskieben (1587-1641) attended school in Kintore which left a lasting impression:

Here first I suck'd the Muses' breasts when young:
It was here first I learned the Latin tongue.
Let Athens by Maeonian songs be raised;
It's fit Kintore be by my verses praised.

KINTORE BURGH

Hard by the slack reaches of the Don which winds behind the kirk, flooding occasionally over the haughs, Kintore became a royal burgh early (*c.*1190; charter renewed 1506). Yet it did not expand, losing out to nearby Inverurie. On the Great North of Scotland Railway, and the junction for the line to Alford. The Keith Lord Kintore owned three-quarters of the parish and the Town House but *under a decree of the Court of Session is bound to give the council a room for their meetings and to pay the municipal expenses of the burgh ...* (Groome).

Aberdeenshire Council

Aberdeenshire Council

Top *Parish Church*
Above *Goosecroft House*

The name ***Goosecroft*** also refers to an area of ground in Kintore granted to the Thains by King James II, who, in his guise of the goodman of Badenreich, had been hospitably treated by the lady of the house who ordered *the hen next the cock* to be dressed for his supper.

Parish Church, 1819, Archibald Simpson
Distinguished Gothic rectangle in granite ashlar, three round-headed, hood-moulded windows on south flank, buttressed and pinnacled west end topped by pyramid-roofed bellcote. 16th-century sacrament house inside, from preceding kirk, carved with angels bearing a monstrance, and some good 18th-century tombs and a double-sided early Pictish stone in the kirkyard. The elegant arched gate in Kemnay granite is the war memorial.

Goosecroft House, The Square, *c.*1784
Good Scots comfort, originally two-storey-and-attic, three-bay granite ashlar house, which may have been raised when the drawing-room wing, in partly pinned squared rubble, was built out from the two west bays. Good 12-pane glazing; additions, 1839. Coped rubble garden wall with cast-iron pedestrian gate.

Town House, 1737-47
Work on this handsome piece of civic pride began in 1737, the year after the Earl of Kintore was elected Provost: the cost was borne

Shepherd

Town House

Left *Place of Origin, Kemnay, 2004, John Maine*
Below *Barra, Bourtie*
Bottom *Inverurie Hospital, classic 1930s entrance*

Shepherd

Shepherd

Shepherd

Greig

Above *House of Monymusk*
Right *Barn o' Braco, 2002, Andy McAvoy, BL@ST*
Below *Echt Tollhouse*

Norman

Shepherd

Shepherd

Norman

Top *Old House of Fetternear*
Left *Field Assembly Unit, 2002, Michael Gilmour Associates*
Below *Dunecht House*
Bottom *Fetternear Garden House, 2000, Michael Gilmour Associates*

Shepherd

Norman

Below *Kemnay War Memorial*
Bottom *Manar Home Farm*
Right *James Mitchell Memorial, Kemnay*

Norman

Norman

Shepherd

by him. It is unusual for its date and is now a fine part of the townscape, with graceful external double stairs and clock-tower with ogee roof. Two-storey, five-window front in rough granite ashlar; burgh gaol under stairs; late 18th century wing at back; 1702 bell for kirk and burgh.

Kintore Arms Hotel, The Square, early 19th century
Solid two-storey, three-window squared granite with coped chimneys.

Clydesdale Bank, The Square, mid-19th century
Unusual arrangement of five-bay ground floor with three windows over. Graced by gently curved angles to broad rectangular windows and prominent quoins.

Kintore Lodge, Kingsfield Road, *c*.1800
Fine, two-storey-and-attic, three-window house in well-cut granite ashlar with (later) wooden porch and good gatepiers with ball finials. Neat dormers, single-storey addition to south-east end.

Kingsfield House, early 19th century
Attractive harled two-storey, L-plan house with skewputs, coped chimneys and (later) two-storey bay to gable; long wing with canted dormer.

Castleton, 1930s
Although the windows have been replaced and the roof pitched, the deeply oversailing eaves, cut-away corners and urbane white render make this a jewel of its time. The arcing pink steps to the main door and the sweeping curve of the garage block form an effective foil to the angularity of the stepped L-plan and the corners.

Crown Hotel, High Street, 1899
Very shipshape, two-storey and full attic, four-window (outer ones double) in granite ashlar with a hipped roof to front and crowstepped gable chimneyhead centre front. Double bands between all floors. Scrolled skewputs; clean lines.

Kintore Medical Centre, Wellgrove Road, 1993, Ron Gauld
Square single storey of bull-faced pink Fyfestone and plain grey Fyfestone above, with wing, dominated by dark-tiled pyramidal

The Keith-Falconers were Earls then Barons of Kintore. The implacable motto of Keiths, Earls Marischal:

They say.
Quhat say they?
Thay haif said,
Lat thame say.

The Town House, which was built on the market stance, originally contained a Council Room, a schoolroom and house, and a meal girnal, where the grain and meal of the Earl's tenants, who paid their rent in kind, were stored.
Al McConnochie, *Donside*

Aberdeenshire Council

RCAHMS

Shepherd

Top *Kintore Lodge*
Middle *Kingsfield House*
Above *Castleton*

Shepherd

Shepherd

Top *Kintore Medical Centre*
Above *Kintore School*

roof with top light. The roof is carried down over the wallhead to rest on slim metal pillars, most prominent at the recessed and glazed angles. A good, practical post-modernist building, similar to the medical centre at Alford.

Provost Lawrence House, Wellgrove Road, 1991
Elongated, L-plan block successfully concealing its bulk by conceits such as a square pyramidal-roofed tower at one end and tall, wooden gables on slightly advanced bays on flank. Articulation of glazed entrance angle less successful.

The huge expansion of Kintore early in the 21st century required a series of external developer-funded excavations which have revealed a wealth of evidence of prehistoric and Roman activity including Neolithic pits and pottery, Bronze and Iron Age round houses, and field ovens of the Roman army.

Kintore School, from 1907
Grown along the main road, a fine example of the former Aberdeen County Council's commitment to education throughout this century. It began with an L-plan, two-storey schoolhouse in squared granite, with neat skewputs to gables and dormers, abutting a U-plan school, set with wings to the road. The south-school gable had a lofty main window set under a broad, depressed arch; the other gable, three plain windows. The area between was filled by flat-roofed block with parapet on a shallow corbel-course. Further along the road was a low, two-storey, post-war school with continuous glazing and two-tone granite, and, behind, the concrete and glass solution of the 1960s; replaced, 2005, by new school to serve the 700 new houses built 1999-2004.

Torryburn Hotel, *c*.1830
Plain, two-storey, three-window house of some dignity in squared granite; good consoled doorpiece with three round-headed glazed lights in door echoed in fanlight. Tall, narrow windows (bay to east is recent) and deep eaves; offices to side.

KINTORE PARISH

61 **Thainstone House**, from 18th century
To a straightforward, two-storey-and-attic granite property, Archibald Simpson added, 1840, an imposing six-window, single-storey (tall) and sub-basement rectangle with a two-storey-and-basement tower (cf Haddo, Forgue, qv) and a pedimented *porte-cochère* with three soaring, round-headed arches, all harled with dressings and with his characteristic oversailing eaves. An exotic Italian flower further embellished by bold plasterwork panels within.

Entrance hall relief panel, Thainstone House

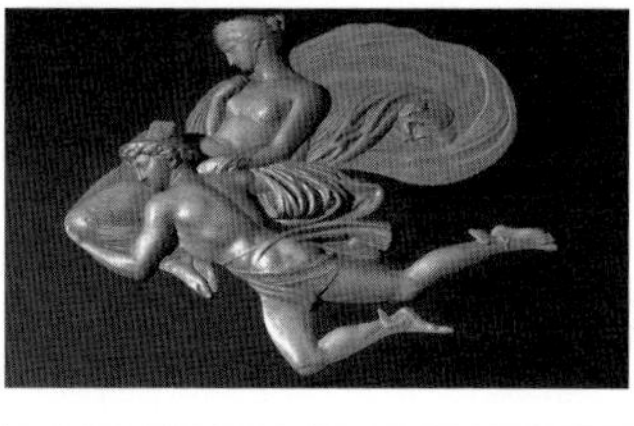

RCAHMS

Aberdeenshire Council

Left *Thainstone House*
Below *Thainstone Gate Lodge*

Aberdeenshire Council

Hotel extension, 1992, by William Lippe, although large, carefully respects style and pre-eminence of Simpson's main house. Home of Sir Andrew Mitchell, ambassador to the Court of Prussia in the time of Frederick the Great. **Gate Lodge**, early 19th century, Archibald Simpson: now severed from its drive and policies by road engineering, this single- and two-storey, chastely harled, edifice with Simpson eaves demonstrates a simplicity of rectangular and square forms and their massing (leaving aside the recent extension) that are enigmatically modern.

62 **Hallforest Castle**, early 14th century
A Keith strength (the Earls Marischal), originally six floors, with walls 7ft thick, the bulk of the tower is taken up by two great barrel vaults, both subdivided by timber floorings to create, in turn, a cellar with kitchen above and a hall with solar above. All windows, such as they are, are on the south side and there is no evidence of internal wall stairs, so timber ladders and hatches must have been required. (Access taken to second

Shepherd

Hallforest Castle, vault exposed

Above *Hallforest Castle*
Right *Aquherton House*

floor.) A remarkable survival of the convergence of medieval military and domestic thinking. One of the earliest towers in Scotland.

Aquherton House, Leylodge,
early 19th century
Plain, two-storey-and-attic, three-window house in coursed stone; rear wing. Renovated sensitively, 1992, Ian J Duncan.

Acid-producing tower, Tait's Paper Mill

Boghead Farmhouse, *c.*1800
Simple, tall, two-storey, three-window harled, no margins, under a slated roof.

Cairnhall Hangar, 1935
Substantial black corrugated-iron shed built in 1935 by local joiner, Reggie Bisset, as a hangar for two de Havilland 89 Dragon Rapides of Ted Freeson's Highland Airways. Freeson, who pioneered flying to the Northern Isles during the 1930s, had been frozen out of Aberdeen by Eric Gandar Dower's acquisition of control of Dyce.

Thainstone Agricultural Centre, Aberdeen and Northern Mart, 1990, Jenkins & Marr
Largest livestock mart in Europe, combining stock pens, auction rings, shops, offices and restaurant around a central *meeting* atrium with *gates* to lean on for the crack. For all the grandeur of its grey, metal cladding, tilted and detailed in red, reassuringly sharny still.

When the present proprietor succeeded, there were more beasts than people, and not one slated dwelling except his own and the Manse.
A I McConnochie, *Donside*, 1901

Tait's Paper Mill, from 1858
Very varied complex ranging from a vast, state-of-the-art mill, 1990, enclosed in a giant metal shed, to an early five-storey brick tower for the manufacture of acid: hand-propelled narrow-gauge railway still.

KEMNAY

The village, enchantingly set on the broad Don, with Bennachie before, developed in two, widely separated bursts; the first the opening up of the granite quarries and the coming of the railway in the mid-19th century, prior to which it had been *a paltry hamlet* (Groome), the second the oil-related expansion of the 1970s and 1980s. Kemnay was the granite core of Aberdeenshire, with quarries at Paradise, Leschangie and Whitestones.

Now augmented by many different styles of timber housing – two-storey, semi-detached, dark browns and muted greens of Fraser Place to the blithe red and dun cabin-styles by the river.

***... it has been so rebuilt** and extended as to become one of the finest villages in the county, and now presents an entirely new and tasteful appearance, with cottages and semi-detached two-storey houses, constructed of granite, roofed with blue slate, and adjoined by garden plots.*
Groome

Parish Church, 1844-5, James Henderson
T-plan, very plain, tall, rubble-built rectangle with canted north and south gables, the latter with elaborated bellcote. Mackenzie's large north window has basket tracery; roof has lucarnes. W A Lawson (Old Aberdeen) bell of 1788; gallery and session house in west. 1871 additions, James Matthews; 1900 alterations, R G Wilson; 1928 general remodelling, A Marshall Mackenzie.
Morthouse, 1831, impregnable: lead-lined and semi-subterranean with granite ashlar front and iron door.

Church Hall
Former Free Kirk on commanding site, Gothic rectangle in squared granite; small detached square tower with steeple.

Kemnay School, 1860, William Henderson
Bright, solid and optimistic group of single-storey-and-attic schoolhouse with advanced, gabled porch, all with deep eaves, and asymmetrical single-storey schoolroom with low pitched roof and three neatly arched windows, all in squared rubble.

Birchfield, High Street, *c.*1840/50
T-plan, single-storey-and-attic house, harled with margins, V-fronted dormers and fancy bargeboards; porch added, 1980.

Burnett Arms, late 19th century
Asymmetrical single-storey-and-attic former station hotel in bull-faced granite with large stone dormer heads, corbie steps and segmental-headed doorpiece; very rustic.

RCAHMS

Shepherd

RCAHMS

Top *Parish Church*
Middle *Burial vault, Parish Church*
Above *Birchfield*

Aberdeenshire Council

Norman

Top *Littlewood Court*
Above *James Mitchell Memorial*

James Mitchell Memorial, 1936
In memory of James Mitchell (1773-1857), carrier, and to provide water for carters' horses, a late symphony in local granites, comprising a well and urn of pink granite with a square grey (Kemnay) granite arched superstructure bearing a sensitive pedestrian statue of Mitchell with roped pack, all in a railed granite-walled enclosure (colour page 132).

War Memorial, 1919
Tall elegant monolith of shimmering Kemnay granite with gabled top, relief carvings of a Celtic cross and saltire and the roll of honour recessed into the otherwise rough surface; all on three steps (colour page 132).

Littlewood Court, 1992/3
Two burly blocks of sheltered housing on corner site in a warm ochrey harl; main block three storeys and monopitched with corner-piece with over-heavy piended roof, sweeping down to glazed wall and recessed entrance with cutaway glazed panels over: all rather unquiet and bulkily urban.

Grove Nursing Home, 1991
Brave attempt at massing two- and three-storey piend-roofed harled blocks with (regrettable) orange metal columns at splayed glazed corners.

Kemnay House, from mid-17th century
Sir Thomas Crombie had a three-storey, L-plan house built with a vaulted ground floor; a three-storey wing with a striking bell-gable was added on the north-west in 1688, shortly after Thomas Burnett acquired the house. The south-east wing was soon remodelled and raised from two to three storeys, and, in 1808, it was given a piend roof. The 1833 work, which may have been by John Smith, includes a plain

Aberdeenshire Council

Above *The Offices, Kemnay House*
Right *Kemnay House*

RCAHMS

porch on the west front, a granite water tower and internal remodelling in classical style. However, the first-floor room in the north-west wing retains its early 18th-century panelled interior with architectural and landscape scenes painted on to the panels. **Offices** (*The Old Laundry*), late 18th century: very pleasing two-storey, five-window rectangular block in squared granite with cherry-cocking; proportions excellent. Converted to dwelling, 1975; extended 1982, with minimal external disruption. **Gazebo** (of old walled garden) at Home Farm, formerly late 17th-century apple house. Rough, squared blocks of granite rubble forming a rustic single-storey-and-attic, piend-roofed structure; fragment of coped garden wall adjoins. (**Bellcote** of old parish church of 1632 in north walled garden: of square ashlar blocks with roll-moulded openings, shafted angles and semicircular pediments topped by finials.)

Granite is a great material *– monumental, strong and enduring ... how beautiful is (its) texture; how pleasant its colour, in almost every case! How clearly the shadows tell and how sweetly shades grade themselves on its bright crystalline surfaces! Subtleties and refinement of modelling are worth doing in granite, as in marble; because they are not lost as they are in a darker material.*
William Kelly, *On Work in Granite*, in *William Kelly: a tribute ...*, Aberdeen, 1949

Kemnay Home Farm, later 18th century (south-east block), house 1861,
James Henderson
Pinned squared rubble south-east block with chamfered openings and a piend roof.

Kemnay Academy, *c.*1980,
Grampian Regional Council
Chunky three-storey hexagonal main block, flat-roofed, with ancillary buildings clustered neatly to one side.

Shepherd
Kemnay Academy

Kemnay Quarries, from 1858
Leased by John Fyfe, an Aberdonian; by 1880, 250 men employed with seven steam cranes and two Blondins (wire lifts – his invention). Blocks 30ft long and 100 tonnes in weight were produced in its heyday. Celebrated for supplying Holborn Viaduct and Thames Embankment, London, and Forth Bridge.

g *Place of Origin, 2004, John Maine: major landscape art (colour page 129)*

Shepherd

63 **(Old) House of Fetternear**, from *c.*1566
The massive footings of the *palace*, built by Bishop Ramsay of Aberdeen in 1226 and extended by Bishop Kyninmond, 1330, are still visible in front of the old house. The lands remained with the bishops until 1550 when a lease, which rapidly became a gift, was granted to John Leslie, eighth Baron Balquhain. They retain a timeless feel. Oldest part is three-storey tower with circular south-west angle tower and vaulted ground floor (to east), built by Leslie on acquiring lands.

RCAHMS

Shepherd

Top *House of Fetternear in its heyday*
Below *1693 armorial panel, House of Fetternear*

Extraordinarily elongated mansion tacked on by Count Patrick Leslie, 1691-3: originally a symmetrical three-storey, six-window house with circular angle towers (that on east belonging to the original house). A one-window wing was also added on the west to balance the original tower. For sheer scale one must look to Fetteresso (near Stonehaven) for comparison. Important 1693 armorial panel over central door incorporating Leslie's coronet of a Count of the Holy Roman Empire, above which is stone carved with sacred monograms (IHS, MRA), part of cult of Holy Name indicating Leslie's adherence to the Counter-Reformation.

The forecourt, with stabling, offices and side wings, was burnt down in 1745 when factor, to whom the estate had been leased, was attempting to strip it bare. Gothicised by Massie in early 19th century by raising the towers and adding corbelling and a heavy, crenellated parapet. A two-storey wing with bow was added in 1818 and a two-storey cross wing in 1850. Burnt out 1919 (colour page 131).

Excellent estate furniture, in particular the huge coped boundary wall and the gryphon-topped gates at Kemnay bridge.

*'...**the Leslies of Balquhain** were building up [at Fetternear] the necessary intellectual and material resources for sustaining Roman Catholic worship ... their property served as the headquarters of the Jesuit mission in Scotland in the late 17th century'.*
P Dransart & NQ Bogdan, *Proc Soc Antiq Scot*, 134 (2004)

Shepherd

House of Fetternear today

Home Farm, 1841
Stable and offices in neo-Tudor quadrangle harled with granite margins; five-gabled east range has a rhythm reminiscent of Smith. Includes a square doocot-tower of ecclesiastical mien with pyramid roof and kennels, cruciform in plan, which are unaltered: a superb complex.

Netherton of Fetternear, 19th century
Strong, single-storey, U-plan steading, cartsheds to rear with decorative brick voussoirs, and a fine two-storey barn of the mid-18th century with steeply pitched roof, skewputs and chamfered openings. Conversion to offices, 1994.

St John's Roman Catholic Church and Presbytery House, Fetternear, 1859, George Goldie
Distinguished group in dark coursed granite with red dressings. West front buttressed and sinuous, rising to a gabled bellcote. Open-trussed rafter roof inside. Presbytery two-storey, L-plan with odd, lean-to porch in angle; shouldered lintels to openings.

Blairdaff Church, 1839
Now sadly roofless, a large kirk in pinned red granite: centre parts of gables slightly advanced with small pinnacles at skew.

Shepherd

RCAHMS

Top *Home Farm of Fetternear.*
Above *The kirk as courtroom: interior, Blairdaff Church*

64 MONYMUSK

Monymusk, with its bowl of low hills, limpid river and fertile haughs, is the Aberdeenshire equivalent of where elephants go to die. It is the secret heart of the North-East (C McKean, *apud ipsem*).

A place of high antiquity
... The proportion under wood ... is very large, the planting of larches, spruces, Scotch firs, and hardwood trees having been begun in 1716, and carried on constantly to the present time.
Groome

St Mary's Parish Church,
from late 12th/early 13th century
Originally the church of the Augustinian Priory (and with beginnings in the earliest *Celi Dei* of

RCAHMS

St Mary's Parish Church

RCAHMS

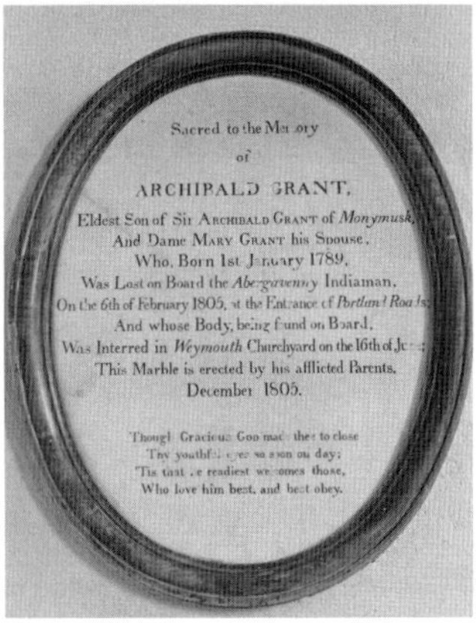

Shepherd

St Mary's Parish Church
Top *Tower*
Above *Grant family memorial*

Aberdeenshire), the priory function is evident in the great length of the first chancel, equal to that of the nave (although three-quarters is now the Grant burial enclosure). From the village green the church is almost hidden; only the slightly squat tower (14ft taken off 1822) with unfortunate crenellations (1891) is visible. An impression of immense age emanates from the thin coursed granite and the sandstone dressings round the simple arched west door with its hood-mould.

The Romanesque church is visible in the round arches to the nave and chancel, the latter with three-shafted columns and cushion capitals. Reformed times wrought many changes, beginning, 1685-93, and continuing with a minister's door and other openings in the south wall in the 18th century. New windows, two large and two small flankers, as well as a north aisle were created in 1822 to form a T-plan kirk, and 14ft of the tower were removed and a spire added. The chancel was given up for a burial enclosure in 1851; the spire demolished in 1891. All this hurly-burly came to an end in 1929 with A M Mackenzie's sensitive restoration which reclaimed part of the chancel, re-orientated the church to the east and converted the north aisle to a vestry.

Now all is white, calm and orderly, with large clear windows to the nave and good recent glass (with local scene) in the chancel. Even the tiers of Grant family memorials divert rather than oppress (eg the aspiring Arthur Henry Grant, 1849-1917, who ... *unsuccessfully contested West Aberdeenshire in 1892, 1895, 1900 in the Conservative interest...*; or the heart-felt plaque to Mr Robert Grant, *d.*1841, who, ... *by a codicil to his will bequeathed a proportion of his property to Lady Grant and her three eldest daughters, which became available on the death of his widow at the advanced age of 92).*

Monymusk Stone is a rare Aberdeenshire example of a Pictish symbol stone with cross, dating from eighth century AD. Clock, 1792, by William Lunan, although face is 1865. Kirkyard enlarged 1900s when earlier stones herded together; one coffin-shaped slab.

1 Monymusk Square

Aberdeenshire Council

Monymusk Village, laid out 1716, Sir Archibald Grant

Although Monymusk is the classic estate village, it was more organically grown than it seems at first sight. When first laid out with a long, rectangular central space, this green was

Shepherd

Monymusk Square

used as a cattle pound by Banffshire drovers and the houses were of clay-bonded stone and heather-thatched. They were rebuilt largely in the 1860s and gradually Tudorised, 1889-1902, by Sir Arthur Grant.

Monymusk Square, *c*.1830/40
No 1 a type fossil: granite ashlar, deep eaves and heavy dormers dignify this little single-storey, two-window and centre-door cottage. Diamond-paned glass is the final archaising – and anglifying – feature. **No 2**, rebuilt 1890, reconstructed 1969: ashlar granite centre gable. **No 3** very similar to No 1 and symmetrical with No 2. **No 7**, *c*.1826, ?John Smith: on site of Moses Morgan's house, possibly incorporating some of its masonry. A double house, two storeys harled with margins, four windows, paired centre doorways and coped chimneys. **No 8** is identical.

Village Hall, 1826, John Smith
Built as parish school, single storey, harled and plain, tucked behind east side of square. Extended 1975.

9,10,11 Monymusk Square, *c*.1830/40, extended 1891: three pretty single-storey granite ashlar cottages, each two window and centre door with diamond-paned glass and wooden canopy gables to doors. **Carriage house** (rear of 13-15 Square), early 19th century: rectangular, in squared pinned rubble with tooled dressings, two segmental arches and with four small loft windows. **Former estate stables** (store of No 16), *c*.1830/40: segmental coach-house arch with loft doorway and stepped gable over. **No 16/17**, 1830/40, Tudorised 1899: single storey-and-attic, granite ashlar; larger than most others in Square, with three windows and two doors with canopy gablets. Also pend arch to stable court.

Below *Former stable, Monymusk*
Middle *Grant Arms Hotel*
Bottom *23/24 Monymusk Square*

Aberdeenshire Council

Aberdeenshire Council

Aberdeenshire Council

Top *Monymusk Post Office*
Middle *Manse of Monymusk*
Above *Monymusk Arts Centre*

Grant Arms Hotel, *c*.1810: good honest ashlar granite two-storey, three-window front, T-plan with consoled and pedimented doorpiece. Quiet and satisfying centre to Square. Good teas.

War Memorial, *c*.1920: tapered classical granite square-plan cenotaph said to have been erected over redundant village well. **No 23, 24**, *c*.1830, altered 1982: originally a pair of three-bay cottages, now one single-storey, six-bay house; original doors with porches now windows.

Library Cottage, mid-19th century, extended 1982: library room has hipped gable and tripartite window; rubble, two-bay cottage. Modern extension carries on dramatic sweep of eaves. **Monymusk Post Office and Shop**, *c*.1830/40: two storey, in large blocks of granite ashlar, with centre door and stepped gable similar to former carriage house.

Manse of Monymusk, *c*.1850
Suitably extensive for such a living: two storey-and-attic, three window, harled with granite margins. Details include consoled doorpiece, large tripartite ground-floor windows with wooden mullions and two canted dormers. Wine cellar included.

Monymusk Arts Centre, mid-18th century
Tree-girt, two-storey structure that began as a lapidary (stone-polishing) mill, with three windows, built by Sir Archibald Grant; it was converted to an Episcopal chapel in 1801 when two round-arched windows were created on the east front and a porch and chancel added. Its interior was rather Presbyterian in layout, with the pulpit on one long wall and the altar in front. After many years of neglect it was deftly restored, 1989, McCombie & Mennie, by the Monymusk Arts Trust as an arts centre, retaining important early organ.

Beech Lodge, *c*.1749
Originally *Bleach Lodge*, this long, double, granite house was for both schoolmaster and (later) factor. Eastern one recast, 1850, has pedimented gablets to first-floor windows.

Braehead Farmhouse

Braehead Farmhouse, *c*.1830
Solid, three-bay, granite farmhouse of some pretension (block cornices to windows and canted dormers) which pales to insignificance against the grandeur of the great U-plan steading adjacent. Remarkably stretched ranges in coursed rubble, with lofts and cart sheds and an

RCAHMS

odd, Tudor-style, detached block with steep roof, hipped at the east and cut back for openings.

House of Monymusk, *c.*1584,
hall restored 1937
In effect, a courtyard palace set on an exquisite bend in the Don, one of the greatest houses of Aberdeenshire, albeit now rather truncated. Traditionally associated with the Priory, it was obtained from the last Commendator by William Forbes who is credited with extending the tower to an L-plan chateau. It was sold in 1712 to the Grants who are still in residence. The prodigious Forbes block was of at least four storeys, with battlements and corbelled angle rounds. It has a vaulted ground floor, the hall at first floor, as usual, and retains its painted ceiling and heraldic panel over fireplace (badly restored between the wars). The tops of the second-floor windows have hoods sitting on sculptured corbels. This block was considerably recast by Alexander Jaffray, 1719-20, who removed the battlements down to the corbel table and added a platformed roof with a high library (with Carolean ceiling) on the west and two storeys of bedrooms on the 17th-century east-north-east wing. He also rebuilt the south wing with its circular tower. A library wing of two storeys and the oriel window were added, 1886, J M Dick Peddie (colour page 130).

The house was once even more extensive, having had a railed courtyard to the south and east with a tower pavilion at the angle to mirror the tower on the south wing and the gates which are now at the entrance to the south drive, thus forming a *claire voyée* facade. These gates, which are by Jaffray, have the piers set diagonally and rusticated in bands. Topped by tall urns. **Walled garden** recently restored.

Aberdeenshire Council

Top and above *House of Monymusk*

Monymusk bought from Sir William Forbes Bt of Pitsligo, 1712, for £116,000, by Sir Francis Grant (1660-1726), elevated to Court of Session as Lord Cullen; he began planting trees in 1716. The second baronet is claimed to have planted 50 million. Now ... *this earthly Paradise, which the Queen has twice visited – need more be said to indicate its beauties?*
A I McConnochie, *Donside*, 1901

RCAHMS

Tollhouse

Pitfichie was owned in the 17th century by the family of Hurry or Urry. The last laird, Sir John Urry, a general of the Covenanting army, was defeated by Montrose at Auldearn and Alford in 1645. Urry changed sides several times but was hanged by Montrose in 1650 while in the royal service. It became derelict after last Forbes of Boyndie, a collector of taxes, vanished with the loot after the 1715 rebellion; he may have been murdered by sailors. W D Simpson

House of Monymusk Home Farm, *c*.1720-50, rebuilt 19th century
The importunate, driving spirit of the Agricultural Improvements, in which the Grants of Monymusk have reason to claim a primacy, is well expressed in this immensely long, single-storey wing set between two coursed granite end blocks. Cartshed range to east with squared granite columns. Fine house conversion from five-window, two-storey block particularly good.

Tollhouse, early 19th century
Single-storey granite in courses; neat three-window bowed end to road; extended 1975.

Milestone (near south gate of House of Monymusk), 1754
Small squared granite stone incised thus FROM THE BRIDGE ONE MILE BY YE YOUNG BUFFS 1754; refers to regiment quartered at Monymusk House after Culloden who had the task of improving the road to Kemnay.

Shepherd

Above *Pitfichie, happed on the brae*
Below *Pitfichie*

Gordon District Council

65 **Pitfichie** *c*.1560-70
Dominated by circular angle-tower to south-west of rectangular block. The collapse of the east wall and south gable in 1936 led Dr W D Simpson to remark, in 1949, that it was an *irremediable ruin*. He could not have envisaged the surge of castle restoring which was to spring up in the north-east during the 1970s and 1980s. Now completely restored, with vaulted ground floor, a small number of wide shot-holes and a pleasing mass of pale harl; spare details and modern services contained in the almost blank east wall. Repaired 1736, unroofed 1769, rebuilt 1977, William Cowie.

Girder Bridge, Pitfichie, 1906, James Abernethy
Two-span parallel-truss bridge with railing of iron rods.

Sir Arthur Grant's School and **Schoolhouse**, 1890
In Monymusk Estate Tudor, the single-storey schoolroom with pair of massive chimneys and big tripartite window is flanked by a single-storey-and-attic house with hipped gable (cf Library). Recently extended and altered for use by differently abled.

RCAHMS

Sir Arthur Grant's School and Schoolhouse

Mosside Cottage (Mosside of Coullie), 1891, altered 1975
Another Estate Tudor house with dormers and lattice windows; good try at extension.

RCAHMS

Left *Ramstone*
Below *Garage*

Aberdeenshire Council

66 **Ramstone**, Lord's Throat, 1889
Rough red granite ashlar in Monymusk Estate Tudor. The piend roof, dormers, and porch and bay with jerkin-head, amount to a concatenation of roofs which are firmly nailed together by a mast-like central chimney. **Garage** addition, 1992, William Lippe, at roadside, a brilliant jewel-box, cubical with hipped gable, heavy-eaved dormer with finial and good wood and granite front.

Ramstone Cornmill, mid-19th century
Rectangular, rubble in courses, with kiln and low-breast wheel in lean-to wheelhouse; masonry wall carries lade.

*... **a road snakes** in a succession of spectacular curves through the pass known as My Lord's Throat, in honour of the Premier Baron of Scotland, Lord Forbes, whose ancestral seat ... stands on the extreme south-western spur of Bennachie ...*
C Graham, *Portrait of Aberdeen & Deeside*, 1980

Suspension bridge, Ord, late 19th century
Harper's patent used to tension main and bracing wire-rope cables; steel pylons on stone plinth and iron rod-suspenders: deckless; crossed the Don to sawmill.

Tollhouse, Tilliefourie, early 19th century
Bow to road, piend roof with stone ridge; large uncompromising flat-roofed extension to rear.

Grant Lodge, Blairdaff, 1827
No-nonsense but pleasing two-storey squared granite villa with symmetrical front topped by a wallhead gable and coped chimneys.

Edinburgh University

Aberdeenshire Council

Top *Place of Tilliefour: proposed restorations and additions, 1884*
Above *Place of Tilliefour*

Place of Tilliefour, 1626; restored 1884/5, H M Wardrop; refurbished 1993-2003, Leslie Hunter Architects
Lying along an almost secret haugh of the Don, the old rubble tower of the Leslies of Wardhouse (1508-1840) was transformed into one of the most pleasing Scots Arts & Crafts buildings. The great length of the low, two-storeyed extension is reduced by the grouping of its elements into gabled, crowstepped and chimneyed blocks, so that the eye is constantly diverted. Fine facet-headed, ball-finialed **sundial** very similar to that at Ellon Castle (c.1717) on shallow plinth in garden.

Tilliefour deserves an important place in Scots architectural history not only on its own, clear merits as perhaps the first restoration of a ruin in the modern period, but also because, on Wardrop's death, his partner, Robert Rowand Anderson, sent as site architect the young Robert Lorimer. The rest is history.

Tillyhashlach

Aberdeenshire Council

Tillyhashlach, Lord's Throat, *c*.1900
Two-storey-and-attic, Arts & Crafts gem with unusual slating on upper walls, sharp gables and good woodwork in windows; excellent kitchen extension, *c*.1992/3, by William Lippe.

CLUNY

The quiet, intensely rural, south end of Gordon, predicated on the great houses of Cluny and Fraser, with burns transecting rolling, semi-bottom land scattered with woodland.

Parish Church (North Church, Sauchen), 1789
On knoll opposite old kirkyard, an Improvement-period rectangle (*a plain old building*) built to accommodate growth of local population. Four round-headed windows; east

wall grey ashlar with cherry-cocking, rest granite rubble. Plain bellcote with Mowat bell. Neatly extended, 1983, with hall.

Fraser Mausoleum, 1808, James Byres
The old kirkyard of Cluny in deepest Aberdeenshire hides a breath of Roman classicism designed with great assurance and executed with extraordinary precision. Miss Elyza Fraser's mausoleum, by her friend James Byres, the classical antiquary, of nearby Tonley, is a drum of fine granite ashlar with a moulded base set on a low square podium; it rises to a dome with oculus. The architraved doorpiece is topped by a fine coat of arms between two swags; the frieze is inscribed: ELIZABETH FRASER OF CASTLE FRASER MDCCC VIII. Miss Elyza left Byers *my carriage and best pair of horses*, but his plans to be interred in a similar mausoleum were later revoked (colour page 95).

There are other treasures in the kirkyard, including the **Linton burial enclosure**, elegant but simple, neo-Greek ashlar, possibly by Archibald Simpson, and an unusual terracotta early Italian Renaissance **monument** to James Reid and his wife Marie Claudine Nardin, probably 1897 (colour page 96). There are also four well-preserved **mortsafes** in front of the Fraser mausoleum.

RCAHMS

RCAHMS

Top *Fraser Mausoleum.*
Above *Mortsafe, Cluny kirkyard*

One table stone reads:
Of Robert Brawny and his wife,
Here ly the bones at rest;
Who of a married state of life
The duties all exprest.

With God sincere, with neighbour just,
They lived from vice sustained
By precept and example they
Their sons to virtue trained.

Manse of Cluny, 1852, William Ramage
Rather grand, two storey-and-attic, three windows broad and very deep, in granite ashlar with classical doorpiece. **Offices** in separate court.

67 **Cluny**, 1604, (?)I Bell
As fantastical a baronial pile as can be found in eastern Scotland, retaining within itself a Z-plan castle represented by the western drum tower – with rebuilt top – the great north-west tower and the rectangular block between – all

Shepherd

Cluny Castle and chapel

Cluny Castle

Shepherd

The mind behind the restless energy of Smith's re-building belonged to Colonel John Gordon, *as eccentric as any member of his family and a good deal less pleasant than most of them.* He amassed a king's ransom in land: the estates of Cluny, Braid, Slains and Kinsteary he inherited, along with property in the West Indies, but he added by purchase the islands of North Uist, Benbecula, South Uist and Barra, as well as the nearby north-east estates of Shiels, Kebbaty and Midmar. He cleared his island properties of 2000 tenants who deservedly cursed his name from their Canadian destination; he died a millionaire in 1858.
H G Slade, *Proc Soc Antiq Scot,* 1981

Below *Stableblock.*
Bottom *Sylvan Cottage*

Aberdeenshire Council

Aberdeenshire Council

refaced in silver-grey granite and refenestrated.

There is something possessed about John Smith's extraordinary rebuilding, 1836-40. This is particularly evident when contemplating the principal frontage: the sledge-hammer symmetry, the repetition of heavy hood-mouldings over all but the ground-floor windows, the sheer height of the towers, the vigour of the machicolation (in fact, deep corbels) and the boldness of the crenellations. The interior is Graeco-Renaissance, in particular the octagonal entrance hall and splendid first-floor corridor. The great staircase is colossal, *c.*1867, with carved wooden balustrade-panels; the drawing room has rich plasterwork and one of the tower rooms has a tent-like ceiling of pleated silk dating, apparently, from the late 1860s.

Long back wings enclose a court with service rooms (there were *137ft of corridors and 14ft of spiral staircase between the kitchen table and the dinner table*); there is also a choice neo-Perpendicular **Chapel**, 1870-3, restored after a fire, 1926, by George Bennet Mitchell, with apse and freestone tracery, including a rose window.

Stableblock, (?)1860: castellated quadrangle with two-storey, U-plan front and central octagonal tower in bull-faced granite. Splendidly cocksure: if it stands still, crenellate it. **Walled garden**, probably 1836-40, is understated rectangle, wall brick with granite dressings. **Gardener's Cottage**, *c.*1864, Gothic, L-plan, in bull-faced granite with lavish detailing: fish-scale slating and traceried bargeboards to eaves. **Sylvan Cottage**, 1836-40, John Smith, fine ashlar; gabled porch with good fanlight, pronounced skewputs. **South Lodge**, 1860, a more austere treatment for the public face of the estate: round-arched gate with crenellated top, octagonal castellated lodge with circular tower and expansive screen walls sweeping in two great convex curves – all, again, in bull-faced granite. **Home Farm**, (?)*c*.1860 – long ranges on an imperial scale, with a machicolated doocot-tower at centre of north front and an unusual circular cattle-court.

Drumnahoy Mill House, 18th century
Quintessentially Scots. Crisp, utterly plain but compelling two storey, three window, harled, no margins and a single-storey wing; good glazing, including pair of tiny square lights high on gable.

Corennie, Sauchen, 1844, (?)James Henderson
A good two-storey, L-plan, harled Free Church manse with round and segmentally arched windows with wooden mullions.

Newmill, *c*.1880
Converted granite grain and sawmill. Rather gentrified: large pyramid roof over former kiln; old sawmill opposite, across millrace, still occupied by all-iron overshot water-wheel.

68 **Tillycairn**, *c*.1550
Substantial four-storey-and-attic, harled, L-plan country house with rounded angles and fine stair-tower in re-entrant angle topped with bold ashlar caphouse. Angle turrets on strong corbels. Almost hidden from the main road, on an elevated site, this is a most rewarding building, particularly in the massing of windows and turrets on the south front, or the interest inspired by the view into the re-entrant. Although referred to as a *bantam cock*, Tillycairn is one of the central Aberdeenshire chateaux whose sheer scale demands a different response than that required of pocket lairds' houses in remoter parts (such as Auchinachie, Forgue). These are big-league players. Ruinous by 1772; restored, 1980-4, Ian Begg, for David Lumsden, whose last act of restoration was to add some heraldry (cf Monymusk).

West Mains Farmhouse, early 19th century
Top-of-the-range estate farmhouse; two storeys, three windows, coped chimneys: solid comfort. Altered 1973-6.

Achath, *c*.1800
Stylish central projection for door with ox-eye window over considerably enhance this simple

Top *Drumnahoy Mill House*
Middle *Corennie, Sauchen*
Above *Tillycairn*

Tillycairn was once held by Matthew Lumsden, *d*.1580, author of *A Genealogical History of the House of Forbes*.

RCAHMS

RCAHMS

Castle Fraser
Top *South-east stack*
Right *Upperworks, north front*
Above *Courtyard*

pinned boulder rubble single-storey-and-attic farmhouse. Canted dormers and back wing are later (see p2).

Shepherd

69 **Castle Fraser**, from 15th century; *c.*1576, Thomas Leiper; 1614, James Leiper; 1617-18, I (John) Bell; 1795, (?)James Byers
The trio of Aberdeenshire finest master-masons has produced an almost perfect Z-plan massing of blocks and turrets combined with an inspired elaboration of upperworks; Fraser is near the peak of Renaissance Aberdeenshire, passing quickly from tower (the earliest work on the bottom of the main block) to palace – complete with U-plan courtyard and laich biggins – and furnished with a colossal asymmetrical bedroom stack of six storeys which yet contrives to balance the whole. As currently presented, far too much rubble is exposed to appreciate the full beauty of the dressed stone, particularly the immense heraldic frontispiece slung high and mighty on the original front and the *Arma Christi*, below and to the right. True, there were many 18th- and 19th-century depredations, including the loss of the ceilings, but the interior retains enough, particularly the high, airy hall (with laird's lug) to savour. Fine **library** by John Smith, 1820, from long gallery (colour page 182). *National Trust for Scotland, open to the public*

Castle Fraser Stables

Aberdeenshire Council

Castle Fraser Stables, 1795
Quadrangular, two storeys to east, one to west, in coursed square rubble with cherry-cocking. Circular angle-towers at once raise the structure and help to pin it to the earth. All in all, remarkably mellow and manorial. Converted to mansion, 1970s; NTS offices, 1994.

Rectangular **walled garden**, probably contemporary, contains 17th-century sundial with complex lectern dial in freestone. **West Lodge and gates**, *c.*1820-30, subdued single-storey ashlar with bow to road and a circular chimney. **Bristow Cottage**, *c.*1825, Tudor, grey and red coursed granite single storey with broad eaves. **Well**, near South Lodge, (?)*c.*1795, vaulted ashlar wellhouse with relief panels of Moses striking the rock and Moses on Mount Sinai.

Leggerdale, *c.*1800
Tall two-storey, three-window farmhouse with single-storey wing and coped chimneys; harl-pointed coursed rubble; well set up.

MIDMAR

A southern frontier, looking partly to Deeside, round the Hill o' Fare, and partly over low hills to the deep-cut Don.

Parish Kirk, 1787
Predecessor at foot of brae dedicated to St Nidan. Archetypal country kirk, a plain Improvement-period rectangle in coursed squared, cherry-cocked rubble, with five generous round-headed windows in south wall. Calm tree-girt kirkyard contains fine recumbent stone circle with canine-like pair of stones flanking the recumbent. West end rebuilt with three lancets and porch, and interior recast, 1885; other additions, 1942.

Manse, 1840, (?)John Smith
Began as two-storey, three-window harled house, porch with round-arched doorpiece and mullions and transoms (cf Kincardine o'Neil and Tarland). Bay window on north-east an addition, 1861, James Matthews.

Aberdeenshire Council

RCAHMS

Above *Parish Kirk*
Left *Manse*

Two distinct varieties of granite were produced from Tilliefourie and Corennie quarries, the blue and the pink. The latter was used for Aberdeen Art Gallery and Gray's School of Art (now Robert Gordon University), Aberdeen. Corennie still available.

Former Free Kirk, west of Bankhead, 1832
A fine example of the fissiparous nature of Scottish religious life post-1707. Began life as Associate Burgher kirk which joined the established church in 1839, only to leave it precipitately in 1843 at the Disruption. Strong, simple rectangle in coursed granite rubble with three good round-headed windows with original glazing in south wall and fine, round-arched bellcote with ball finial on top. Porch and hall later.

Mains of Shiels, 1742 (skewputs)
Notably complete small mansion-house of mid-18th century, the residence of Charles MacKay of Shiels (*d*.1794) who commanded a merchant ship in the West India trade from the Port of London (stone in St Nidan's kirkyard). Muscular, simple and very pleasing T-plan main house with two-storey, ashlar granite front. Openings chamfered; bellcast roof with skewputs and ogee-coped chimneys; first-floor rooms panelled. Single-storey outbuilding probably earlier – large hearth with ingle seats. Large walled garden.

RCAHMS

Mains of Kebbaty

Kebbaty House, mid-18th century
Very plain, harled, three-window, two-storey front; central gable-head on north. Garden walls coped and crenellated. Additions.

Mains of Kebbaty, late 18th century
Comfortable two-storey-and-attic, three-window granite ashlar house with later wooden bays and substantial single-storey, one-window granite wing.

Mains of Kebbaty Steading,
probably 18th century
Imposing Improved quadrangular steading in squared rubble with good details such as broad segmental-headed pend arch, columned cartshed and cobbled north range.

70 **Corsindae House**, (?)1484;
recast 16th century
Vivid, grandiloquent house harled for unity. Began, apparently, as three-storey, L-plan tower with circular stair-tower in re-entrant; plain two-storey-and-basement, three-window wing added on west in early 18th century; back wing with squared stone bow, *c*.1800, when circular tower heightened. Major reconstruction, 1840, John

RCAHMS

Corsindae House

Smith, when old house was doubled to form an approximately symmetrical U-plan court with centre gable. Porch and dramatic quoins added to west wing shortly after this.

Rectangular, (?)18th-century, rubble-built **walled garden** whose west wall was lowered in 1840 to provide material for Smith's reconstruction of the house. Small, late 17th-century sundial. **Doocot**, rubble-built, late 17th century, square plan with rat-course, neat skewputs and double-pitched roof.

Mill of Corsindae,
late 18th/early 19th century
Robust T-plan, boulder rubble with ashlar at wheel gable; sensitive conversion to house, 1988, Burnett & Reid, Surveyors Dept, including harled extension; now cruciform in plan; wooden details less good.

Old Schoolhouse, Corsindae,
late 18th century
Inn originally, became schoolhouse in 1861 with addition of single-storey schoolroom in rough ashlar; broad-eaved, low-pitched roof. House two storey, three window in harl-pointed rubble. Porch later.

Corsindae Croft, by Waterridge, 1802
Burgher church and manse, the former represented by a much-altered single-storey cottage with high coped chimneys and shed, the latter by two-storey, three-window house, harled with porch and outset to rear.

St Nidan's Kirk, 1677
On site of earlier church, on knoll opposite Cunninghar motte – the medieval village presumably lay between them. Ruin of rubble-built church with fragment of bellcote and a quadripartite east window with masonry transoms and mullions. Centre of south wall

Below *Mill of Corsindae*
Bottom *St Nidan's Kirk*

Aberdeenshire Council

Shepherd

Good collection of early stones in kirkyard, including memorial to George Bell, master-mason of Midmar: HEIR LYIS GEORGE BELL DECEISIT IN BALOGY (old name for Midmar Castle) ANO 1575.

*... **deep shadows** and strong lights lie upon it; a dashing burn flows down the glen, dark with overshadowing trees; and above all, it has a green, secluded garden where grow old-fashioned flowers and where there are holes in the sunny walls for bee hives ...*
A Leith-Hay, *Castellated Architecture of Aberdeenshire*

was raised to admit pulpit, *c.*1730, when internal plan was changed.

Right *Midmar in 1961*
Below *Midmar today*

71 **Midmar**, 1570-5, George Bell
One of the largest and most harmonious of Aberdeenshire's many châteaux. On terrace above the Gormack Burn, Z-plan formed from massive square, four-storey central block with six-storey circular battlemented bedroom stack and four-storey-and-attic square tower with turrets – prototype of Fraser? Precious survival in being almost continuously uninhabited from 1842 to 1977, although kept wind- and water-tight. 18th-century interiors, particularly *c.*1733 panelling, intact, including the elegant 1796 dining room.

Anciently, Ballogie, one of sublime family of Bell châteaux in Gordon – Cluny, Fraser, Craigievar, Pitfichie(?), Lickleyhead – characterised by sure-footed massing of blocks, lightness and airyness of upperworks. Squinch arch at level of corbel table of main block carries upper part of stair of great bedroom stack: all remarkably spare and light for its bulk, eschewing the exuberance of the upperworks of Fraser.

Recalcitrance of George Gordon of Midmar and Abergeldie (Deeside) at nearby Battle of Corrichie led to forfeiture of land, 1562. It was restored three years later and G Bell worked from 1565 to his death 10 years later. Lower floors at least hint of the earlier tower (gunloops) destroyed by Mary; attacked again, 1594, after Gordon defeat at Glenlivet. Repairs post-1602. In 1728 bought by Alexander Grant and became known as Grantsfield: 1730 remodelling, two low wings added to north (north-west wing probably 17th century judging by stone dormer-heads) to create small courtyard, terraced owing to fall of land (cf contemporary work at Castle Grant, Grantown on Spey). Restored for dwelling, 1977-80.

Battle of Corrichie, 1562
Another Gordon débâcle, in which Queen Mary, having sought to trim the power of the Earl of Huntly, witnessed the death of Huntly from apoplexy on the field, *the said erle of Huntlie was tane be ane Andro Reidpeth, one of our souerane ladies gaird, quha put him vpone his horse to haue brocht him to the quenis majestie; bot howsein he was set vpoun horsback, incontinent thairefter he bristit and swelt, sua that he spak not ane word, bot deceissit – Diurnal of Occurrents* and, five days later, the beheading of his son, Sir John Gordon, in the Castlegate in Aberdeen. The sequel was even more bizarre: *Upon the dead Earl's pickled body, standing upright in its coffin, the Scottish Council, solemnly sitting in judgement seven months later, pronounced the doom of forfeiture.*
W D Simpson, *Earldom of Mar*

Early 18th-century, hollow-dialled **sundial** with ball finial and, in garden, two-storeyed gazebo with elaborate broken-pedimented bee-skeps adjacent. Imposing outbuilding, mid-18th century, originally two storeys in coursed red granite with cherry-cocking, skews and skewputs.

Barnyards of Midmar, *c*.1796
Harled quadrangular courtyard block in castellated Gothic with front centre archway and drum angle-towers. Rear courtyard reconstructed as mansion-house, 1965-6. The first steading conversion?

Marionburgh Smithy, early 19th century
No-nonsense single-storey rectangle in pinned squared rubble enlivened by horseshoe-shaped doorway.

Old Kinnernie
Abandoned, 1740, when parish united with Midmar; rubble-walled churchyard enclosure with footings of rectangular church, two mortsafes and some old stones.

Linton House, probably 1835, Archibald Simpson
Superb, severely classical, harled with granite dressings, asymmetrical front with two-storey advanced pedimented porch and low-pitched, broad-eaved roof; main part three window.

Mains of Linton (former Home Farm), 1835, also by Simpson, part perhaps completed, 1866, by J Russell Mackenzie; quadrangular, single storey including farmhouse, front symmetrical with centre blind-arched screen flanked by semi-elliptical arches; doocot with small pyramidal-roofed tower, almost church-like.

Murn, ye heighlands, and murn,
ye leighlands!
I trow ye hae meikle need;
For the bonnie burn o Corrichie
His rin this day wi bleid ...

I wis our quine had better frinds,
I wis our countrie better peice;
I wis our lords wid na discord
I wis our weirs at hame may ceise!

Shepherd

Left *Linton House*
Below *Arch, Mains of Linton*

Aberdeenshire Council

Much of Aberdeenshire's landscape carries the signatures of individual lairds: Monymusk, its trees, Fraser, its hedges. No part is more extensively stamped with the owner's wishes than Dunecht, whose estate houses, offices, steadings, and especially its drystane dykes intersect in a grand net pattern.

ECHT

Kirkton looks, like neighbouring Midmar, partly to Deeside; the location of thronged horse fairs, hiring fairs and cattle marts which were regularly held here during the 19th century. Whole dominated by rounded bulk of the Barmekin of Echt, crowned by an ancient fort.

RCAHMS

Below *Cowdray memorial*
Right *Echt Parish Kirk*

Shepherd

72 **Echt Parish Kirk**, 1804, William and Andrew Clerk
Real quality: striking west frontage, three bay, centre advanced, with elegant elliptical window, curved gablet and bellcote, to Gothic four-window rectangle, harled with margins and original basket-tracery glazing. Original gallery inside with Doric columns bearing arms. (St Machar-type ceiling, pulpit, lectern, communion table, 1930, William Kelly.) In all very like Skene, and old Crathie: 600 sittings.

Kirkyard includes War Memorial, 1921, a bronze infantryman by William Macmillan atop a granite plinth; David Morris of Estate Office; and singular monument to Viscount Cowdray (*d*.1927), William Kelly, a superlative version of a Greek *temenos* in rural Aberdeenshire: a vast granite sarcophagus with pediment and volutes guarded by lions atop obelisks.

Glenecht (old manse), 1805
Behind ball-finialed gatepiers a fine, spare two-storey-and-attic, three-window ashlar granite house. Rear addition, 1855, William Smith; dining room and drawing room altered, 1877, John Smith II. Extensive offices.

The Neuk/Auchendryne, *c*.1900, partly G Bennet Mitchell
Striking cottage-style, single-storey-and-attic, L-plan block in coursed granite; two heavy, piended dormers and gabled porch on one face almost mirrored on other; reconstructed and formed into two houses, 1932, Cowdray Estate Office, from sketch designs by Dr William Kelly.

The Terrace

Aberdeenshire Council

The Terrace, early 1900s, G Bennet Mitchell
Six single-storey-and-attic, cottage-style houses with prominent dormers and glazed porches, very much the pattern for Dunecht Estate houses now mirrored in development of new houses at west end of Dunecht.

Shepherd

Tollhouse, Garlogie, early 19th century
Single storey in coursed rubble with bow to road, extended and heightened, *c*.1970.

Tollhouse, Echt, early 19th century
Excellent single storey in large, squared granite blocks, T-plan with bow to road and corbie-stepped porch. Rebuilt, 1932, when circular windows inserted in bow (colour page 130).

Left *Tollhouse, Echt*
Below *Greentree Lodge*
Bottom *Mill of Echt*

Aberdeenshire Council

RCAHMS

Greentree Lodge, *c*.1840
Standing tall on full basement, a single-storey-and-attic house, harled with margins, invigorated by prominent pedimented porch and broad eaves. Dunecht Estate dormers, early 1900s, G Bennet Mitchell.

Mill of Echt, early 19th century
Sizeable two-and-a-half-storey, piend-roof mill in coursed rubble; rectangular, five-windows wide with kiln wing at right angles; diminutive attic windows immediately below eaves. Converted to lavish house, 1979.

Monecht House, 1851
Former Free Church manse; pleasing broad-

gabled, three-window, two-storey house, harled with margins and pediment-hood over doorpiece.

Kinnernie Tollhouse, early 19th century
In squared rubble; single storey, piend roof and coped chimney, with typical bow to road; porch later. Turnpike formed, 1803.

Aberdeenshire Council

Aberdeenshire Council

Top *Dunecht House*
Above *Dunecht House terrace*

73 **Dunecht House**, 1820, John Smith; 1859, W Smith, G E Street
Architecture as the working out of strong intellectual imperatives: a rare and potent example of strength of conviction allied to enormous wealth. Began as neo-Greek, two-storey, basement and attic square block for William Forbes, as replacement for Housedale, the 18th-century mansion whose remains still survive to the north. In 1845 the seventh Earl of Balcarres bought the house as a Scottish seat for his family, the Lindsays, who had been amassing wealth from the Lancashire coalfields. Three years later the house was conveyed to his heir, Lord Lindsay, the polymath book-collector and author of *Sketches of the History of Christian Art*. William Smith was commissioned, 1855-9, to produce a large two-storey, coursed granite extension to west, over a deep basement (forms south side of present court), a 100ft-long gallery with rooms to south and remodelling of the old house with *porte-cochère*, belvedere over entrance, bay windows (*porte-cochère* removed to lochside, 1877) and an emphatic four-storey Italianate tower at junction with old house. The south front is particularly striking, with tall, blind arches, balustrades and extravagantly chequered top parapet. Lord Lindsay's concern for fire-proofing led to the use throughout of

rolled-iron floor joists; the remodelling of the old house included the insertion of a grand square staircase decorated by Italian artists with Raphaelesque figures and scenes.

George Edmund Street was commissioned in 1867 to design a great **library** and chapel. The intellectually pre-Raphaelite Lindsay had chosen an arch Gothic revivalist who responded with two extraordinary spaces. The 120ft-long library is of railway-station proportions, but in the non-pejorative sense, in that these were the cathedrals of the Victorian age. A vast iron-framed space, barrel-vaulted with roof lights and lined with two great galleries, it contains a most spectacular chimneypiece in Italian marbles. The **chapel** is equally stunning, a colossal barrel-vaulted expanse, 50ft high, 100ft long, French-Italian Romanesque with great round arch to chancel. Not created without much heartache, caused by Street's assertion of total supervision.

Death of Lord Lindsay abroad in 1880 halted building work. Theft of his body from vault under new chapel, 1881, led to advertising of estate for sale in 1886, eventually sold, 1900, to A C Pirie of Craibstone, who employed G Bennet Mitchell (then of Davidson & Garden Advocates) to design additions to house (new dining room, conservatory) and a large scheme of estate improvements. Estate let in 1907 to Lord Cowdray who purchased it, 1912, and commissioned Sir Aston Webb to make extensive additions, 1913-20 (Bennet Mitchell dining room and conservatory removed, boiler-house wing, gates and lodges, terraces, loggia, **gazebo**, 1913, with early Italian Renaissance doorpiece etc). Further internal changes, *c.*1924-32, William Kelly. Library, never filled with Lindsay's incunabula, became ballroom (colour page 131).

Offices, *c.*1820, (?)John Smith, quadrangular, two-storey, eight-window front in squared granite with sharp dormer-heads and new pend arch with clock over; now flats, garages. **Dunecht Lodge**, 1820, John Smith, single-storey, temple-form with Doric front, harled with granite dressings and broad eaves.

RCAHMS

Dunecht House Chapel

... I call it quite too d—d provoking *for there is the place exactly as it was last year, not one thing done ... I shall see Master Street when I go to town and then I think I may possibly let loose the pent up bowels of wrath upon his devoted head.*
Letter from Ludovic, Lord Lindsay's son, 1 October 1880

Aberdeenshire Council

Dairy Cottage (offices), Dunecht House

Aberdeenshire Council

Above *Tower Lodge and boathouse*
Below *Housedale*
Middle *Dunecht Estate Offices*
Bottom *Heraldic panel, Estate Offices*

Aberdeenshire Council

Aberdeenshire Council

Aberdeenshire Council

Main gate, 1924-25, William Kelly: set back as drive sweeps off main road, pair of rusticated granite piers with gryphon tops and fine wrought-iron work. **South Lodge**, *c*.1820, probably John Smith: very plain single storey harled, with low, broad-eaved piend roof. Gates, 1859, probably William Smith. **West lodges**, 1912, Sir Aston Webb, remarkably subdued (compared with main gate), but finely detailed, pair of single-storey lodges, harled with prominent granite margins and canted bays to drive. Gates supported on four fine piers with urn finials. Smaller version at **north lodges**, *c*.1912, also Webb. East gate (tower lodges and gates), 1922-3, A Marshall Mackenzie & Son, grandiloquent entrance formed by pair of symmetrical four-storey tower-houses in fine granite ashlar with battlemented parapets, caphouses and circular stair-towers. Massive plain gatepiers topped by gryphons support gigantic wrought-iron gates. Screen walls of bull-faced granite running down to Loch of Skene flaunt square angle-turrets and a boathouse with portcullis gate. Immensely witty and assured fantasy.

Housedale, 18th century
Mansion layout survives, front wall of centre of house represented by moulded doorpiece and fine, 1795, cartouche over – formerly five windows. Short quadrant links to north (gardener's house) and south (reconstructed, with Venetian window in east gable) wings. Fine two-storey outbuilding, dated 1723 I.F.M.F., harled with chamfered margins and skewputs, outside stair. Large **walled garden**; west gate, *c*.1820, John Smith.

Dunecht Works Yard, 1922, David Morris (Dunecht Estate Office)
Rustic ashlar range, end wings project for yard-like steading; U-plan in bull-faced granite with corbie steps to gables and shouldered lintels.

Dunecht Estate Offices and **Hall**, 1925-7, Dr William Kelly, harled, two-storey offices emboldened by colossal heraldic frontispiece at centre to intimidate the tenantry. Hall on east with large Venetian window; internally, a fine survival.

The Terrace, early 1900s, G Bennet Mitchell
Attractive example of estate village showing owner's control from beginning of the century to development of sizeable cottage-style houses,

with large projecting porches and dormers, at west end. Generally, single-storey-and-attic cottages with some variation. Shops, 1923, and garage, 1936, David Morris. Village originally called Waterton – hence farm – most built by A C Pirie during his ownership of the estate. **Jasmine Villa**, *c*.1880, in style of Pirie and Clyne, Gothic single-storey-and-attic in ashlar granite with bay windows. **Bridgend**, late 18th century, U-plan cottage group in coursed granite, around a sunken court. Largely single storey, reconstructed with thatched roofs, 1925, to sketches by William Kelly. Thatch replaced by slates, 1950, and detail changed considerably.

Aberdeenshire Council

Above *Jasmine Villa, Dunecht*
Left *Bridgend Cottages, Dunecht*

RCAHMS

Sandyhillock Rifle Range, 1860
At 400yd marker, a small vaulted building in pinned rubble with very steep roof and straight skews. Star-shaped marker(?) stone dated 8th A.R.V. (? Aberdeen Rifle Volunteers), 1860.

SKENE

Formerly bleak and barren, being part of the badlands, agriculturally speaking, round Aberdeen. Now under development pressure owing to its proximity to Aberdeen, it retains a rural feel around the, in north-east terms, extensive Loch of Skene.

Parish Kirk

Shepherd

74 **Parish Kirk**, rebuilt 1801, (?)William and Andrew Clerk
Very similar in detail to Echt Kirk; rectangular, harled with margins and piend roof, retaining original glazing: two windows to east and west, with centre circular window and doorway. South frontage grand with four windows, the centre two advanced with gable quatrefoil and bellcote, 1840, John Smith. Session room, 1884. Interior remodelled with west gallery, 1932, G Bennet Mitchell. **Kirkyard** contains

Aberdeenshire mortsafe and lavish red granite copy of Tolquhon Monument (see p. 179) to McCombies of Easter Skene and Lyntурk, 1890.

Kirkstane House, from 1779
Formerly Manse of Skene, front and remodelling, 1840, John Smith, creating a plain but pleasing double house; the later crowstepped with centre bay gabled and advanced with round-headed doorpiece and plain stepped hood-mould. Offices. **Sundial**, 1810, very fine incised square freestone table dial with inscription *Manse of Skene* 1810.

Kirkton House, 1825, John Smith
Muted neo-Greek, single storey and full basement in muscular granite ashlar (basement bull-faced) with broad eaves. Doric portico in white-painted wood at centre of east front; twin bows west front, canted bay centre of south front. North part, 1848, J & W Smith. **Walled garden**, 1819, brick rectangle with granite dressings and slim square doocot, (?)1825, harled with pyramidal roof.

Auchinclech, 18th century
Former mansion-house of small estate; south part a harled cottage, early 19th-century extension on west; new north front three-gable with deeply recessed arched central doorpiece. **Steading**, early 19th century, quadrangular, open at south, west side two tall storeys with three cartsheds; east, bizarre single storey battlemented with splayed corners corbelled to square with centre doocot. Harled, no margins.

Easter Skene House, 1832, John Smith
Choice, sustained essay in Smith's Tudor, four-bay, L-plan asymmetrical front with two-storey porch, harled with margins and crisp, sharp dormer-heads. Back wing similar but with circular conical-roofed tower in re-entrant angle;

Aberdeenshire Council

Aberdeenshire Council

Aberdeenshire Council

Top *Kirkstane House*
Middle *Kirkton House*
Above *Auchinclech Steading*

Aberdeenshire Council

Easter Skene House

diamond-shafted chimneys. **Walled garden** with central stone tempietta on six Doric columns; dome pointed with saucer capping.

Aberdeenshire Council

East Lochside Farmhouse

East Lochside Steading, 1927, William Kelly and David Morris
Excellent remodelling of earlier structure in Dunecht Estate rustic; crowsteps at out-turned ends and roll-moulded archway centre. Substantial L-plan, single-storey-and-attic **farmhouse**, 1931, with prominent corbie-stepped gables and large dormer-heads.

Aberdeenshire Council

Skene House
Left *The house*
Below *Door detail*
Middle *Arcade*
Bottom *Stableblock*

Aberdeenshire Council

Aberdeenshire Council

Aberdeenshire Council

Skene House, from 14th century
King Robert (Bruce) granted the barony of Skene to Robert Skene in 1318; it was held by his male descendants until 1827, during which time was erected one of the largest tower-houses in Scotland (early 14th century - reputedly the first stone-and-lime castle in Mar). Originally having three vaults, it was massive and brooding, was gutted and remodelled, 1680, and is now largely obscured by later work; a south wing in ashlar, c.1745; and, 1847-50, an extensive baronial mansion by Archibald Simpson and (?)William Ramage for the Duke of Fife (north wing includes original tower). This scheme, reputedly on Simpson's drawing-board at his death, involved extension of the south wing, a single-storey entrance hall with twin slim towers at gate and the replacement of the austere Georgian fenestration with larger lights and oriels.

Stableblock, *c*.1860, Archibald Simpson: sizeable two-storey baronial in coursed granite with machicolated centre tower, battlemented and caphoused; converted, 1984, to form five houses. **Walled garden**, 1847-50, with twin ogee gazebos; rustic **lodge**, *c*.1840.

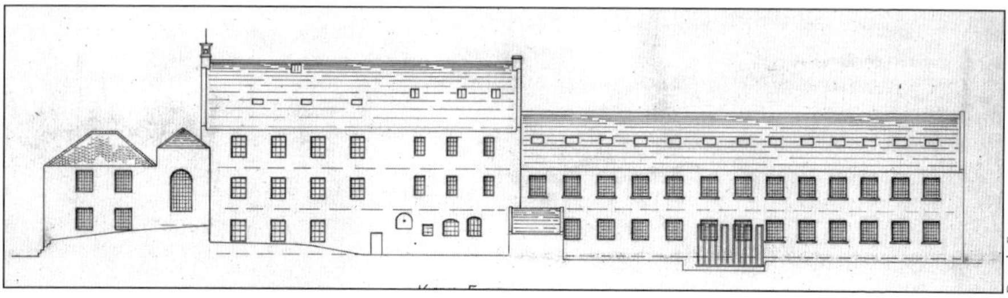

Dunecht Estate

75 **Garlogie**

Dundee-scale woollen factory, began with water-power, then, from *c*.1830, it was driven by a gigantic beam-engine with elegant Doric column at centre and a 16ft flywheel. This is still *in situ*, in brick-built engine-house to rear of rubble-built factory (of which 16 bays demolished) for Haddens of Aberdeen. It ceased operation in 1904 and became site for water turbine, 1923, Escher Wyss, which provided electricity to estate and grid until 1960s. It was served by lade from Loch of Skene (surge-tank and out-take works still extant).

Surviving south wing converted to village hall, 1931, David Morris, extended 1989. Museum of Power conversion of engine-house and turbine-hall, 1994-5, Douglas T Forrest Architects for Gordon District Council and North-East Scotland Museums Service.

Full-scale, early 19th-century rural industrial settlement all around, including **Mill House** (former office and counting house), solid two storey, five-on-four windows; converted to semi-detached houses, 1935. **Nos 1-3 Garlogie**, low, sturdy coursed rubble cottages. **Garlogie House**, former factor's house, *c*.1840/50, T-plan, harled with gabled centre projecting.

RCAHMS

Aberdeenshire Council

Garlogie
Top *Elevation, woollen mill*
Middle *Beam engine*
Above *Mill House*

Westhill Garden Suburb, from 1972, layout T Findlay Lyon, final design Thomas Cordiner Cunningham & Partners with Findlay Lyon This, in many ways, one of the few extensive and coherent legacies of the oil boom in the north-east, began as a developer-led proposal, 1966-8, of an *article 10 departure* to Aberdeen County Council for 30 houses. By 1972, following planning permission, 80 acres were envisaged for a residential development of 2000 houses. The guiding principle was to *jump the green belt* around Aberdeen and provide an integrated community in open country. *The estate is to be laid out as a garden suburb with* *great emphasis on landscaping* and with church, schools (3 primary, 1 secondary) and an element of municipal housing integrated. Now a successful major settlement rising up tiered, south-facing slopes, with views to Deeside; **Elrick School**, with pitched roof, is pleasing, and **Medical Centre**, Westhill Drive, 1985, Ron Gauld, a single-storey plinth in red stone carries two opposed, monopitched roof sections of some size: very plain and functional.

Shepherd

Shepherd

Top *Medical Centre, Westhill*
Above *Peregrine House*

Westhill Industrial Estate
Contains several challenging buildings, including **Peregrine House**, 1993, an angular, post-modernist, three-storey U-plan in Fyfestone for Stewart Milne Group. Main elevation fully glazed in dark glass and green metal frames; triangular outshots topped by triangular eaves flank the entrance; altogether understated and refreshing. **Stena House** has a certain attractive austerity derived from its two-storey system-build with flat roof and expressed square towers. **Dowell Schlumberger Technology Centre**, a high-tech, metal-framed, black box beside rather ordinary office range.

76 **KINELLAR**
Scattered between the Don and the A96, with the (former) distillery village of Blackburn, once called Broadford of Glasgo, sprawling up the den.

Pictish stone, Kinellar Kirk

RCAHMS

Former Parish Church, 1801
Broad rectangle, harled, no margins, with two large round-headed windows on west wall, porch and bellcote at north gable and session house at south, standing isolated on a ridge. Oddly domestic dormers on east side. Original furnishings include two lairds' pews at west corners and one in upper gallery (this last carried on cast-iron columns). Pictish stone in porch. Altered 1977; converted to house 2005.

Old Manse, 1778 (at skew)
A tall narrow house, squared granite to front, two storey and basement; three windows, with staircase window at half-landing. New porch in harmony. Garden wall rubble-built and contemporary with house (incorporates datestone of 1615). Alterations 1977.

Aberdeenshire Council

Old Manse

Westwood House, 1844, James Henderson
Former manse; harled generous cottage-style, single-storey-and-attic. L-plan front with

round-arched doorpiece with stepped hood-mould (cf Learney House and Skene Manse, James Smith).

Kinellar House

Kinellar House
Kinellar House, (?)mid-18th century or earlier
Anciently, Glasgoego, a U-plan house formed by three blocks, the wings attached to the main part only at angles. Main block two storey, harled with margins, four window with slightly advanced centre gable, coped chimneys. Extensive **offices** including laundry; garden wall incorporates a good 19th-century circular gazebo. Additions, 1780; altered mid-19th century. Restored, 1993.

Below *Woodhill*
Bottom *Tertowie House*

Woodhill, (?)late 19th century
Notable for imposing square three-storey-and-attic entrance tower, in stuccoed brick with sandstone dressings to twin lancet windows; denticulated stringcourses between each floor and mock machicolations below pyramidal slated roof. A baronial surprise.

Tertowie House, 1867, James Matthews
May incorporate parts of earlier house. To Matthews' slightly lugubrious baronial two-storey-and-attic block, William Kelly added a lively single-storey-and-basement crowstepped wing with strong dormers and a confident round angle-tower in 1905. The central unifying tower projected for the east front was, unfortunately, never built. Nuclear bunker created in late 1980s.

Kinaldie House, *c*.1800
The lower part of the bold, broad-eaved house with the grand tetrastyle Doric pedimented portico front is from *c*.1835, perhaps by John Smith. It has a simple interior with domed

Aberdeenshire Council

Kinaldie House

circular central hall. Around 1880 the upper floor and broad eaves were added; the whole sits at right angles to a single-storey-and-basement house of *c*.1800 with bays to east and west. **Doocot**, early 18th century? Although the double-pitched roof is modern, still a good plain example in boulder rubble with a single rat-course.

Kinaldie Home Farm, early 19th century
Rectangular farm group (court originally open) with low two-storey angle pavilions with ox-eye windows at first floor; rubble on ashlar basecourse. Small bow-ended bothy.

77 **FINTRAY**
Rising in gentle knolls and rounded eminences flanking the north bank of the Don.

Parish Kirk, 1821
Broad, harled, Gothic rectangle with granite margins and pinnacled buttresses, set diagonally on gable angles. Gable of **old kirk**, 1703, abandoned 1821, with bellcote stands in old burial ground. **Morthouse**, 1830 (lintel), partly subterranean, with massive vault at ground level and iron door in granite gable.

To facilitate the administration *of their lands beyond the Mounth, and for the ingathering of their teind sheaves and other dues, the Abbots (of Lindores Abbey in Fife, see Garioch, p. 102) erected a hall and a grange on their land of Fintray. It is from this that the present village of Hatton (Hall-Town) of Fintray gets its name; and the surroundings have all that air of ancient culture and well-tended husbandry, that* insita sibi species venustatis *which seems inseparable from an old monastic site. Small wonder that this pleasant place became a favourite point of call for wayfarers coming over the eastern Mounth passes northward through the Laich o' Mar and the Garioch. Thus James IV was three times here, in 1497, in 1501, and again in 1504.*
W D Simpson, *The Earldom of Mar*, 1949

Haughland Farmhouse, Hatton of Fintray, early 19th century
Imposing two-storey, three-window house in granite ashlar, foursquare and utterly plain, yet appealing. Pedimented wooden porch carried on tree-trunk columns more common on Deeside.

Haughland Farmhouse

Aberdeenshire Council

Milton of Fintray, early 19th century
Pleasing complex of ashlar granite comprising two-storey, three-window farmhouse with low wings at right angles to rear.

Wester Fintray Farmhouse, *c*.1800
Good rural Georgian house, two storeys on basement, three windows (with astragals), harled

with margins; two wings to rear; altered 1975. Fine, slightly later, steading to rear.

Disblair House

Cothal Mill was a large woollen factory with steam- and water-power and upwards of 100 hands. Superseded by larger works downstream near Grandhome.

Disblair House, early 19th century
Unusually ponderous single-storey-and-basement, U-plan granite house with broad eaves, piended roof and symmetrical wings with blind round-arched windows. Belonged to Revd Dr Morrison; armorial panel IB BF. Picturesque **doocot** on knoll, sub-rectangular, with single, heavy rat-course and saddle-backed, slated roof.

St Meddan's (House), 1804
Old manse: restrained proportions of traditional three-window, two-storey design aggrandised by pair of bay windows. Harled with granite margins and rear wing.

St Meddan's, medieval
Magical ruin, hidden in dark trees on terrace overlooking broad sweep of the Don, plain rebuilt rectangle with remains of sepulchre and several enigmatic medieval gravestones.

Newmill Farmhouse

Newmill Farmhouse, early 18th century
Thackstanes show early origins, but neatly elaborated by skewed dormers and sharp porch with skews and skewputs. Early wing to rear. Windows enlarged, 19th century.

Mill of Fintray, from 18th century
Old granite mill at heart of large, later complex, jammed tightly into a deep-cut den hard by the Don.

Fintray House, mid-19th century
A large modern mansion in the Tudor style (Groome): estate acquired, 1610, by first of Forbeses of Craigievar. Formerly belonged to Lindores, until the Reformation, at which time it was called Lamington. A cut-down version of John Smith's Forglen (see *Banff & Buchan* in this series), the skyline was all gables and diamond chimneys. The gabled front, in granite ashlar, had tripartite windows and a fine *porte-cochère*. Demolished, sadly, 1956.

Fintray House

OLDMELDRUM

Clustered tightly on its little hill (from Gaelic, *meall-droma*, hill of the ridge), looking south and west over the Garioch to Bennachie, the town was once the real megalopolis of the Garioch: in the 1690s there were 16 merchants here against four in Inverurie and one each in Insch and Kintore. It received its charter as a burgh of barony in 1672 but had been running since at least 1634. In those days you entered from the south by Mill Road or from the north by Cowgate (the sweeping highway to Banff is a late-20th-century implant). The nucleus of the 18th-century town can still be found in the network of little streets and lanes debouching on the Market Square (itself truncated in the 19th century by the row of houses and shops built on its north side). Oldmeldrum was superseded by Inverurie in the early 19th century following the construction of the canal and the turnpike. This decline was confirmed by its branch-line status, 1856 (colour page 184).

Coincidentally, Oldmeldrum also the birthplace of William Forsyth (1737-1804), the arboriculturalist who gave his name to the shrub, Forsythia.

RCAHMS

Parish Church

Greig

Oldmeldrum from the air

Parish Church, 1684, enlarged 1767
Steep, tree-lined brae leads to this plain T-plan kirk, harled with old surface-granite dressings at jambs and dark granite voussoirs above. Three pointed windows on north side. Partial reconstruction, 1861, William Smith; alterations, 1886, Matthews & Mackenzie; organ installed, 1897, William Kelly; interior recast, 1954, George Bennet Mitchell & Son; some good stained glass.

7 Kirk Street

Aberdeenshire Council

7 Kirk Street (south side)
Good 18th-century group, harled with margins, skewputs and coped chimneys; 19th-century bay on South Road side.

Aberdeenshire Council

Shepherd

Top *Meldrum Arms Hotel*
Above *Sailor, Meldrum Arms Hotel*
Right 4 *Market Square*

Sailor statue in freestone, early / mid-19th century, outside hotel: engaging, near life-size with large head, said to have been carved for a sailor's widow who came from Kingsford, near Alford. It was rescued from a rubbish dump near Craigievar by the collector *Postie Lawson* and moved with him to Oldmeldrum in 1938.

4 South Road
Double house; north gable 18th century with chamfered windows, rest good 19th-century rebuild. Single storey and attic, harled with sandstone dressings: three windows and two consoled doorpieces and three pedimented dormers; in all, crisp and trig.

Auquharney, South Road, *c*.1840
Solid single storey, basement and attic, harled with granite margins.

Meldrum Arms Hotel, late 18th century (central part)
A very linear hostelry, the central part two-storey, three-window, harled with skewputs. Splay corbel at set-back of north wing which has a small circular window by door and tripartite one above. Low office wing to south. The glazing is largely original and has been reflected in the modern continuous dormer. Hall, of mid-18th century, extended 1978/9, originally had stabling below and a hayloft above. Harled with ball finials at apices.

Market Square, reduced to present form in 19th century by row of shops on north.

Meldrum Motors, late 17th century, reconstructed early 19th century
Front block, two storey, five window, almost totally transformed by 20th-century garage conversion.

4 Market Square (Free Church manse), 1843, James Henderson
Imposing two-storey-and-basement, three-window house harled with granite margins and dressings. Good doorpiece, consoled and

Shepherd

pedimented with steps up to door. Plain belt courses at ground-floor level and at top of wall; refitted 1978.

Former **Free Church** also by Henderson – a large simple classic rectangle, closed 1954.

Shepherd

The Square, east side

6, 7 Market Square, mid-19th century, 1981 reconstruction
Business-like tenement, two-storey-and-attic, L-plan, granite front; three windows with two canted dormers. **Glenfoyle Cottage** (7 Market Square), mid-18th century, reconstructed 1981, tiny single storey, two window and central door.

7 Market Square, mid-18th century, remodelled 19th century
Gable to square, a sizeable two storeys, harled with chamfered margins, skewputs and coped chimneys. Late 19th-century splay at north-east angle; interior reconstructed, 1981.

Aberdeenshire Council

Above *Morris's Hotel*
Left *Town Hall*

Morris's Hotel, Market Square, 1673
Former coffee house; captivating two-window gable to square, with pairs of windows reducing in size; a rare survival of this date. On side a late tripartite doorpiece and dormers.

Town Hall, 1877, William Smith
Much burgh pride expressed in its two-storey, five-bay façade in rough granite ashlar, with

Shepherd

slightly projected centre. The arched doorpiece therein is said to approximate to that of the previous building. Rises to a consoled clock-stage with ogee-capped timber and lead bell-turret above (noted as having *illuminated clock*, 1899). Well-executed details include curved angles corbelled to square above.

Advertised as alterations in the *Aberdeen Journal* of 5 May 1877, but the work involved the complete demolition of the old town house. The fine Urquhart coat of arms on the present building with WU MDCCXLI came from that building, which had a tall, ogee-capped tower of 1741 with a single-storey-and-basement block behind whose simple narrow-gabled form suggests a yet earlier date.

18 Market Square, mid-18th century, altered 19th century
Two-storey, three-window house and shop, harled with chamfered margins, skewputs and coped chimneys. Shop inserted last century: raise the eyes to appreciate the earlier form.

Below *3 Baker Street*
Bottom *6/7 Urquhart Road*

Aberdeenshire Council

Aberdeenshire Council

3 Baker Street, 1829, but ground floor older? Solid municipal comfort in a two-storey, three-window house in mixed rubble, incorporating much re-used material; converted, 1984.

Former Brewery, Urquhart Road, east block late 18th century
Good, two-storey, two-window gable to street; gable harled, rest rubble. The parallel western block is later. Converted to shop, 1984.

1 Major Lane, off Urquhart Road, (?)1741
Classic two-storeyed, 18th-century town house, gable to street, harled with some chamfered openings.

6, 7 Urquhart Road, 1727 (south part); late 18th/early 19th century (north part and long north-east wing)
Former inn; 1727 gable of No 6 (shop) refaced in quarried granite (earlier, surface granite above); very trig. (Bay window in courtyard is later.)

1 King Street, late 18th century, converted 1983
Two houses, two storey, three windows harled with greenstone margins; interlaced arch fanlight. **18 King Street**, late 18th century: solid two-storey, three-window, harled house.

5 King Street, earlier 19th century
Now part of sheltered housing, 1980, Gordon District Council. Excellent reconstruction of single-storey-and-attic cottage of five bays. Good squared and pinned granite rubble gable, rest harled.

Broombank, 16 James Street, late 18th century
Substantial two storey, three window in rough dark granite ashlar with red granite dressings. Tall coped rubble wall of (?)1733. Clever extension, 2002, Leslie Hunter Architects.

Aberdeenshire Council

Above *Broombank*
Left *Kirkhill House*

Aberdeenshire Council

Kirkhill House, Albert Road, (?)1850s, William Smith
Grand, for Oldmeldrum, almost exotic, two-storey house dominated by paired Dutch gables drawn up to dramatic ogee-points, complemented by wooden bay windows. Harled with red sandstone dressings: very successful.

Below *Cromlet Bank*
Bottom *Cromlethill*

Aberdeenshire Council

Aberdeenshire Council

Cromlet Bank, South Road, *c*.1820
Solid two-storey, three-window block with broad, heavy gables. Harled with surface granite margins and consoled doorpiece. Quarried granite bay windows; side screen walls.

Cromlethill, South Road, early 19th century
Restrained centre block, two storeys, three windows, stuccoed with wooden Doric-columned porch and piend roof. One-window wings set back. Restored 1983.

Memorial on roadside outside Cromlethill: Birthplace of Sir Patrick Manson, GC, MG, MD, FRCP, DSC, LLD, FRS, 1844-1922, *the father of tropical medicine* ... erected by the London School of Tropical Medicine founded by him in 1899.

Glengarioch Distillery, Distillery Road, from 1797
Earliest is the malt floor and store, by Ingram, Lamb & Co, a chunky four-storey, 11-bay range of maltings in granite rubble, attractively functional. Cast-iron columns within. Still-

Glengarioch Distillery

Aberdeenshire Council

house three storeys with attached boiler-house with brick chimney. The bonds, with nine immense granite bays, are mid-19th century as are the coped rubble walls to the rear of the pyramidal-roofed kilns.

Oldmeldrum Station, 1856
By Inverury & Old Meldrum Junction Railway off Great North of Scotland Railway at Inverurie; was a one-platform terminus with a single-storey wooden platform building and brick goods shed still surviving.

Meldrum Mausoleum, Bethelnie
In ruins of old parish church, dedicated to St Nathalan (parish known as Bethelnie until parish kirk moved into village in 1684), a square, rubble-built enclosure with three slits on each side, inscribed: *Beneath this building rest the remains of many generations of Meldrums, Setons and Urquharts of Meldrum / AD 1236 to 1863.*

Bethelnie Steading

RCAHMS

78 **Bethelnie Steading**, 1872, James Duncan
Double quadrangle, pinned dark granite with light granite dressings; south front symmetrical with real rhythm to gablets, dormers and cart-shed arches. Pends under gables; dormers of (comparatively) lavish bothies at either end. Lies within one of the most intensively farmed landscapes in Scotland, largely created in the century running up to Bethelnie's construction, just on the onset of the great agricultural depression. In many respects, agriculture has never been as confident again.

Meldrum House

Aberdeenshire Council

Hillhead of Glengarioch, 19th century
Real, and necessary, feeling of enclosure in courtyard of simple two-storey, three-window farmhouse, extended by conversion of adjacent block, linked by tall angle-tower, 1993, John Campbell.

Meldrum House, from 1625, 17th and 18th century
Baronialised mansion with much earlier nucleus, hinted at in vaulted ground floor and

RCAHMS

history of *weel-connectit* families involved (Meldrums, 1236 – mid-15th century; Setons to 1670, then son of Urquhart of Cromarty). Symmetry of Archibald Simpson's recasting, 1836-9, a neo-Jacobean three-storey block with two-storey advance pavilions and centre porch to south-west, was lost in W L Duncan's alterations of 1934-7 in which the top storey was removed, the south-east pavilions and porch demolished and a new entrance constructed at the north-west. Now dominated by grandiose (?)17th-century external stair to first floor, with balustrades, Simpson's slender angle-towers and the pair of Dutch gables on the opposite façade. There is a tradition that the stair came from Castle Fraser where it had given access to the original, first-floor, entry. The upper floor was once occupied by a row of four posters for the unmarried sisters of the family.

Many good structures in policies, including a pair of circular, 17th-century **garden houses** originally entered from the first floor off a little wooden bridge. **Outer gate and stable and coach house** of 1628 (altered ?1777) consists of a U-plan into which coach house inserted in the late 18th century; **doocot** in upper floor; fine royal arms on north-west face. Tunnel-vaulted ground floor, bosses on vault. **South Lodge**, 1851, restored 1982, Marion Fraser (also known as Chain Lodge). Tudor, single-storey dark granite with fancy bargeboards and lattice glazing; roofline pierced by four diagonal chimneys and spiky finials. **South gates**, 1851 *presumably*, restored 1986. Tudor-Jacobean, harled with dark granite dressings, at middle a four-centred arch with keystone and octagonal piers with *double globule* finials; footgates in flanking screen walls. **Farm** and semicircular **kennels** wing are excellent.

Aberdeenshire Council

Aberdeenshire Council

Top *Meldrum House in the 19th century*
Middle *Garden House*
Above *Gate piece*

St Matthew's Episcopal

Shepherd

St Matthew's Episcopal, 1863,
Ross and Joass
Pleasing granite Gothic (early Decorated) with striking chequered voussoirs to west window. Simple nave and chancel with angle buttresses and an almost detached spire rising from square to hexagonal cross-section from beside porch. Tendril-like freestone tracery carved with real freedom. Inside collar-braced roofs, glass by Hardman and an intricate Arts & Crafts monument to Beauchap Colclough Urquhart of Meldrum, *d*.1898. A fine ensemble.

Below *Mill of Foresterhill*
Bottom *Kilblean*

Aberdeenshire Council

Aberdeenshire Council

Mill of Foresterhill, *c*.1800 on earlier site
Strong two-storey-and-attic L-plan in pinned boulder rubble; converted to dwelling, 1976-9.

Kilblean, 1827
Built by the Mansons, Oldmeldrum merchants and distillers, a pleasant two-storey, three-window house in pinned boulder rubble, with quoins. Garden wall incorporates cheese press.

Cromlet House, mid-18th century
Almost identical to (old) Manse of Bourtie but harled with margins. T-plan, two-storey, three-window, with late canted dormers and conservatory, but intrinsically fine.

FORMARTINE

The level eastern end of Aberdeenshire where it finally meets the sea in the links and dunes of Belhelvie. A land of vast fields and domed skies.

TARVES

Village set on gently rising ground, a cluster of granite walls and trees in an open, rolling landscape of corn and kail. Bartol Fair (Bartle – St Bartholomew) is an old established fair for cattle, horses and sheep.

Shepherd

Forbes tomb, Tarves

William Forbes, who extended the château of Tolquhon and erected his tomb at Tarves, founded a hospital *hard by the church ... for four poor men, who were to eat and lye here, and to have each a peck of meal, and three shillings, a penny, and two-sixths of a penny Scots weekly, also some malt, peats etc. The meal and money they have (1730) but their hous, which is slated, is neglected, and quite waste.*

Dr Arthur Johnston praised Forbes in a Latin poem for his improvements at Tolquhon, for the erection of the burial aisle and for founding the hospital. The last two lines are:

Quantulus! exuvias si spectas corporis alti
Si pensas animi munera, quantus homo est.
(Look at his ashes, and you'll say, 'How small a man'
His lofty mind's gifts ponder, you'll exclaim, 'How great!')

Parish Church (St Englat), 1798
Rather grand, if uncomplicated, ashlar granite rectangle with cherry-cocking and four large round-headed windows in south wall (glazing mostly original) and door and arched windows in each gable. Undersized ball-capped bellcote on west gable. Organ-chamber apse formed at third south window (James Cobban). Very complete furnishing inside, with excellent original horseshoe gallery, pews and good pulpit of 1825. Bell, 1855, J Warner. **Churchyard**, which contains Craig slab of 1583 and some 18th-century stones, also houses the Tolquhon Monument of 1589 (Thomas Leper). For William Forbes of Tolquhon and his wife, Elizabeth Gordon, it is all that survives of the south aisle of the old kirk. A marvellous blend of Gothic and Renaissance motifs, a worthy reflection of the life of the builder of Tolquhon. (Pediment over probably 1798.)

79 **Tolquhon**, late 14th century; 1584-9, Thomas Leper

AL THIS WARKE EXCEP THE AULD TOWR WAS BEGUN BE WILLIAM FORBES 15 APRIL 1584 AND

Entrance detail, Tolquhon

Shepherd

Tolquhon
Right *Courtyard*
Below *Entrance (Billings)*

ENDIT BE HIM 20 OCTOBER 1589 proclaims the datestone of one of the most characteristic châteaux of the Scots Renaissance. Very similar in sequence and plan to that other grand Forbes work, Pitsligo (see *Banff & Buchan* in this series), it began with the Preston Tower, a dour rectangle with walls 7½ft thick, now reduced largely to its vaulted ground floor. This functional block was enfolded within the courtyard plan of the new building created for the Renaissance man, Sir William Forbes.

Entry to this new wark was by an arched pend surmounted by a rich frontispiece set between two central semicircular towers. These are distinctly unmilitary in the thinness of their walls and the decorative Leper triple shot-holes and stringcourses. Harled, with its gilded frontispiece, the effect would have been stunning. Quality living was at the first-floor level: the gatehouse and west wing consisted of galleries, the latter a formidable 57ft by 14ft, starting from a bold flanking round tower, incorporating the main stair and ending at the south range. This, two storeys and attic, with commodious hall and private rooms, is enlivened by a central circular stair-tower corbelled to the square above. By Thomas Leper, the similarity to nearby Schivas is clear. A small south-east tower creates a hollow Z-plan encompassed by enclosures; these enclosures, in the manner of Pitsligo, include a large hexagonal outer forecourt with 12 bee-boles in its wall, a walled garden to the north and a pleasaunce around the main mansion (colour page 182).
Historic Scotland; open to the public

Shepherd

Shepherd

RCAHMS

RCAHMS

Shepherd

Top *House of Formartine, 1995, Morris & Steedman*
Middle *Balgrian, Pitmedden, 2002, Richard Murphy*
Above *The great Avenue, Haddo*
Right *Haddo House interior*
Bottom *War Memorial, Udny Green*

McKean

Shepherd

Greig

RCAHMS

Top *Château of Tolquhon restoration by Charles McKean*
Middle *Methlick Bridge, restored 2004, Aberdeenshire Council*
Bottom *Tolquhon*
Above *Castle Fraser*

Greig

Shepherd

Shepherd

Shepherd

Top *Collieston Harbour*
Left *Old Slains Castle*
Middle *Oceanlab, Newburgh, 2002, George Watt & Stewart*
Above *Straloch House*

Shepherd

Pitmedden: the Great Garden
Above *Gateway and stairs*
Right *Pavilion*
Insert *Detail*

Shepherd

Below *Station Road, Newmachar, 2004, David Murray Associates*
Bottom *Oldmeldrum and the Garioch*

Shepherd

Greig

Old Inn, *c.*1800
Foursquare, two-storey, three-window hostelry (now house) in coursed granite with belt-course.

Aberdeen Arms Hotel, *c.*1810/20
Two storey, three window: very plain but serviceable. Pinned granite front set in Aberdeen bond; rest rubble. Rectangular fanlight.

Shepherd

Aberdeenshire Council

Above *Aberdeen Arms Hotel*
Left *Tarves Manse*

Tarves Manse, 1847, John & William Smith
Restrained Tudor in coursed granite; L-plan front with flat-roofed porch in angle, mullions and transoms to windows and pronounced flat skewputs to gables and gablets. Similar to their other manses at Tarland and Kincardine O'Neil. Elaborate chimneystack to gable.

Bede House, probably 18th century
Long, low, single-storey cottage in coursed rubble; originally thatched.

Shethin Farmhouse, *c.*1830-40
Very perjink, compact two-storey-and-basement, three-window house in pinned mixed rubble. Good consoled doorpiece; steps up to door. At sides, screen walls set back with doorpieces and cornices.

South Ythsie Farmhouse, *c.*1840 (centre)
Good group in granite ashlar. Two-storey, three-window with belt-course and symmetrical piend-roofed, single-storey wings. Altered 1981.

North Ythsie Farmhouse, late 18th and early 19th century
T-plan: front early 19th century in granite ashlar, single-storey-and-attic (with basement in part owing to sloping site). Nicely detailed

Below *Shethin Farmhouse*
Bottom *North Ythsie Farmhouse*

Aberdeenshire Council

Aberdeenshire Council

front elevation with central door and railed steps, 12-pane sash windows. Slightly advanced, lower piended wings have circular front windows. This, the original house, is now the back wing of an undistinguished large house of the early 19th century.

Bridge of Auchedly, 1901, William Davidson
Solid, in pinned red granite, with two hexagonal arches.

RCAHMS

Right *House of Schivas c.1932*
Below *House of Schivas today*
Bottom *Gatehouse*

Aberdeenshire Council

RCAHMS

80 **House of Schivas**, *c.*1585 or slightly earlier, Thomas Leper
Lands originally held by Scheves family, a succession of owners has wrought many changes and additions. Remarkably complex with some of the massing of Barra, but many links in plan and details to Tolquhon (eg triple gunloops). A lofty, L-plan, with square stair-tower and a stair-turret in the re-entrant – for George Gray, fourth laird. North-east wing added, 1750, by Forbeses; 1780, main block extended to west; before 1851, north wing built by Irvines of Drum; 1900 burnt; 1902 rebuilt, A G Sydney Mitchell (executed James Cobban); from 1931 much internal work, A H L Mackinnon; 1934-7 restored, Fenton Wyness, Scots 16th-century style for first Lord Catto of Cairncatto, a Buchan loon turned merchant banker. Wyness remodelling very effective in unifying the various surviving fragments; in particular the courtyard wall and jewel-like **gatehouse** are admirable. Plasterwork of great hall by Mitchell, modified by Wyness; that of drawing room, also by Mitchell.

Sundial, 17th century, probably from the townhouse of the Earls Marischal in Aberdeen, transferred to the old house of Rubislaw, *c.*1789; 9ft 5in. high with two hollow-dial blocks. The balusters are not original. **Howff of Schivas,** 1783-90, possibly including older work: ship-like burial enclosure initialled HF

(Hugh Forbes) and CG (Christian Garden) with coped walls, obelisks at the angles and a segmentally arched entry.

Mains of Schivas, late 18th century (west block), high-quality granite ashlar on west side, includes three arched sheds.

METHLICK

Very much the estate village of Haddo (eg patronage of church bought by the Earl of Aberdeen from King's College (which had acquired it from St Machar's), and who continued to act as patron until patronage abolished in 1874): more than usual number of stimulating buildings.

Old Parish Church (St Deavanach/Devenick), 1780, repaired 1840
In old kirkyard, roofless rectangle in split-boulder rubble with cherry-cocking. Simple round-headed openings throughout, bellcote on west gable, stair to former loft at south-east corner, north wall blind. South section of old kirkyard wall incorporates a good collection of 18th-century tomb sculpture.

War Memorial, *c.*1920
Cenotaph-like in gleaming ashlar granite; a truncated obelisk with simple sword-like cross in relief and insignia, atop a corniced plinth bearing names in narrow panels.

Below *New Parish Church*
Bottom *Manse*

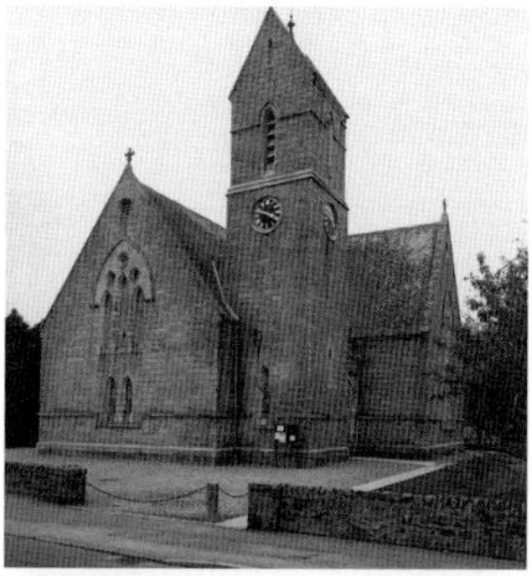

Shepherd

RCAHMS

New Parish Church, 1865-7, Brown & Wardrop; 1908, Gillot & Johnson Bell
Good early pointed Gothic in tooled ashlar; L-plan formed by south transept, angle filled by tower and porch; north end three-sided. Strong, saddleback tower with clock. Forms an important feature, crisp and strong, in the long, slightly straggly village.

Free Church, 1847-8, James Henderson; additions, 1881, William Clark
Austere harled Gothic on hill to north, with elaborated, angular gable to road; converted to dwelling, 1994.

Manse, 1860-1, William Smith
Sober Tudor, two storeys of pinned granite with steeply pitched porch and dormer-heads, all with corbelled skewputs. L-plan front with bay window. Wood mullions and transoms to all other windows. Similar to earlier Smith manses at Tough, Tarland, etc.

RCAHMS

Bridgend

Bridgend, *c.*1850
Former schoolmaster's house, slightly institutional in feel but in good granite ashlar. Single-storey-and-attic dominated by pedimented centre porch; paired, round-headed windows with original glazing.

Opened by W E Gladstone, 16 September 1884, thus uniting two enthusiasms of *We Twa* (see Haddo): Liberalism and the welfare and education of girls destined for, or already in, domestic service. (Ishbel, Countess of Aberdeen, also founded the distinctly maternalistic, but well-intentioned journal *Onward and Upward* for them.)

Ivy Cottage, 1875, William Clark
Built as Female School which was purchased by Lord Aberdeen when the schools in Methlick were amalgamated and refitted as Training Home for Girls. U-plan, single storey, harled, with south-east section a cottage-style house with consoled doorpiece in the centre of an advanced gable.

Beaton Public Hall, 1908
Sub-baronial four-bay frontage with gable above roll-moulded doorpiece, square corner tower, crenellated, and broad corbiesteps, in granite ashlar. Adjacent **Ythan Villa** has similar doorpiece and excellent asymmetrical front.

Below *Beaton Public Hall*
Bottom *Little Ardo Farmhouse*

Shepherd

Aberdeenshire Council

Bank House, *c.*1900
Asymmetrical two-storey front with two-bay piend roof, centre recessed and massive splayed bay with consoled windows, all in grey squared granite. Suitably uncompromising for a farmers' bank.

Ythan View Hotel, late 19th century
Two gabled wings with oversailing eaves, recessed and gabled centre to two white-washed storeys; pleasing and rustic.

Little Ardo Farmhouse, early 19th century
South section is plain but pleasing, two storey, three window, harled with margins. Good instance of estate improvement by fourth Earl of Aberdeen shortly after 1805.

Methlick Bridge (River Ythan), 1844, J & W Smith
Low, workmanlike squared granite arches flank a central span of six perforated cast-iron arched girders with lattice parapets above and splayed granite walls to either side. Excellent example of early Victorian engineering put to local use. Rebuilt [on wider plan] 2004 by Aberdeenshire Council (colour page 182).

Shepherd

Tanglandford Bridge

Tanglandford Bridge, 1864, James Abernethy engineer
Sole two-span, parallel-girder, cast-iron bridge in Scotland; wooden deck supported by cross girders, and the main girders borne by stone abutments and circular cross-braced columns. Whole, spare ensemble once finished with trim cast-iron railings; so pleasingly functional.

North Lodge, Haddo, *c.*1845
Slightly understated single-storey Tudor in rough granite ashlar with good central chimney-shafts, hood-moulds and original glazing. The **laundry**, *c.*1845, *style of J & W Smith*, perched at edge of first terrace above the Ythan, taking advantage of fall in ground for an additional half storey (as well as proximity to water). In pinned rubble with granite dressings; low-pitched, broad-eaved roof. Suitably plain and functional; 1975 extension.

Below *Laundry, Haddo*
Middle *Library*
Bottom *Haddo House*

Aberdeenshire Council

Shepherd

81 **Haddo House**, 1731-6, William Adam (with John Baxter); kitchen court, 1843, J & W Smith; interiors, 1879-81, Wardrop & Reid
Reticent Palladian mansion of three-storey, seven-window main block with slightly advanced and pedimented west centre and single-storey quadrants running to two-storey, five-window wings, all in granite ashlar. Urns, parapet and piend roof above.

In 1822, Archibald Simpson replaced the staircase from first to second floors and heightened the quadrants. The original first-floor entrance was replaced by James Maitland Wardrop in favour of the ground-floor colonnade, and major internal redecoration (by

Shepherd

We Twa
The title of the joint autobiography of John Campbell Hamilton-Gordon (1847-1934) and his wife, Ishbel Marjoribanks, daughter of First Lord Tweedmouth (*d*.1939), seventh Earl and Countess (and first Marquess/Marchioness) of Aberdeen. *It is impossible to distinguish 'Johnny's' public appointments from her expansive influence.* Appointed Viceroy of Ireland by Gladstone in 1886, he went on to become Governor-General of Canada, 1893-8, and again, Viceroy of Ireland, 1905-15. *In both Ireland and Canada they left permanent marks and these two countries are perpetually evident at Haddo.* Her first book was *Through Canada with a Kodak* (1903); she was President of the International Council of Women from 1893 to 1936 and set up health clinics and rural industries in Ireland during the second Viceroyalty. *Both halves of the partnership were subjected to ridicule, scandalous gossip, lampoon and official criticism ... They soon learnt to shrug off hostility from Conservatives, Irish gentry, powerful North Americans and smart Londoners*, although during their lifetimes the Haddo estate shrank from 75,000 acres to about 15,000 acres.
Archie Gordon, *A Guide to Haddo House*, 1981

Wright and Mansfield of London) in an early Adam-revival style took place. The Ante-Room is the only room to retain its Adam/Baxter scheme, apart from a portrait bust of Queen Victoria presented by Herself.

Excellent Early Decorated **chapel**, 1876-81, by G E Street, with wooden barrel-roof and Burne-Jones glass. Haddo was the first great house in Scotland to be opened to the public by advertisement (*The Scotsman*) on one day in 1883, by *We Twa*; 96 years later the property passed to the National Trust for Scotland. Wonderful treasure-chest of James Giles's watercolours of Aberdeenshire castles.
National Trust for Scotland; open to the public

Fountain, mid-19th century; part of landscape furniture of park, which includes **The Avenue**, with the Golden Gates, *c*.1847, J & W Smith; delicate cast-iron work including an oversailing coat of arms; four rusticated gatepiers (colour page 181). **Pair of Stags**, (?)*c*.1847, J & W Smith, lightness of the rendering of the roe deer contrasts with the monumental granite plinths on which they appear to have momentarily alighted. **Urn** (terminates avenue and closes long vista from house), 1847, J & W Smith, truly massive granite urn on large square plinth, inscribed GEORGIUS MES ABREDON ENSIS. MDCCCXLVII HAUD IMMEMOR: George, the fourth earl in sorrowful reflection?

Sundial, 17th or early 18th century, cube type, on later base. **Balustrades**, mid-19th century, granite piers, flanking south-east avenue. **Sundial**, late 19th century, circular marble shaft with lions in relief at base and an open spherical copper dial and gnomon. **Stable and coach-house block**, 1822, probably Archibald Simpson, quadrangular, two-storey U-plan in pinned split-boulder rubble with granite dressings, eight-window south-west frontage with flat centre arch. Two tall linteled coach-house openings in each of advanced ends. Broad-eaved piend roof certainly suggests Simpson. **Obelisk**, shortly after 1815, tall ashlar granite obelisk with long inscription, a monument to Colonel Sir Alexander Gordon who was killed at Waterloo. **Walled garden**, early 19th century, gates 18th century, probably by John Baxter, rubble-built wall, with fine mid-18th-century wrought-iron gates; rusticated piers with panelled pilasters topped by urns. Probably formerly on west axis of house. Victorian half-column Peterhead granite sundial in garden. **Gardener's cottage**, *c.*1843 or earlier, single storey with Tudor porch, deep eaves and diagonally shafted chimneys. **Icehouse**, early 19th century, granite entrance, brick dome. **Burial enclosure**, 1884, Alfred Walterhouse, Gothic, with freestone enclosure walls on a buttressed plinth of bull-faced granite and a pointed granite archway. **Butler's House**, *c.*1860, T-plan, single-storey-and-attic, rustic log-cabin porch and (?)palm-leaf chimney pots.

Shepherd

i *House of Formartine, in walled garden, 1995, Morris & Steedman (colour page 181)*

RCAHMS

Left *Butler's House*
Below *Theatre*
Bottom *The Peatyards*

Shepherd

Aberdeenshire Council

Theatre (Haddo House Hall), 1891, timber, of Canadian inspiration from *We Twa*'s sojourn as Governor-General; opened by the American evangelists, Moody and Sankey. *Its remarkable acoustics* assisted the Haddo House Choral and Operatic Society (founded 1967; now part of Haddo Arts Trust). **The Peatyards**, Haddo House Hall, 1993, Douglas T Forrest Architects (partner in charge, Leslie F Hunter). New rehearsal rooms and bar in cunning metal-and-glass roof pavilion above extensive storage and workshop areas contained within massive granite plinth, which also supports a terrace for guests: refreshingly direct yet ageless. Impressively large coat of arms on main wall frontage, 1905.

South Lodge, Haddo House, (?)*c.*1845
J & W Smith
Rough granite ashlar in same restrained Tudor Gothic as the North Lodge. Modest eaves and good central, diagonally shafted chimney. **Haddo House Lodge and gate**, Keithfield, 1878, rather heavy-handed, sub-baronial, L-plan, single-storey-and-attic in coursed rubble with ashlar dressings. Crudely crowstepped gables with ball finials. Solid central chimneystack in ashlar (modern dormer in re-entrant). Dwarf gatepiers with balls; original timber footgates; low screen walls.

Opposite *Stag, The Avenue*

Top *Mains of Haddo*
Above *Prop of Ythsie*

The old castle of Ardgith, on the Hill of Ardgirth, was held by the Kennedys of Kermuck, hereditary Constables of the Castle of Aberdeen; it was plundered by royalists in 1644 and passed to the Forbes of Waterton after a bitter confrontation over the building of a mill in 1652 during which Thomas Forbes was killed by John Kennedy. In 1706 it was bought by Bailie James Gordon who was a rich Edinburgh merchant. The whole of the present layout dates from this time. In 1752 the castle and lands were sold to George, third Earl of Aberdeen, *The Wicked Earl*, who installed Penelope Bering of Pett, Sussex, and their two children in a largely rebuilt mansion. He also kept a mistress and children at Cairnbulg Castle and Wiscombe Park. George died in his eighties, in 1803, at Ellon Castle, and the property passed to his second son, the Hon William Gordon MP, who let it decline. It then passed to his half-brother, Alexander Gordon, son of Penelope, who completed the work with explosives.

Mains of Haddo, *c.*1822, Archibald Simpson (or *c.*1845 Smith?); altered 1890 and 1980s
Originally symmetrical about a segmental pend arch with circular window over flanked by two-storey, three-window houses with porches, and low, three-bay block beyond. All harled with granite margins capped by a heavily eaved, Simpson-style, piend roof. **Farmhouse**, *c.*1822 (or 1845?), later additions: two-storey, three-window house with a slightly truncated look perhaps from its beetling eaves and moderate pitch to roof. However, the glazing is good and the harl, with granite margins, crisp. Porch may be later, as is the single-storey-and-attic, single-window wing.

Prop of Ythsie, 1861-2; restored, 1992
Gordon District Council
Like a giant chesspiece abandoned in rolling farmland; to the Prime Minister, fourth Earl of Aberdeen, who become embroiled in the Crimean War. A square tower in coursed red granite rising from a steeply battered lower stage to a corbelled parapet cut by a single deep crenel in each face.

ELLON

Riverside gateway to, and ancient capital of, Buchan; from Gaelic *eileann*, meaning an island. It began as seat of justice for Comyn earldom of Buchan but was burned during Bruce's *heirschip* or harrying; motte, now gone, marked by plaque above river. Medieval kirk gifted by David I to Kinloss Abbey, Moray, whence the confusing name Kinloss-Ellon. Although at key crossing-point of Ythan, just above its tidal limit, its 19th-century development was constrained by landowner Alexander Gordon's refusal to let off reasonable feus. Now transformed by enveloping oil-related housing, which began in the mid-1970s and is continuing apace.

Ellon Castle (Old), late 16th century; reconstructed, *c.*1706-15; 1781-5, John Baxter; ruinous post-1801, demolished 1851
Only south wall remains of an impressive and complex château. Baxter retained only the square tower with its circular south-eastern angle-tower as part of a four-storey, U-plan block (130ft by 75ft), open to the east, which had twin three-window bows. West front was seven-windowed with the centre three recessed. Fluted stone pilasters survive of the stairhall at the west end.

RCAHMS

Gordon District Council

Above *Old Castle*
Left *New Castle of Ellon from postcard*

Castle gatepiers, *c*.1715. Ellon Academy now sits astride the avenue originally laid out as an approach to Ellon Castle; the piers of the gate which terminated this avenue have been relocated to the east of the Academy. They are elaborate, with alternate pulvination and double-diamond treatment and are capped by solid, globular finials. **Castle park wall** and **deer dykes**, *c*.1715: the park was a grand 400 by 300 yards enclosed by a rubble-built wall. The east gate has alternately fluted and rusticated gatepiers topped by ball finials, and the south gate (Castle Road) has square piers with angle rustication and ball caps, flanked by much repaired footgates. Much rebuilt, 1850s. **Sundial**, *c*.1717, cubical, with three cherubs' heads on top, said to have been erected in memory of the two elder sons of Bailie Gordon who were murdered in 1717 by their tutor, Robert Irvine, for having related *some liberties they saw him take with their mother's maid*. Irvine's wrath was wreaked in public, he was apprehended by an angry crowd and hanged two days later.

*... **it is accounted here** a very great house, the great hall having two rows of windows, and being twenty-eight foot high.*
S Forbes, *Book of Bon Accord*

Garden house and **terrace stairs**, 1715, adapted 1851, James Matthews. What began as a sizeable three-storey block in pinned rubble set into an escarpment was adapted by Matthews who replaced the upper storey with a neo-Tudor parapet reached by a handsome flight of stairs. **Walled garden**, 1715 (datestone above gate leading from garden to village), repaired 1851, a rectangle dominated by a great terrace at the north into which the garden house is set and above which lours the old castle. Bailie Gordon's garden was extended southwards in 1851 to cover five acres in all, with great yew hedges adding to the sheltering walls. **Sundial**, *c*.1700-15, marked original centre of garden, standing on a podium of three moulded steps and supported on a sculptured square shaft, a fine facet-headed dial with hollows on all 24 faces, topped by a ball finial.

Garden House

Aberdeenshire Council

Aberdeenshire Council

Ellon Castle (1927 offices conversion)

*... **Ellen**, the small town on the river Ythan, supposed to be the **Ituna** of the new map close to which town Lord Aberdeen has a large old House (Udny), and a great plantation of fir trees ...*
Pococke's *Tour Through Scotland*

Ellon Castle (new), 1725; rebuilt, 1781-5, John Baxter; incorporated in new house 1851, James Matthews, Mackenzie & Matthews
Began as offices, rebuilt on H-plan. Baxter's front door is inscribed *George Earl of Aberdeen 1785* and bears a grand segmental pediment broken by an armorial panel from the old castle. The 1851 mansion had a grand Fyvie-like recessed arched centre flanked by tall bay windows and angle turrets, all crisply done in white granite. The 1927 conversion of the offices produced a two-storey house, harled and crowstepped, with low eaves and a small baronial round-tower. Main house demolished, 1927.

St Mary's Parish Church, 1776-7; repairs, 1828/9, George Clerihew, builder; renovated, 1876, George Marr; apse on south front, 1884, G Marr & W Davidson
The materials of the old (cruciform) church being given with unsentimental economy, a simple rectangular church capable of accommodating 1200 was constructed in coursed granite, with keyblocked window arches. It has undergone a series of radical alterations, including the addition of an organ chamber, the three-sided *apse*, now a memorial apse, the removal of the horseshoe gallery and the emplacement of quite the ugliest porch imaginable, in stark grey concrete. Early Christian cross in centre of east gable. Alterations, 1907, William Kelly; *modernisation*, 1967/8, D Kinghorn, H G West & Associates.

Shepherd

j *Drill Hall, Ellon, 1936, Leslie Rollo*

Annand Memorial, early 17th century
Formerly in old kirk; three pilastered panels with elaborated ogees and armorials of Annands of Auchterellon over (central one has pairs of fine gryphons); cornice oversails all. Other stones in kirkyard date from 1713.

Shepherd

Detail, Annand Memorial

Riversfield, 6 Castle Road, (?)late 18th century
Former manse with large granite-edged windows set in harled walls dominated by substantial bowed gables. Doric porch in angle; original house lies north-south; enlarged 1826 (probably west wing); additions 1860, D MacAndrew; divided in two, 1978; high garden wall with gatepiers.

Aberdeenshire Council

Riversfield

The Square is now a slightly incidental offshoot of the road, but retains some grace.

Old Bank House, Square/Market Street, 1845-7
A more regular, two-storey-and-basement, three-window house, harled with granite margins, a belt-course and fine consoled doorpiece. The west wing is lower and slightly angled back. Eastern part is later.

Bank of Scotland, Square, late 19th century, (?)A Marshall Mackenzie
Pleasing sandstone two-storey-and-attic, three-bay block, quoined, asymmetrical front having one slightly advanced gable with large tripartite ground-floor window with balcony over and an imposing central doorpiece, consoled with balcony over. Balconies are fronted with cast-iron foliage work; neat attic dormer window.

Shepherd

Bank of Scotland

Tolbooth, 18th century; demolished 1842
Handsome, with outside stair like Kintore, it stood on or close to No 7 The Square; now only represented by fine segmental dormer-head with what has been claimed to be Bailie Gordon's coat of arms set in gable of shop. The motto reads VENIUNT FELICIUS UVAE (*Grapes come with good fortune*), the grapes appearing on the achievement.

War Memorial, 1920
On square battered plinth of Kemnay granite, near life-size infantryman.

16 The Square (formerly North of Scotland Bank), 1937/8
Remarkably late, low but intriguing granite ashlar block of three bays, two with double windows, the third, the door, with strong horizontal planes created by band course, and blind course rising to cornice. (Built for *c.*£1000, of which more than £400 spent on the safe; much of the rest must have gone on its superb granite frontage.)

16 The Square

Shepherd

Veterinary Surgery

Shepherd

20, 21 The Square
The former a three-window, two-storey, granite ashlar building with skewputs and a consoled doorpiece, the latter (Murisons') two storeys, harled with dressings, with a two-bay gable to the Square; neat round-headed window high on gable, beneath coped chimneyhead.

Trough, 1895
For the refreshment of weary beasts, a plain, pink granite water-trough backed by a pedimented panel with inscription.

Veterinary Surgery, The Square,
late 19th century, 1980 extended to east
Cottage-style L-plan in squared granite rubble, with double gable to Square, the eastern one set back and harled. Both are bargeboarded. Pair of attractive low cottages to west.

33 The Square, early 19th century
Formerly blacksmith's workshop, low range converted to offices, 1993, Taylor Design Services.

Ebrie Cottage, Castle Road
Solid, rubble-built, two-storey, two-bay house with prominent skewputs and two pedimented dormers; hood-moulds over ground-floor windows and central chimney cluster.

Olrig

Aberdeenshire Council

Old School, Smiddy Lane, 19th century
Long, asymmetrical, two-storey rubble block with large, skewed gable to front, containing school and band rooms; attractively converted to dwelling house, 1993, Taylor Design Services.

Olrig, Station Road, 1847, D MacAndrew
Former Free Church manse. Apart from the curiously forbidding round-arched porch, a not unsuccessful composition with broad eaves,

low-pitched roof, and an advanced and gabled centre front with concave-roofed bay window.

RCAHMS

Ramornie

Ramornie, Craigs Road, 1914, J G Young (Offices of Works)
Charming Scots-style house: two storeys of pinned boulder rubble with pairs of bay and oriel windows, dormer-heads and corbie-steps; a solid delight.

Ellon Academy (and Community Centre), 1980s, Grampian Regional Council
Bold horizontals of glass and concrete deal effectively with the building's great mass.

Old Bridge of Ellon, 1793; disused 1944
Sturdy, no-nonsense in pinned rubble with granite dressings and three segmental arches (central the largest), keyblocked, and V cutwaters. The elongated southern approach has a flood arch. Built at cost of third Earl of Aberdeen.

Old Tollhouse, early 19th century
Single-storey, bowed end to brae; now harled.

Aberdeenshire Council

St Mary on the Rock

St Mary on the Rock, 1870-1, G E Street
On rising ground, hard by the river, sophisticated early middle-pointed design in dark granite with lighter dressings, freestone windows and stringcourses. The sense of height is enhanced by steeply pitched roofs and, on west, a lean-to narthex with five lancets enclosed in a depressed arch above. Organ chamber on south wall, narrow apsidal chancel, vestry on north and, at the junction of nave and chancel, a neat spirelet which transforms itself imperceptibly from square to octagonal to circular plan. Inside is a pointed waggon-roof with tie rods, a good original stone pulpit, coloured marble reredos, two-seat sedilia and piscina. Sacrarium with brass door by Hardman; good glass, by Clayton & Bell, on north side of nave and chancel, more, by Lavers & Barreau, on south side of nave.

The original decoration, now plastered over, was by A E Street, to designs by his father. Rectory by Butterfield, sadly added to and recast, *c*.1926.

Auchtercrag, Commercial Road, 1894
Built for William Smith, owner of Boot and Shoe Factory (to the north, now demolished). Coldly baronial dominated by three-storey,

Neil Ross Square

The hinterland of Ellon, running back from the north bank of the Ythan, rises to *pretty enough hillocks that yet command far-away views to Bennachie and the Grampians.*
Groome

The Formartine & Buchan Way
Formed from redundant railway line, 1987, Aberdeenshire Council, allowing walking and cycling from Dyce to Peterhead and Fraserburgh.

crenellated, square entrance-tower and stack of canted four-light bays. Neat candle-snuffer turrets with fish-scale slating. Gatepiers are two massive monoliths in granite, ballcapped.

Neil Ross Square, Bridge Street, 1991
Pleasing recessed opening in street flanked by single-storey shops with substantial piended dormers and ridge tiles over and larger, harled blocks, set gable-wise to Square.

Modley Court, 1991,
Grampian Regional Council Architects
Remarkably disciplined sheltered housing of real elegance: two storeys, U-plan and strictly symmetrical, centred on slightly advanced harled block with large porch, red-tiled piend roof with cupola and plain windows: all around a formal garden.

Royal Mail Sorting Office, 1988,
Lyon & McPherson
Wonderfully surreal articulation of two, low, slightly offset, windowless blocks, by means of massive glazed-tube rooflight, like giant toilet-roll dispenser.

Ellon Station, 1861
For Formartine and Buchan Railway; was three-platform through station, main offices on down platform in low, harled building with awning. Boddam branch served from additional island platform, 1897, with large wooden structure and iron-framed awning all round; granary in goods yard.

82 **Nether Ardgrain**, 1664
Successive dates taken from royal arms in centre gable, plus CR and JEB (John Edward Bean) at lintel. One of the crispest, sparest and most truly Scots houses in the north-east.

Nether Ardgrain

Ardgrain was erected to a barony by royal charter in 1528 and was purchased by John Kennedy of Kermuck in 1629 who is credited with building the house; the extent to which Bean subsequently refitted it is a matter of some debate.

Two storeys and attic, harled with skewputs, thin jambs and a central, slightly projecting, one-window gable which is the pleasing focus. Steeply battered walls (including the centre gable), roll-moulded doorpiece and chamfered jambs to all front windows are 17th-century work. The doorpiece is crowned with an arched panel inscribed HOW HAPPY WOVLD THE HVSBANDMAN BE IF HE KNEW / HIS OWN GOOD (VIRGIL) LET IMPROVEMENTS AND LIBERTY FLOVRISH which could stand as a text for the whole Improving Movement, and there is a **sundial** over. The interior woodwork is all 1751. A single-storey kitchen-wing abuts at right angles. Conversion, 1982/3.

Aberdeenshire Council

Turnerhall Doocot

Turnerhall Doocot, 1787
Square and stumpy with battered walls, single rat-course and pyramidal roof; wood and brick boxes inside.

Turnerhall, 1861, D MacAndrew
Owes its name to the wish of John Turner of Birse, merchant in Danzig, to perpetuate his name. (In the 17th century the name of the area went from Hilton to Rosehill to Turnerhall.) The sixth laird built a *striking if not very attractive* house of two storeys with gabled wings, deep eaves, round-headed double and tripartite windows and a four-storey square entrance-tower, off centre and slightly institutionalised. Demolished, 1933, walled garden and kennels left.

83 **Hilton of Turnerhall**, *c.*1800
A remarkably tall, narrow farmhouse in coursed granite on three floors and with three windows set on a ridge. Sashes original; tall, single-storey back wing; adjacent to **Hilton Windmill,** (?)1787 or 1825. Lower part octagonal, 30ft high, top 20ft circular and tapering. Rubble-built in pinkish granite and with dressed quoins and a slab walkway reefing-stage carried on granite corbel-spurs at the angles. Originally four floors to spiral stair. The barn is two storeys high, the lower storey being below the level of the base of the tower.

The sails were blown off on 28 December 1879 in the same storm which did for the Tay Bridge; this led to the capping of the windmill and the installation of a three-horse gin in front of the tower to power the adjacent threshing barn. (This itself was replaced by a stationary engine in the base of the tower which caused a fire which destroyed the original timber-work and fittings of the windmill.)

Hilton of Turnerhall Windmill

Aberdeenshire Council

Aberdeenshire Council

Aberdeenshire Council

Top *Nethermill*
Above *Boat of Ardlethen Bridge*

Hilton Steading, mid-19th century
Good, almost symmetrical courtyard layout, centred on windmill and open to the south. Boulder rubble with granite dressings.

Nethermill, 18th-19th century
Former L-plan grain mill which began as a low, pinned boulder rubble building which was first raised at the kiln with a gable, then with a jerkin-headed (hipped) roof and red granite dressings. Single-frame start-and-awe wheel, 10ft 4in. in diameter at north-west.

Boat of Ardlethen Bridge (River Ythan), 1893
Plain but pleasing with three segmental arches with simple pilaster strips at cutwaters. In rough red granite ashlar whose courses slope with the roadway.

84 **Esslemont House**, 1769
Of the original 1769 house only sections of masonry remain, principally in the north front where the fenestration and eaves-course are partly original. (Old photograph shows a two-storey, two-basement, five-window house with piend roof, big chimneys and a centre Doric porch.) J Russell Mackenzie's transformation is big, baronial but somewhat uninspired. An asymmetrical composition in squared granite, of two storeys, basement and attic with a four-storey crenellated tower at south-east with an ogee-capped bell-turret. Staircase reconstruction, *c*.1958, A G R Mackenzie.

Aberdeenshire Council

Esslemont House

Castle of Esslemont, 15th century, burnt 1493, new tower in south-east angle, 1570-90
The original L-plan tower was demolished and replaced by a five-sided artillery castle, the south-eastern angle-tower later being used as the base for the slighter, two-storey-and-attic house on a stepped L-plan, corbelled to square; now much robbed. (Passed to Errolls, 1625, bought by Gordons, 1728, abandoned 1769.)

Aberdeenshire Council

Above *Castle of Esslemont*
Left *Arnage Castle*

Mill of Esslemont, 19th century
Substantial three-storey L-plan in coursed granite rubble, with kiln at right angles. Cast-iron-framed 14ft overshot wheel.

Aberdeenshire Council

85 **Arnage Castle**, late 16th century, Thomas Leper; partly remodelled (gables) late 17th/early 18th century
The pinned rubble, now so laboriously exposed, was once decently harled to emphasise the fine details such as the triple Leper shot-holes, so similar to Tolquhon and Schivas. Other probable Leper work includes the original door, now blocked, in the south-east re-entrant, the vaulted ground floor and the engaging double stair-turrets in the angles. Matthews' 1860 baronial entrance is more institutional than domestic; his addition on south, remodelling of north-east wing and infilling of north re-entrant are of varying success: addition to Matthews' wing, 1964, D C Stewart.

Built by Cheynes *from whose hands it passed c.1630; purchased by Rosses of Auchlossan 1702 ... [it] is a castellated rather than a Gothic building, and, with a few judicious alterations in harmony with its original style, would hold a prominent place among the houses of distinction in the neighbourhood.*
J B Pratt, *Buchan*

Hillhead of Fechil, 19th century
Former steading converted to five dwellings, 1992-3, Taylor Design Services.

Waterton, early 19th century
Bone mill, warehouses and quay dominated by two-storey, seven-bay store with outside stone stair and arched entry. Waterton was the end of

navigation from Newburgh and saw the comings and goings of the coastal trade, including coal lighters; it closed *c*.1920.

86 UDNY

Centred on the secret jewel of Udny Green, Monymusk-like in its atmosphere but translated to the very edge of Buchan and set atop a ridge sloping gently to the south. The fine tall beeches fringing the fields of the surrounding Udny estate give a welcome sense of enclosure and a hint of what could be achieved in the vast open acres to the north. The village is grouped around an asymmetrical village green dominated by the kirk and war memorial, with intriguing views to the truncated cone of the morthouse.

Aberdeenshire Council

Parish Church

Parish Church (Christ Church), 1821, John Smith
Fancy south gable in rough ashlar with sturdy tower, crenellated, pinnacled (clock top added 1895) and diagonally set buttresses to tower and nave. Four windows have original glazing, although the south ones are blind. Interior open-roofed with gallery carried on quatrefoil piers; remodelled, 1890, A Marshall Mackenzie; vaulted porch beneath tower; north window, 1927; Thomas Mears bell of 1821 (inscription).

Morthouse, 1832, John Marr of Cairnbrogie
A sophisticated response to the resurrectionists, completed in the year the *Anatomy (Scotland) Act* rendered it obsolete by the simple expedient of appropriating the unclaimed bodies of the poor. Coffins were placed within the circular, windowless, rough ashlar granite chamber on a platform which

Shepherd

Morthouse

was ratcheted round in a minimum of seven days (although the regulations permitted coffins to remain for up to three months). A strong oak door with a lock requiring four separate key-holders and an inner iron door completed the defences. The mason was Alexander Walker and the wright, Thomas Smith. Used as a rifle store in the Second World War.

Kirkyard includes the Pitmedden (Setons) and Pittrichie burial enclosures.

War Memorial, *c*.1919, Frank Coutts
Calm granite infantryman atop square plinth; one of the finest examples of Aberdeen granite carving (colour page 181).

Udny Schoolhouse, (?)1867, George Marr-Trig two-storey, two-window house, harled with granite margins and good details such as gablet dormer-heads and wood-mullioned windows.

Udny Arms Hotel, *c*.1800
Plain but strong, like the hotel in Tarves, in rough granite ashlar; three bays, two storeys with piended single-storey wings (and a pair of canted dormers).

Primrose Cottage, mid-19th century
A classic Improvement-period cottage in pinned granite, small in scale, simple and direct in style, with wooden porch.

Old Library, *c*.1912
Crisp single-storey L-plan in squared granite, wooded gable to front, deep eaves and broad, tripartite windows; formerly library presented to village by local farmer (plaque); good conversion to house, 1960s.

Self-build Housing, Udny Green, 1991
On rising site, an intimate grouping of single-storey-and-attic houses, some harled, others rough-faced granite with porthole windows to porches.

Manse of Udny, 1851, J & W Smith
High and box-like in pinned granite rubble but distinguished by an advanced and steeply gabled centre with ashlar-faced porch with finials. Bold windows with wooden mullions and transoms (cf Slains); interior altered, 1885, J R Mackenzie.

RCAHMS

Udny Schoolhouse

Udny Academy, founded 1786: sons of gentry boarded with the schoolmaster (cf Fordyce); well-known son of founder succeeded to role of dominie at age of 17 and four years later became minister of Bourtie. **Academy Court**, west of Green, now pleasing small-scale development as old people's homes.

Below *Old Library*
Middle *Self-build Housing*
Bottom *Manse of Udny*

Shepherd

Shepherd

Shepherd

Aberdeenshire Council

RCAHMS

Above *Udny today*
Right *Udny Castle in 19th century*

Earliest recorded Udny was Ranald of Uldney who received a charter from David II. Twelfth Laird of Udny retained Jamie Fleeman/Fleming (1713-78) as his *feel* (fool or jester) who was renowned for his riposte to an enquiring aristocrat, *I'm the Laird o' Udny's feel, fa's feel are e?* Saved the family when Castle of Knockhall went on fire, 1734. Buried at Longside under a memorial raised by public subsription (see *Banff & Buchan* in this series).

Udny Castle, 16th century
Rising sublimely from a cocoon of greenery, the richly detailed upper works lighten the gravity of this truly imposing, tall (four storeys and attic), harled tower. Particularly fine on south side where a corbelled and cannon-spouted wall-walk is slung between two twin angle-turrets. The large caphouse is corbie-stepped and the chimney coped. Many mural chambers including the pit. Large baronial mansion added, 1874-5, H M Wardrop; additions demolished and tower restored, 1964-7, by G Bennet Mitchell (John Lamb).
Deserted, *c*.1775, some repairs, 1801, but of Wardrop's efforts only the good plasterwork on the hall vault survives.

Udny Castle Lodge, *c*.1875, Wardrop & Anderson, lurking behind elaborate late 17th-/early 18th-century gatepiers, rusticated with console-crowns, the lodge is all angles – particularly in the heavy bargeboarded eaves which follow the asymmetric front and the narrow gable. Good, strong double chimney in centre of roof.

Udny Bridge, *c*.1800
Rubble-built with dressed voussoirs to the two segmental arches.

Udny Mill Business Centre, 19th century
Conventional low steading in rough granite with dressings, converted discretely, 1991, with minimal additional openings and good woodwork.

Pitmedden House

Aberdeenshire Council

Pitmedden House and **Great Garden**, 17th-century house
An apparently guileless building, but substantial, plain, part-harled, part corbiestepped, with pedimented windows rising above the first-floor wallhead. Fire-damaged, 1818; *c*.1853 (?)William

Henderson; remodelled, 1954-5, A G R Mackenzie.

Garden, 1675, Sir Alexander Seton; recreated since National Trust for Scotland acquisition in 1952 to designs of Dr J S Richardson, executed by George Barron: the greatest Renaissance example to survive in Scotland, consists of a massive rectangular enclosure, 190 yards by 160 yards, divided into an upper and a lower garden. There are fountains in both parts. The upper area contains Sir Alexander's fountain and the lower one created from fragments of Robert Mylne's Linlithgow Cross fountain (designed to commemorate the restoration of Charles II) as well as some stones from Pitmedden. Entrance to the lower, eastern garden is through a gateway with pineapple-topped piers and down a double stair with rustic decoration (including font recess). There are two very grand twin ogee-roofed pavilions with quoins at angles and groin vaults to ground floors; the upper room in the north one has panelling of 1686. Terraces to north and south permitted viewing of the parterres or borders planted out with formal patterns and heraldry. The **sundial**, *c*.1675, in the centre has an octagonal facet-head and ball finial; it originally stood to the north-west of the house (colour page 184).

Great Garden created by Sir Alexander Seton, Lord Pitmedden, one of the Court of Session judges removed by James VII for opposing his growing catholicism. His initials, and those of his wife, Dame Margaret Lauder, appear in the foundation inscription (*Fundat 2 May 1675*), while the bleeding heart in the family coat of arms and the melancholy Latin inscriptions picked out in low hedges in the garden are references to the death of Seton's father, Bonnie John Seton, fighting on the royalist side, at the battle of the Bridge of Dee in Aberdeen in 1639.

Shepherd

Left *Great Garden: aerial view*
Below *Museum of Farming Life: farmhouse*

Shepherd

The **Museum of Farming Life** is based on the old farmhouse, now restored, and adjacent buildings, all crammed with tools and equipment from last century. The dank bothy is an excellent evocation of the living quarters of those whose toil created the modern farming landscape of Aberdeenshire. Another vital factor in the Improving Movement, lime, would have been provided from the massive limekiln and pit still visible across the road. *National Trust for Scotland; open to the public*

Aberdeenshire Council

Aberdeenshire Council

Norman

Top *Atholhill Farmhouse*
Middle *Pittrichie House*
Above k *Balgrian, 2002, Richard Murphy (colour page 181)*

Pitmedden (former) Free Kirk
(now Church of Scotland), *c*.1860s
Prominently placed on raised ground in middle of village, early Gothic rectangle in pink squared and stugged sandstone with finely dressed margins, six bays divided by wall buttresses and lit by single lancets. Pointed arched entrance on front gable; elaborate, rectangular-plan, four-stage flighty clock-and-bell tower at angle about to rise, unaided, to the sky; decorative band of red and green slates in middle of steeply pitched roof. Interior U-plan timber gallery on Egyptian-style cast-iron columns. Remarkable survival.

Atholhill Farmhouse, *c*.1830-45
A degree of elegance is imparted to this single-storey pinned granite farmhouse by the railed steps with curved splay to door and the height lent by its basement and attic. Dormers later.

Pittrichie House, 1818, for J W Mackenzie
Late T-plan, two-storey mansion with three-window recessed centre bay and a belt-course at first floor, now gutted. **Pittrichie South Lodge**, 1818-25, plain single-storey with piend roof and central chimney, distinguished by two fine Gothic windows; porch recent. **Doocot,** *c*.1818-25, unusual square-plan in dark pinned granite, rising two storeys to a pyramidal roof. Striking arches with red voussoirs. **Home Farm**, 1823, elegant symmetrical layout, now much decayed; original parts in dark granite, later extensions in red. Datestone: INVIDOS VIRTUE TORQUEBO 1823. Two-storey, pyramidal-roofed bothy in centre of east range.

87 **Tillycorthie Mansion**, 1911, John Cameron
For James Rollo Duncan, a renowned Bolivian tin magnate. Not quite the earliest concrete mansion to be built in Britain (Beachtower at Dundee, 1874 ... also Hydropathic at Melrose are earlier still), it is a bewildering amalgam of the high-tech and the sub-baronial. The symmetrical front has as centre a thin battlemented tower (with chimneys rising from the merlons) flanked by gabled, crowstepped wings with pencil-slim turrets, with glazed screens between. Oak panelling in entrance hall and drawing room; chimney of heating plant rises in adjacent field, served by long underground flue; ice-rink on roof of power house; artificial lake. Converted to three (large) flats, 1980s.

Tillycorthie Mansion

Shepherd

LOGIE-BUCHAN

A fine mixture of rolling fields open to the sky and the secluded policies of Auchmacoy. *The river Ythan here navigable at full tide for small sloops ...* (Groome). Downstream from Ellon, precipices of gneiss rock flank the river.

St Andrew's Kirk, 1787
Undistinguised externally, porch 1891, inside original ceiling with Adam-like centrepiece and two-light Gothic windows, part of 1912 recasting, William Ruxton. Pulpit was originally in the centre of the north wall with a horseshoe gallery bearing the Buchan coat of arms (George Reid, Peterhead, carver. Monuments to Thomas (*d*.1819) and Robert (*d*.1825) Buchan). Bell, 1728, Robert Maxwell. Church bought by Captain David Buchan to ensure access and survival. **Kirkyard**, plain ashlar granite gatepiers and rubble walls; some table tombs.

Aberdeenshire Council

St Andrew's Kirk

The Buchans of Auchmacoy had a burial place within the old kirk, whose patronage was given by David II to Cathedral of St Machar. Major General Thomas Buchan (son of laird of Auchmacoy) succeeded Viscount Dundee in command of army, 1689. Supported the Old Pretender in 1715 Rising; buried here, 1720.

Manse of Logie-Buchan, 1775
Much grander and more lavish than kirk: two storeys and attic, three-window T-plan. Harled with margins including chamfered doorpiece; dormers Victorian; extension to rear. Clearly the residence of the second citizen of the parish.

Mains of Rannieston, *c*.1780-1800
Remarkably municipal in appearance, for its date. Effect comes from height of two storeys, attic and basement added to steep piend roof and pair of coped chimneys. Also cherry-cocked granite ashlar adds to the severity of its appearance. Three-window south front with two-light centre windows on each floor. Piended stair projection on north wall has doorway in angle. Plain, late 18th-century woodwork and large square stairwell with cantilevered stair.

Below *War Memorial bridge, Auchmacoy, 1935*
Middle *Manse of Logie-Buchan*
Bottom *Mains of Rannieston*

RCAHMS

Aberdeenshire Council

Aberdeenshire Council

88 **Auchmacoy House**, 1831, William Burn
A Scots Elizabethan fantasy for James Buchan, built near the site of two previous houses. Two storeys, harled with granite dressings and shafted chimneys; the south front is gableted and symmetrical about a projecting gabled centre with bay windows. The east (entrance) front has everything – bay window, porch with Tudor doorpiece, ogee gable and pencil-slim, conical-roofed tower with lower north wing. Interior simple neo-Greek.

Top *Auchmacoy Doocot*
Right *Auchmacoy House*
Above *Mission Hall and House*

In the grounds, a Tudor **mausoleum** for Thomas Buchan (*d*.1866), with diagonal buttresses and a gabled porch. Also **estate office**, using part of earlier house, and **doocot**, also near previous house site.

Auchmacoy Doocot, 1638 (although Leper-like, therefore ?late 16th century)
Like an improbable giant stone barrel, squared-off and corbie stepped, in pinned split-boulder rubble. Two pronounced rat-courses encircle its squat, friendly body and the two east-facing skewputs bear weathered carvings of faces.

Oldyard, *c*.1780-1801
Good, plain, Scots two-storey, three-window house with coped chimneys, in pinned rubble, once harled. Originally only one little window on back wall, high up, to light the stair; poor modern additions.

During the civil and religious contests *between the Covenanters and the Loyalists which unhappily mark the annals of Scotland during the greater part of the 17th century, the parish of Logie Buchan seems to have had its full share of suffering. The proprietors generally were firmly attached to the royal cause, and the dominant party took care that they should feel the consequences. On 23 February 1644, forty musketeers were sent from Aberdeen to plunder the lands of the Lairds of Rainieston, Tipperty, Tarty and the* Guidwife of Artrochie, *non-subscribers to the Covenant. Mr William Innes of Tipperty ... and other gentlemen, to the number of eighty horse, met the Covenanters on the bounds of Tarty, defeated, disarmed and dispersed them, to the great offence of Earl Marischal and committee.*
J B Pratt, *Buchan*

Mission Hall and **House**, Denhead, 1891
Gothic group; the hall rectangular with porch and three-light windows; harled with strong red sandstone dressings. The house sports half-timbering at first-floor level and a sympathetic modern addition. Built by Buchan sisters.

South Artrochie, *c*.1800
Finely detailed two-storey, three-window house with droved dressings to window and other margins, bold skewputs and coped chimneys.

SLAINS

In the windy bents and lunar dunes of Slains, Aberdeenshire finally achieves the sea. One of only three coastal parishes of Gordon and the most maritime in feel, this ancient parish boasts the ever-changing Sands of Forvie and the cliffs with *deep ghastly chasms* that edge the land to the north.

Parish Kirk, 1806
Plain rectangle with birdcage bellcote set high and sure. Porch and session house later. Originally interior had horseshoe gallery, rearranged with single west gallery, 1882, recast 1927. **Kirkyard** contains some 18th-century stones, a small morthouse at the north-east and the **Erroll Aisle**, perhaps 1599, which contains a 1758 slab to Mary, Countess of Erroll.

Aberdeenshire Council

Aberdeenshire Council

Top *Parish Kirk*
Above *Doocot, Manse of Slains*

Slains House (old Manse of Slains), 1876, William Smith
A tall, gaunt two-storey-and-attic house, harled with margins, whose gabled centre front is very slightly advanced for a Tudor-arched doorpiece with ball finials. Tripartite ground-floor windows and square gatepiers.

Manse of Slains Offices (The Glebe), early 19th century
Low, single-storey offices and later gig house. The little circular **doocot** is mid-18th century, as is the surrounding wall which incorporates a ramped duck-walk to the stream; converted to house, 1974.

Slains Lodge, 19th century
Crowning the highest point in the village, plain sub-baronial mansion of two storeys with long gabled frontage terminated in three-storey round tower; now subdivided into apartments.

Collieston Harbour, 1894
Aberdeenshire's only formal link to the sea, angle granite pier and quayed shore; notable for *tunnel piercing foundations of break-water-pier near the present end of its walkway, evidently designed for the flushing-out of silt like those recommended by Smeaton* (1770) *at Dundee* (A Graham). In 1696, 36 fishermen lived in *Collestowne*, one of the largest fishing

Smuggling was frequently carried on in the district (termed an *hereditary propensity*). Grave of Philip Kennedy (*d.*1798, aged 38) survives. He was caught by the Excise along with his brother; his skull was laid open by a stroke from one of the excisemen who was tried for murder but acquitted.

Collieston Harbour

Shepherd

Revd James Rust was minister, 1840-74; interested in local antiquities, principal work *Druidism Exhumed* (Edinburgh 1871), *contains theories and etymological speculations which are probably more ingenious than useful* (Jervise). However, he was percipient regarding *black rain showers* in Scotland, 1862-3, which he attributed to the eruption of Vesuvius.

Aberdeenshire Council

Above *Old Slains Castle*
Right *St Fidamnan's, Leask*

St Catherine's Dub, the dark, cliff-girt, bay at Collieston, is traditionally the site of the sinking of a Spanish Armada ship. It was, in fact, a ship from the Spanish Netherlands gun-running for Francis, eighth Earl of Erroll's Catholic uprising in 1594. He died in 1631 and was buried *upone the nicht* in the kirk at Slains. His body was *convoyit quyetlie with his awin domesticks and countrie freindis and with torche licht.* It was the Earl's wish that the expense saved should be given to the poor. He was celebrated by Arthur Johnston thus:

Nascentem placido te vidit lumine Pallas,
Mens apta est studius prurit in arma manus.
(Pallas with kindly eye looked on thy birth,
Fitted is thy mind for learned pursuits - thy hand in deeds of battle excels.)

House of Leask

Aberdeenshire Council

communities north of the Tay; by the 1880s, there were over 100 fishing for *prodsing speldins* (dried haddock) or *blauvin fishies* (whiting), yet the community moved, almost wholesale, *c.*1900, to Torry as a result of *the stone*, an incurable malady. The Lang Reel o'Collieston used to be danced by the whole community on Forvie Sands after each fisher wedding (colour page 183).

89 **Old Slains Castle**, 15th century
Crowning a steep peninsulated rock (Groome), represented by stark fragment, *c.*8ft thick, of south-east angle of a vaulted tower of the Hays, which was blown up on the orders of James VI in 1594 in return for eighth Earl's support for the Earl of Huntly's rebellion that year (colour page 183).

Mains of Slains Farmhouse, late 18th century and additions
Severe, but good proportions (three windows, two storeys), harled with coped chimneys and moulded skewputs.

RCAHMS

90 **St Fidamnan's Chapel** (St Adamnan's), Leask, probably 15th century
Ruinous rubble-built rectangle in wooded corner whose eastern gable, sporting a large tracery-less pointed window, is relatively entire. Piscina and aumbry, otherwise very plain.

91 **House of Leask,** 1826-7, Archibald Simpson
A formerly harled, two-storey granite rubble mansion-house comprising a main block and lower service wing. Dressings of basal and stringcourses are very fine; five-bay main elevation with central door and extravagantly tall ground-floor windows. Originally had a piended slate roof with Simpson's characteristically deep eaves. Burnt 1927.

Doocot, mid-18th century, actually belonged to the original Pitlurg House. Notable for its height and spare, square plan, it rises to a row of flight holes just above an improbably elevated rat-course and is crowned by a ball finial. Reslated 19th century, restored 1981.

Forvie Kirk, medieval
Given by James VI to King's College, Aberdeen, 1574; annexed to Slains. Very plain, ruined rectangle with door at west end of south wall. Dug out of covering sand by local doctor at end of 19th century when the piscina was unearthed.

Bridge over Ythan, c.1988, Grampian Regional Council
Immensely simple forms: flat deck springs from new plain landforms and is carried on two unobtrusive stone piers.

FOVERAN

The farmland, open and arable, rolls down to the coast; a fringe of bents and sky.

Parish Church, 1794
Plain rectangle of surface granite with round-headed windows, skewputs, red dressings and west gable crowned by a ball-capped birdcage bellcote. Repaired, 1852, William Buyers; reseated 1871; galleries renewed, 1877, William Christie; organ-chamber apse added, 1900-1, (?)Jenkins & Marr. Good monuments, including a fine marble with portrait cartouche to George and Alexander Udny, *d*.1788, by John Bacon RA, a Mears and Stainbank bell, 1760 (recast 1905), and the **Turing Slab**, a fine medieval stone bearing two incised armoured figures (cf Kinkell, qv) beneath a canopy.

92 **Foveran House**, 1771
Cold, angular, two-storey-and-basement, five-window mansion in quoined granite ashlar with central wallhead gable on the front. The porch and set-back wings are later, as is the regrettable first-floor addition over the porch. Courtyard with offices to the rear, dominated by a grandiose harled tower with Jacobean angle-turrets each ogee-capped. Considerably altered, 1885, Matthews & Mackenzie. **Lodge and gates**, late 18th century (piers), early 19th century (gates), late 19th century (lodge – A Marshall Mackenzie). Good ball-capped gatepiers with strong cornices. Lodge single-

Aberdeenshire Council

Doocot, House of Leask

House of Leask began as Leask, a Cuming property in the early 18th century, became Gordon Lodge on marriage of Barbara Cuming to Dr Alexander Gordon of Hilton and Straloch, a descendant of the Gordons of Pitlurg in Banffshire. Their grandson, a major-general, renamed it Pitlurg after the ancestral lands, but his son, Captain Gordon Cumming Skene of Pitlurg, Dyce and Parkhill, commissioned Simpson to build the House of Leask, returning it to the original name.

Tower, Foveran House

Aberdeenshire Council

storey, T-plan and harled with margins. Neat, pedimented entrance bay, canted bay window on gable and central chimney; all very agreeable. (Antique-looking tower at rear replaced *Turing's Tower*, which fell about 1720 and was part of an early castle, now gone.)

Aberdeenshire Council

Above *Mill of Foveran Farmhouse*
Right *Knockhall Castle*

Tradition of three heiresses defrauded of property by near relatives and cast adrift in a boat; they pronounced the following malison:

If evyr maydenis malysone
Did licht upon drye lande,
Let nocht be funde in Furvey's glebys
But thrystl, bent and sande.

This is part of the tradition, common to other coastal settlements (eg Culbin, Skara Brae) of a sudden and catastrophic influx of sand; truth is more prosaic – Forvie was transformed into a *wild and lonely scene* with a *weird* feeling of profound *solitude* by gradual incursion of blown sand on to the simple fields.

Mill of Foveran Farmhouse, (?)1609 at north-west skew
Formerly girnal; intriguing, long and substantial. Original openings, where surviving, were in sandstone, chamfered and barred; saltires in skewputs. The mid-19th-century remodelling added dormers, a central door with steps and curious consoled *cornice* which is in fact a gutter. (Mill has datestone of 1720; raised in height then gutted.)

RCAHMS

93 **Knockhall Castle**, 1565
A classic L-plan, three-storey place (with staircase tower at centre of north side) of some grace. Door in southern re-entrant has two mouldings above for armorial panels and the windows on the south and east fronts are finely moulded. Remains of circular **doocot** adjacent; once fine with conical roof and entrance cupola. Reconstructed late 17th century, burned 1734.

Ythan Lodge

Aberdeenshire Council

Ythan Lodge, 1775
Solid two-storey-and-attic, three-window front with several projections to rear. Harled and cream-washed margins to front and angles. Good skews; original part of west gable fine with tiered pairs of windows, diminishing in size, and a large chimneyhead. Offices attached at north-east. Restored, *c*.1965, D Turnbull extended 1975.

On the spreading estuary of the Ythan, **Newburgh** was a significant port for fish and Ellon-bound cargo; also resort of retired seamen.

Shanghai House, 31 Main Street, *c*.1850
Suitably trim and neat for Captain Thomson, clipper master. Straightforward two-storey, three-window layout, harled with margins and granite dressings. Door unusual, flanked by panels of plain ashlar enclosed in wide architrave. Glazing original.

Newburgh House, Main Street, *c*.1800
Slightly box-like but grand two storey, attic in rubble with surface granite dressings. Turned to south to catch the sun, with large two-window gable to street. Key-blocked and quoined south doorway with rectangular fanlight; plain parapet and canted dormers above.

Old Kirkyard, 18th century
Dominated by Udny family vault, a harled rectangle with straight skews, a tall, steep roof and blind gablet at back. A few 18th-century stones around.

94 **Tillery House**, 1788
Estate was bought from Udnys of Udny in 1788 by John Chambers (formerly Chalmers), a retired planter from the southern USA, who built a plain three-window, two-storey house. This was added to substantially by his grandson, William Chambers-Hunter, who commissioned a Greek-revival mansion, 1826, Archibald Simpson, burnt 1950s; of two storeys with a three-window west front dominated by a four-columned Doric porch and a restrained cornice and blocking course. The south front had a grand three-window bow.

RCAHMS

Aberdeenshire Council

Top *Shanghai House*
Above *Udny family vault*

***Ranks as a subport** of Aberdeen; and carries on commerce chiefly in exporting grain, and in importing coal, timber, lime and bones: extensive manure works.*
Groome

Our hills may be laigh,
and our trees may be few,
An our bents may be bare in
the Highlandman's view;
But the bonnie braid acres we
hae under plough
An sic craps an sic cattle
he'd fain hae, I trow.
William Forbes, *The Newburgh Salmon Dinner Song*

Aberdeenshire Council

Tillery House

Norman

Shepherd

Top l *Holyrood Chapel, Newburgh, roof refurbishment 1906-7, John Robertson*
Above n *Oceanlab, 2002, George Watt & Stewart (colour page 183)*
Right *Culterty Quay and Mill, 1970*

Mill of Minnes, early 19th century
Two-storey-and-attic rubble rectangle; short *Aberdeenshire* kiln vent and overshot wheel 12ft in diameter.

RCAHMS

Culterty Quay and **Mill**, from 18th century
Mill three-storey in brick, kiln at end; also three-storey, 20-bay, wood and iron-framed, corrugated-iron-clad granary, 1897, by Spencer & Co of Melkham, Wiltshire. Concrete-faced quay with some rubble warehouses, two-storey-and-attic, eight-bay rubble.

BELHELVIE

Sand-fringed and undulating, Belhelvie rises to rocky spine of former moors and mosses.

Parish Kirk, 1878, William Smith
Plain Gothic grey granite rectangle with belfry 70ft high.

Aberdeenshire Council

St Columba's

St Columba's, 17th century
Now slightly below the sweep of the modern road, T-plan predecessor, represented by high west gable in coursed granite crowned by muscular bellcote (dated 1762) and part of south aisle containing fine but weathered monument to Innes of Blairton. Unusual in having two **morthouses**, one a turfed and vaulted chamber of uncertain date, the other more finished, 1835, rectangular, with ashlar granite front, oak door with bar over keyholes and, internally, two shelves with rollers each side.

95 **Orrock House**, 1781
Austere three-storey, five-window gabled main block in dressed granite with single-storey piend-roofed wings, dominated by upward sweep of roof. The London banker, Alexander Fordyce, who acquired the property of Over Blairton in 1770, may have begun the building but his spectacular bankruptcy later that year

RCAHMS

Orrock House

would have given him little time. The property was acquired by John Orrock, *late captain of ships trading in the East and West Indies*, who transferred the name from the family lands in Fife which had been lost. The large Os above the attic-gable windows are his imprint. Original woodwork inside; porch later 19th century. Circular **doocot**, *c.*1782, with ogee-arched doorway, cherry-cocking and high rat-course.

Aberdeenshire Council

Above *Orrock doocot*
Left *Balmedie House*

RCAHMS

Balmedie House, 1878, (?)Peddie & Kinnear
Rather pedestrian Jacobean Baronial for William Harry Lumsden, incorporating walls of single-storey Regency house; two storey and basement in local rubble, with sandstone dressings, dominated by asymmetrical four-storey tower with singular porch; dining room good. **Lodge**, *c.*1820-40, harled with eaves, behind 18th-century gatepiers with ringed ovoid finials.

96 **Belhelvie Lodge**, *c.*1783
Centre block for Harry Lumsden, advocate in Aberdeen, who had bought the forfeited Panmure estate from the York Buildings Company in 1782. A two-storey-and-basement, three-window house

Belhelvie Lodge

Aberdeenshire Council

in squared granite with margins and piend roof; arched and key-blocked porch early Victorian. Two-storey east wing, *c*.1800; west wing, 1969, on site of former low wing.

Aberdeenshire Council

Above *Ardo House*
Right *Menie House*

Ardo House, from *c*.1756
Pleasing L-plan group, original plain house and granary built shortly after 1756 by Dingwall of Rannieston; petite granite mansion at right angles, *c*.1850, for Peter Harvey, to which an excellent neo-Greek porch was added in 1921, its calm precision suggesting William Kelly. Greenhouse, 1913; office court.

RCAHMS

Menie House, *c*.1835, John Smith
Out of Auchmacoy (qv) but more ponderously Jacobean; two storeys with dormer-heads in pinned granite with freestone dressings and diagonally set chimney-shafts; symmetrical south-west front enlivened by central bay with curvilinear gable flanked by octagonal angles with sharp finials. North-west front has Tudor porch and circular angle-tower. Earlier (1782-3) two-storey, L-plan house incorporated at south-east.

Below *Timber house, Potterton*
Bottom *Kilrenny*

Shepherd

Mill of Blairton, 18th-19th century
12ft-diameter wheel in rectangular single-storey-and-basement rubble building.

Shepherd

Potterton
Village edges main road with denticulation of single-storey timber housing of Scandinavian inspiration, *c*.1975, similar to some in Kemnay (qv).

97 **Kilrenny**, 1970, David Taylor Architect
Uncompromising flat-topped living space projecting dramatically from the slope of the ground, poised on a slim black plinth incorporating the entrance, and severely clothed in full-length glazed and white panels. An outstanding contemporary *jeu d'esprit*.

Eigie Road, Balmedie, *c.*1988, SSHA
Good feeling of enclosure and variety from placing of two-storey, cheerfully harled houses, further brightened by occasional balcony or canopy and little pends between.

Aberdeenshire Council

Eigie Road, Balmedie

Balmedie Country Park sand dunes enlivened by good, timber **visitor centre**, *c.*1988, poised, boat-like, on stilts. Drunken Second World War pillbox at edge of sand-plain to north.

NEWMACHAR

Once under the deanery of St Machar, known as Upper Parochine of Oldmachar, then New Machar, the ancient focus was on the Monykebbock barony.

Shepherd

o Sustainable housing, Station Road, Newmachar, 2004, David Murray Associates (colour page 184)

Parish Kirk, 1791
Large restrained rectangle in squared granite with four well-proportioned, round-headed windows on south side, birdcage bellcote with ball finial on west end and tall, narrow session house to east. Fine Douglas Strachan window marking connection with bishops of Aberdeen and deanery of St Machar's.

Aberdeenshire Council

Parish Kirk

98 **All Saints Episcopal**, Whiterashes, 1858, James Matthews
Nicely judged country church in granite; modest, steeply pitched nave and small chancel; with buttressed and skewed porch set asymmetrically on gable (itself topped by strong gabled bellcote) and rectangular windows with (good) glass, these last, 1890, by Sir Ninian Comper. Internally, all is very chaste: open timber roof, plastered walls. (In use as school from 1858 to 1885 when it was dedicated; in 1889 it was consecrated as a church.)

Shepherd

All Saints Episcopal

Newmachar House (former manse) 1781, with low wings to rear

Norman

Gordon District Council

RCAHMS

Above *Straloch House*
Right *Straloch House last century*

Straloch comes from Strathloch, earliest record 1348, charter granted to Henry Cheyne; Cheynes owned Straloch for over 250 years; in 1600 sold it to Gordons of Pitlurg. John was followed by Robert, the *Great Straloch*, owing to his fame as a cartographer and historian; it was his grandson, another Robert, who founded Robert Gordon's College. Gordons sold Straloch in 1758 to John Ramsay ... Mary married Francis Irvine of Drum and their eldest son inherited Drum from his father, and the second, Quentin, Straloch. Ramsays of Straloch became Irvines of Barra and Straloch without change of line.

99 **Straloch House,** 1780
Serene five-window, two-storey-and-attic centre block with pair of end wings at right angles, set back; distinguished by slightly advanced pedimented centre, prominent blocking course and elegance of curved gables, double on main house, single on wings (colour page 183). **Walled garden** and policies laid out, *c.*1750, with great garden wall, *c.*15ft high. **Home Farm**, late 18th/early 19th century, massive two-storey main front in coursed rubble: nine bays with central segmental pend arch and tiny square upper windows, lurking under the eaves.

Elrick House, late 18th century
Crisp, if a little bland, five window, two storey and basement with two low end wings in granite ashlar, with pronounced quoins and small wooden portico. Panelled interiors. **Doocot**, a granite drum with single rat-course, (?)16th century; **Home Farm**, 18th and 19th century, U-plan in coursed squared rubble.

Parkhill House
West Lodge with its neat columned verandah and piend roof all that survives of sizeable 18th-century mansion of Skene of Dyce, now demolished.

Aberdeenshire Council

Above *Parkhill House Lodge*
Right *Parkhill House*

Bogdan

Without the charm of Charles McKean I would never have embarked upon this painful, but ultimately delightful task. I am grateful to him, and to David Walker, for much incisive and useful criticism along the way. Without the list of Buildings of Architectural and Historical Interest, the facilities of the then Gordon District Council and the Sites and Monuments Record of Grampian Regional Council (now Aberdeenshire) the guide could not have been written. For the first edition, Helen Leng and Wendy Gardiner of RIAS were models of supportive patience and stern encouragement. The staff of the RCAHMS were unfailingly efficient and helpful as were those of the North-East of Scotland Library Service.

The late Geraldine (Ges) Scott, Director of Planning of Gordon District Council, was instrumental in getting the book started; many of the buildings submitted for the Design Awards which bore her name are here. I am indebted to many of the staff of the Planning Department of the then Gordon District Council for their interest and assistance over the years, principally Bob Tinch, Jonathan Young, Andrew Carruthers, Alyson James, Elaine Hare, Bob Knorr, last but not least, Douglas Law, and to the Members of the Council for their considerable commitment to the volume. I should also like to thank my then director, Dr Howard Fisher of the Economic Development and Planning Department of Grampian Regional Council, for his support and encouragement. To the late Nicholas Q Bogdan and Ian B D Bryce I owed a particular debt of gratitude for sharing their deep knowledge of Aberdeenshire castles with me over many years.

Many thanks are due to all those who helped with the production of this second edition, in particular to Shaun Norman for his photographic support and to him, Moira Greig and Bruce Mann for the tremendous help in the last stages when I was *hors de combat* within the NHS. Thanks also to the staff of the RCAHMS, in particular Philip Graham and Rebecca Bailey, and to Ann Dean and Iain Gray who provided invaluable detailed comments. Finally I am most grateful to my family, to Lek, Bryony and Sunniva for their huge support sustained over the years and most importantly to my father, James P Shepherd (1911-93), who cheerfully and efficiently did much of the initial collection of material for the short column entries and who first showed me the kirks and castles of Aberdeenshire and beyond.

References

The North East Lowlands of Scotland, J R Allan, 1952; **The Baronial and Ecclesiastical Antiquities of Scotland**, R W Billings, 1852; **Circuit Journeys**, Lord Cockburn, 1888; **Antiquities and Scenery of the North of Scotland**, Charles Cordiner (in a series of letters to Thomas Pennant), 1780; **Inverurie and the Earldom of Mar**, John Davidson, 1878; **A general description of the East Coast of Scotland**, Francis Douglas, 1782; **The Beauties of Scotland**, R Forsyth, 1806; **A Pictorial History of the Garioch**, Garioch Heritage Society, 1991; **A Portrait of Aberdeen and Deeside**, C Graham, 1984; **Ordnance Gazetteer of Scotland**, Francis Groome, 1888/96; **Epitaphs and Inscriptions**, A Jervise, 1875, 1879; **Life and Labour on an Aberdeenshire Estate, 1735-50**, Henry Hamilton (ed), 1946; **The Donean Tourist**, Alexander Laing, 1828; **The Castellated Architecture of Aberdeenshire**, A Leith Hay, 1849; **Donside**, AI McConnochie, 1901; **The Book of Ellon**, AI McConnochie (ed), 1901; **The Castellated and Domestic Architecture of Scotland**, David MacGibbon and Thomas Ross, 1897; **Grampian Battlefields**, Peter Marren, 1990; **Buchan**, J B Pratt, 1858; **Exploring Scotland's Heritage: Grampian**, I A G Shepherd, 1986; **The Earldom of Mar**, W D Simpson, 1949; several articles on north-east châteaux by H Gordon Slade in the **Proceedings of the Society of Antiquaries of Scotland** Vols 99, 109, 111-13; **Fermfolk and Fisherfolk**, J S Smith (ed), 1989; **The Queen's Scotland; The Eastern Counties**, N Tranter, 1972; **Antiquarian Gleanings from Aberdeenshire Records**, Gavin Turreff, 1859; **The Land o'Lonach**, R Winram, 1986; **The Making of 19th-century Aberdeenshire**, S Wood, 1985; **Sand and Silence: lost villages of the North**, D Wylie, 1986.

INDEX

PICTORIAL GLOSSARY

1. Ashlar (dressed stonework in smooth blocks).
2. Balustrade (line of small columns usually along a balcony or parapet—in this case in ironwork).
3. Bow (projecting semi-circular bay).
4. Buttress (Stone column supporting the walls, usually of a church).
5. Cherry-cocking (small stones set between larger blocks of stone).
6. Corbel (stone supporting a projection above, one end embedded into a wall).
7. Cornice (projecting top of a wall).
8. Crowstepped gable (a gable in the form of a series of steps).
9. Curvilinear gable (wavy-shaped gable).
10. Cupola (roof light).
11. Dormer window (window projecting through the roof plane).
12. Drum tower (circular one-bay tower, usually for staircase).
13. Eaves (overhanging edge of roof).
14. Fanlight (patterned glazed window above a door).
15. Finial (crowning feature e.g. of tower).
16. Keystone (centre stone ot an arch).
17. Palazzo (a building in imitation of an Italian Renaissance palace).
18. Pavilion roof (piended, or hipped—sloping on all four sides).
19. Pediment (triangular feature).
20. Pilaster (flattened column attached to a wall).
21. Quoin (long and short protuberant stones emphasising the corner).
22. Stringcourse (stone course or moulding projecting from the surface of the wall).
23. Tracery (window pattern, usually in churches).
24. Venetian window (three-part window, the centrepiece raised and curved).
25. Wallhead or nepus gable (gable rising through the roof in the front of a building).

Aberdeenshire:
Donside and Strathbogie

Buildings added to this edition are shown by lower case letters a – o

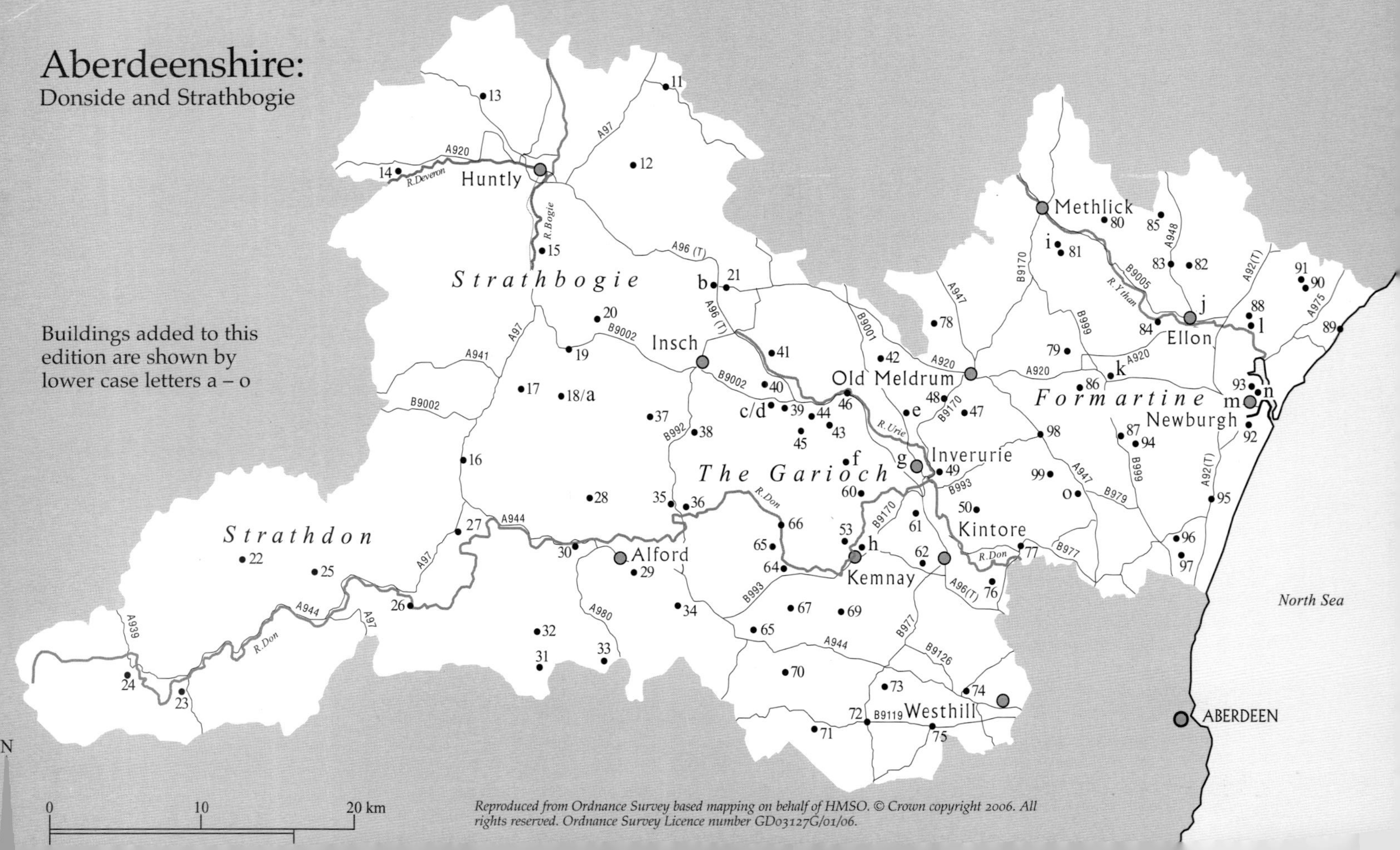

Reproduced from Ordnance Survey based mapping on behalf of HMSO. © Crown copyright 2006. All rights reserved. Ordnance Survey Licence number GD03127G/01/06.